SELLING TO THE BRAIN

THE NEUROSCIENCE OF BECOMING A SALES GENIUS

Robert G. Best

with J.M. Best

Best Wishes

Rob

Parts of this book appeared in different form on Robert G. Best's blog site, *Mindframewithrobb*

Audio book link available at *BestMindframe.com,* a division of Giant Pivot Table LLC.

Cover & book design by Vincent Skyers of UmbraSolutions.com

Internal artwork by Lauren Carter Best

Edited by Casey Best and Jessica Best

Printed on acid-free paper.

2022

First Edition

DISCLAIMER

This book details the author's personal experiences with and opinions about cognitive science. The author is not a licensed medical doctor.

The author and publisher are providing this book and its contents on an "as is" basis and make no representations or warranties of any kind with respect to this book or its contents. The author and publisher disclaim all such representations and warranties, including for example warranties of merchantability and specific advice for a particular purpose. In addition, the author and publisher do not represent or warrant that the information accessible via this book is accurate, complete or current.

The statements made about products and services have not been evaluated by the U.S. government. Please consult with your own legal, accounting, medical, or other licensed professional regarding the suggestions and recommendations made in this book.

Except as specifically stated in this book, neither the author or publisher, nor any authors, contributors, or other representatives will be liable for damages arising out of or in connection with the use of this book. This is a comprehensive limitation of liability that applies to all damages of any kind, including (without limitation) compensatory; direct, indirect or consequential damages; loss of data, income or profit; loss of or damage to property and claims of third parties.

You understand that this book is not intended as a substitute for consultation with a licensed medical, legal or accounting professional. Before you begin any change your lifestyle in any way, you will consult a licensed professional to ensure that you are doing what's best for your situation.

This book provides content related to cognitive science topics. As such, use of this book implies your acceptance of this disclaimer.

Contents

Prologue

When I first got into sales, I was eager to learn as much as I possibly could. I began my sales career in a showroom and listened intently to my fellow salespeople, attempting to emulate the ones that seemed to have a gift for putting their customers at ease and into the mood to buy. Each salesperson I studied seemed to be good at selling certain kinds of customers and not necessarily good with others. I always wondered why that was the case.

In the early days, I read all the books about selling I could get my hands on. Over time, I noticed something about them: their prescriptions for selling were all over the place, often in direct opposition to each other. Yet, if you were to take the authors' words at face value, each had been wildly successful with their particular methodology.

All of this might not seem so strange when you realize for the longest time, sales has been considered an art form, more magic than science. The successful salespeople seemed to practice their own brand of alchemy, a self-taught, trial-by-error, school of hard knocks approach. If there was one thing everyone agreed on, it was that perseverance was at the heart of success, but beyond that, the recipe for the secret selling sauce, if there was one, remained elusive.

All of that started to change in 1978, when researchers Ian Robert Young and Hugh Clow produced the first MR images of the human brain using a machine that today we call a magnetic resonance imaging machine, or MRI. The MRI has changed our understanding of the brain and how it functions. It has led to enormous breakthroughs and helped catapult neuroscience into one of the fastest growing fields of medicine.

Scientists are using MRIs and other new technologies to help unlock the keys to basic brain function, decision making, rational or irrational thinking, new habits, and a host of other topics at the very essence of modern sales.

For the last twelve years, I have traveled nationally and internationally, and had the great privilege to read and talk to pre-eminent scientists in the field of neuroscience and psychology in order to help demystify the selling experience.

This book represents the fruit of our labor: a practical guide to becoming a Sales Genius, someone who demonstrates exceptional sales and customer experience, without raising their stress level.

The book is composed of five sections. The first section dispels the standard sales myths. The second section lays the groundwork for the fundamentals of brain research, and how that learning helps us understand your customers' decision making. The third section expands on this idea and offers specific selling techniques built on the back of brain research. The fourth section focuses on science-based closing methods, and the last section outlines how the customer's experience is at the heart of making your customer happy, and salespeople successful. I hope you enjoy this brain-based approach to sales.

Robert G. Best, with J.M. Best

Sales Myths

part

1

Sales Myths

The end of World War II brought with it a wave of new sales and marketing techniques as GIs came home from the war and new consumer products and goods began to flourish. Pent-up demand created no shortage of selling "experts" or sales literature that purported to have the power to turn you into a certified selling machine.

Old-school sales books from that era are rich in personal selling anecdotes that, while entertaining, are often poor on practical application for today's fast-paced sales environment. Before we look at some cutting edge 21st century brain science it's important that we dispel four common sales myths.

Myth 1: Sales ability is something you're born with— you either have it or you don't.

This is among the most common of sales misconceptions. The story goes that great salespeople are the winners of the genetic lottery. In other words, they were born with a gift for gab and the natural ability to sell ice in the dead of winter to the good people of Fergus Falls, Minnesota.

The problem is that Albert Mehrabian's pioneering work on body language shows that when it comes to getting a message across, only roughly 7% of the impact comes from the actual words spoken. 38% stems from things like vocal tone and inflection, and the other 55% is nonverbal[1]. So much for "the gift of gab."

Myth 2: The harder I work, the more I'll sell.

Hard work is a key to good selling, but there are plenty of salespeople out there burning the midnight oil with little to show for it. Burnout is common in this profession.

It's not so much about how hard you work, but more about your ability to create an emotional experience that resonates with your customer. Understanding the basics of brain research on decision-making allows you to capitalize on human biases to significantly improve your selling abilities. It's not only about hours logged, it's also about creating a quality experience for your customer.

Myth 3: It's all about choice; the more options I can offer, the more likely I'll sell.

This is a pervasive idea in today's sales and marketing. Companies are constantly generating new versions, and variations, based on the belief that consumers have an unending appetite for variety. (How many flavors of potato chips do we really need?) This might seem counterintuitive, but more product offerings doesn't necessarily equal more sales. An overload of choice can kill a sale.

Why?

Choice is important, but when choice occurs outside of a choreographed selling experience (for instance, when too many options are offered at once), choice leads to mental overload, overload leads to frustration, and frustration is not a winning buying formula.

Myth 4: The Holy Grail to Selling is out there somewhere, I just need to find it.

Like the Spanish explorer Ponce De Leon on his failed search for the Fountain of Youth, you're going to come up empty-handed on your quest for a magical selling program. There is no singular selling system or sales strategy that will pay off with infinite rewards. Neither this book nor any book on sales has a lock on selling technique, and claims to the contrary should give you pause before you drop your hard-earned cash on them. You will need a variety of strategies to be effective.

Which brings us to what can be described as selling systems.

Selling Systems

A selling system is a definitive singular process or methodology for acquiring a sale. Selling systems generally fall into four categories.

There is the "aggressive sale," where the goal is to get an upfront contract or commitment, and usually some kind of deposit right off the bat. There is the "buddy system', where the goal is to bond with your customer and work the sale from a friendship position by becoming their new BFF. There is the "expert sale system," where the goal is to overwhelm with expertise in order to convince the customer to trust the salesperson's recommendation. And there is the "scripted sale," where the goal is to carefully guide the customer through a predetermined dialogue designed to logically bring them to a favorable selling conclusion.

So which system is the best? The answer is all of them, and some of them, and sometimes none of them. It all depends on the customer. Humans' needs, wants, beliefs, habits and desires run the gamut, and as we will see in the coming chapters, you have to learn to be a sales chameleon, employing a host of strategies to succeed. And those strategies are dictated by your customer, not you.

Any one of the aforementioned systems by themselves might have great or a deleterious effect on your chances of selling. Unfortunately, just like with clothing, there is really no such thing as a "one size fits all" approach.

The promoters of selling systems generally tout the incredible results they have personally had with the proprietary-based system they are trying to sell you, and by adopting their system, they assert that you will finally achieve your true selling potential.

We don't necessarily doubt a promoter's sincerity or that they have radically outperformed their own expectations in sales over the course of their career. What we do doubt is that there is only one viable way to achieve sales mastery.

Like in sports, music and a whole host of endeavors, there are basic fundamentals in sales that can be identified, practiced and mastered. We believe that understanding the basics of brain research, and building a strategy around that knowledge, serves the core of any legitimate selling program.

Furthermore, once you understand some basics of the brain's operating strategy, and how that translates into real life behavior, you are free to pick and choose the best practices from any selling methodology. Then you will be able to offer a creative selling experience tailored specifically to the vagaries of each specific customer, no matter who that person might be.

Will you be able to sell every customer your product or service? Realistically, the answer is no. This is not to say that sales is a total crapshoot. On the contrary, learning scientific fundamentals about the brain will give you an incredible ability to connect, sell, and create the ultimate experience for your customer. But that said, it's impossible to sell every prospective customer no matter your level of confidence or mastery, and importantly, there is no singularity to selling.

The Why of Sales

So, why are some people phenomenal at selling? Why do these same salespeople succeed over and over again?

When these super salespeople happen to be in your own organization, they are using the same ordering software, warehousing, delivery system, and selling the exact same product or service as you. If you ask them what they are doing differently, they will probably tell you something like this:

"I don't know what to say. I work hard, try to listen to my customer's needs and then try to deliver our products and services on-time and complete."

The problem with this response is that's also your game plan, but with results that sometimes fall short.

So why the difference, and what is your brain's role in all of this?

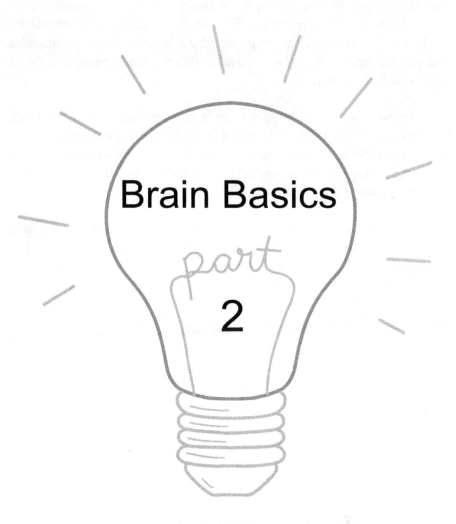

Brain Basics

part 2

Origins

Your brain is a three-pound pile of electrified meat, responsible for every decision you ever make. This amazing piece of biochemistry might not be the first thing you consider when you think about sales and marketing, but it all begins and ends with the roughly eighty-six billion neurons in your brain.

Neuroscience has made huge strides in understanding how the brain is governed by connections between its cells and the consequences of those connections. Neurons can fire in clusters of up to 10,000 in the blink of an eye, and when operating properly, they allow you to walk and chew gum at the same time.

The Homo sapiens brain has gone through countless iterations, and as our ability to trace DNA sequences has increased, the story has only gotten more complex. Although the human brain is incredibly complicated, its mission is in some ways simple. It is primarily designed to keep you alive by anticipating the next event based on your past experience. In other words, the brain is a life-sustaining, data-driven prediction machine.

Understanding the fundamentals of the brain's predictive decision-making strategy is the gateway to understanding how to sell. If you can optimize your own brain behavior, you can train yourself how to recognize and guide your customers' decision-making machinery into buying your product or service, and create a positive customer experience.

Sales Geniuses and Flow

Research in brain science is rewriting everything we thought we knew about how sales and selling actually work. Top performers probably do much of what you do, but they make tiny choices along the way that lead to far different outcomes. It's those incremental decisions which spell the difference between mastery and mediocre results.

Up until recently we didn't understand the science behind superior selling. Today, based on an explosion in our understanding of the brain, we have a good idea.

The Yerkes-Dodson Law

The Yerkes-Dodson Law is named after two guys not surprisingly named Yerkes and Dodson. They get their own law because they were the first to identify the distinct link between stress and performance.[2]

Before we jump right in to superior sales performance, it's important to understand how the brain manages stress. It might seem counter-intuitive that in sales, stress can be positive, but we will see that in some cases stress serves more than a useful purpose. It turns out that superior sales performance depends on it.

Your brain has a specialized system of cells known as your HPA axis, which is short for the hypothalamic-pituitary-adrenal system. The hypothalamus is a gland that is situated just above your brain stem and sends signals to your pituitary gland which sits just below it. When your brain senses a stressful situation ahead, your hypothalamus sends a distress signal to your pituitary gland, which then releases hormones into your bloodstream that travel down to your adrenal glands, located just above your kidneys.

Your adrenal glands, once they get the signal from your pituitary gland that there might be trouble ahead, produce the stress hormone called cortisol. The hormone cortisol is then released into your bloodstream and does things like mobilize glucose (your brain's fuel), to prepare for the possibility of a long siege of stress. This is just one of many defensive tactics your brain employs to keep you alive and thriving.

The Yerkes-Dodson Law, or arc as it is sometimes called, follows a typical bell-shaped curve for gauging the effect of stress on performance. At the bottom of the curve is the state of *boredom*, where lethargy is the soup du jour, a direct result of low levels of cortisol in the bloodstream. In this brain state, everything seems like an endless chore, sales performance is lackluster, and salespeople tend to struggle to get motivated.

At the other end of the curve is what scientists call *frazzle,* where your adrenal glands have produced an excess of the cortisol stress hormone. A frazzle brain state can trigger a whole host of negative outcomes, including, but not limited to: a loss of sleep, loss of appetite, and loss of focus (which hinders your ability to remember and learn). This is because too much cortisol affects the hippocampus, where short term memories are converted into long term memories. Ruminating on a problem or a situation that you can't seem to shake loose from thinking about can be a sign of frazzle.

An overload of cortisol due to chronic stress, technically called "allostatic load," can even eventually have a caustic effect on your immune system, making you more susceptible to illness and disease. Aside from all those undesirable results from prolonged stress, in sales, "frazzle" often leads to burnout, and burnout is the gateway to unhappiness, frequently ending in a career changing decision.

The good news for all of us, particularly salespeople who have mastered their selling domain, is what happens at the top or apex of the Yerkes-Dobson arc, when the relationship between cortisol production and performance are in perfect balance. This is where "good stress" kicks in, and with it comes motivation to hit a deadline, or increased focus on getting an important customer to close, and your selling skills begin to shine like never before. When the brain gets its stress recipe just right, frequently other hormones like adrenaline and dopamine show up. This potent mix of neural chemicals drives the brain to operate at peak performance.

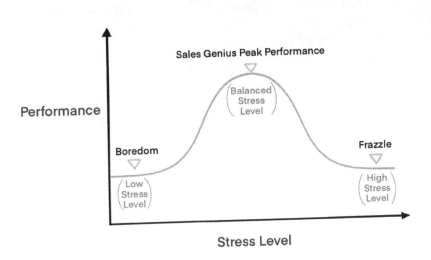

A Sales Genius, what we will describe in this book as the best of the best, achieves an important consequence—sometimes intentionally, but just as often unintentionally. What separates a Sales Genius from the rest is not some preordained ability to sell. Whether these sales experts know it or not, they are operating in a special balanced brain state where just the right amount of cortisol serves to enhance their selling abilities.

This in turn creates a kind of neural harmony where cognition is maximally efficient and sales performance reaches its zenith. This brain state is called *flow*.

Flow

If you've ever played improv games, sports, or jazz music, you may have experienced flow firsthand; it's sometimes called being "in the zone."

Time vanishes and so does your ego. Every thought, every movement seems to follow naturally from the one before it. Self-consciousness and anxieties melt away and the rest of the world seems to disappear. While in flow, you are simply able to perform at your absolute best.

To be clear, flow is not pseudoscience or the latest Internet fad, but is grounded in thousands of hours of well documented cognitive research by highly regarded scientists like Arne Dietrich PhD, author of *Introduction to Consciousness*, and also *How Creativity Happens in the Brain*, and Mihaly Csikszentmihalyi PhD.

It may sound a little fantastical, like an extension of The Force, but flow is a very real brain mechanism, spurred by a combination of brain chemicals triggered in a particular order.

During a flow experience, blood flow decreases in the dorsolateral prefrontal cortex (DPFC). Among other things, this area is responsible for controlling impulses, monitoring behavior, and analyzing actions. The result is a loss of one's sense of self—not in a terrifying way, but in a freeing way. The inner critic is gone. Instead, there is increased blood flow in the medial PFC, which pertains to self-expression and creativity. This state is called hypofrontality.

Flow unlocks the door to in-the-moment flashes of insight and creative problem-solving. This is where Sales Geniuses leave most in their dust. It's an exhilarating feeling, and because it doesn't tax the effortful, analytical systems of your brain, it's also energy-efficient, a high-achieving state in which your brain doesn't consume much fuel.

"The essence of flow is the merging of perception and action, the smooth, rapid-fire integration of sensory input and motor output that cleanly bypasses the centers of higher thought and consciousness," psychologist Arne Dietrich told us when we interviewed him in our previous book, *Brain Apps: Hacking Neuroscience to Get There*.

How can *you* get there? Although there is no guaranteed route to achieve it in every sales transaction, the road to flow involves operating just on the edge of your ability, with supreme focus on perfection. It is like operating in autopilot at the highest level possible while at the same time conserving mental energy, and balancing stress.

You must start with a clear goal, break down the action into small pieces, and practice each piece until you've got it polished, and the entire action becomes second-nature. Regardless of strategy or system, relentless incremental improvement is the essence of all great selling, and this will help lead to achieving a state of flow.

Automation is key.

Dietrich explained the technical side of flow this way: "The motor output from the sensory input, the flow experience, has to be completely automated. Only then can you produce the sequence...otherwise it cannot be in flow. If you have to engage your explicit system your flow is gone. Because obviously, that's the whole point—that your consciousness is disengaged." In other words, if you're "thinking" about what you're doing while you're doing it, you aren't operating in flow.

Still, flow is not zoning out; it's born of intense concentration and dedication—almost a sort of meditation. You see this all the time in professional sports when, for example, the game is on the line and an NBA superstar player stands at the free throw line and coolly, almost robotically, sinks the shot to take the game into overtime. All done with hundreds of thousands watching it play out via telecast. In many ways what makes the game so exciting, and what we are paying for, is the chance to watch that superstar's lack of "nerves" on vivid display, to see *flow* firsthand from the comfort of our recliner.

Each of us has experienced the opposite feeling, when we become incredibly aware and self-conscious of our actions. In those moments, whether trying to sink a putt in a friendly golf game, standing up in front of co-workers to give a presentation, or trying to close a sale, we all know that creeping feeling of doubt and loss of control, with a dose of impending doom thrown in for good measure. In sales, the ability to focus and reach the ultimate state of flow that Dietrich describes is at the heart of super performance.

One way to enhance your selling skills is by practicing a well-documented and scientifically researched brain strategy called meditation. Learning to meditate will improve selling ability? The simple answer is yes. Meditation creates good mental habits that enable more focus and better flow states. Neuroimaging studies conducted by Harvard-affiliated researchers at Massachusetts General Hospital have shown that meditation changes the wiring in your brain after just 8 weeks of practice. If you're not already meditating, it may be time to give it a try.

What happens to the brain during meditation?

When researcher Wendy Hasenkamp was at Emory University, she and her team ran experiments on focused meditation aided by the fMRI[3]. In the end, the researchers came to recognize a distinct pattern among their subjects, a four-phase process involving four distinct brain areas.

As subjects entered the fMRI scanner, they were told to focus on the sensation of their own breathing. The subject's insula, the part of the brain registering present moment awareness, would default towards mind wandering. When that happened and the subject became aware of the fact that they had lost focus and were no longer concentrating on their breathing, they were instructed to press a button.

When the subjects tried to refocus on their breathing, their salience network would take over. This is the part of the brain that registers sudden attention shifts, alerting you to nearby distractions. Your salience network might be more aptly named your distraction network, and for many of us, this network is frequently on high alert. Just attempting to concentrate on your own breaths, something you don't regularly do, becomes a challenge—especially when you're crammed inside an fMRI as the subject of an experiment.

In the third phase, the test subject would attempt to decouple their salience network and wrestle back focus from distraction in order to renew their concentration.

Finally, in the last stage, the prefrontal cortex's executive control center would reestablish its dominance and restore focus on the subject's breath, moving that focused breathing back into awareness.

Regardless of whether we're talking about an experiment on breath concentration or just living our daily lives, this four-stage process of focusing, mind wandering, decoupling and reestablishing focus is a ritual that we practice over and over all day long. The speed at which you can regain and hold focus has enormous implications for everything you do, specifically in learning, and especially in selling.

The good news is anyone can learn to meditate and thereby increase their level of attention and focus. It's not uncommon to hear people say that they've tried meditation and they couldn't keep their mind from wandering. That's actually the point; when your mind wanders, the act that researcher Hasenkamp describes as the third phase of meditation, attempting to wrestle back your focus from distraction, is how your brain builds new pathways.

It's like lifting weights; each time you do a bicep curl, you are technically breaking down the muscle fiber to be rebuilt later, and the end result is a stronger bicep. The practice of forcibly redirecting your attention is building stronger focus and thus new powerful neural pathways. The more you practice meditation, the more incremental improvement you'll see in your ability to focus.

So, it's completely okay in the beginning to struggle with maintaining your attention. In fact, that's exactly what would be anticipated. Practicing daily breath-focused meditation, and constantly forcing yourself back to focus, even for just twelve minutes a day, has been demonstrated to improve willpower, which is a prerequisite for flow and as an added bonus, can lead to an increase in your level of happiness.

Meditation also has an interesting side effect: many people who meditate experience up to an additional hour of quality sleep at night. This additional hour of rest has all kinds of health benefits, including lowering your general level of stress and anxiety. Besides, who couldn't use an extra hour of sleep? Good sleep and practicing focus meditation help lay the groundwork for the flow experience.

To achieve flow, Sales Geniuses operate in a constant state of open mindedness, adopting a regimen of growth through learning, and automation through deliberate practice.

That last paragraph is a mouthful, so let's break it down. To reach Sales Genius status requires setting aside time for learning and practicing in an unending pursuit of selling excellence. As you're well aware, carving time out of an already hectic day is no small undertaking. It brings into balance the difference between what you know you should do, and actually doing it.

From exercise to diet to learning new selling protocols, the hard part is in the doing. The willingness to devote adequate time to learning and improvement—that's where the rubber meets the road, and that's what separates the Sales Geniuses from the "pretty good.'

The ABCs of Selling

In *To Sell is Human*, writer Daniel Pink makes a bold declaration: regardless of our official job title, the majority of us are in sales. After all, if you define "selling" as "an act of persuasion," then don't we all spend our professional lives pushing products, ideas, or advice on someone?

But in addition to rethinking what sales is and who does it, Pink also seeks to overturn our notions of how to do it. In an era of Yelp and ubiquitous online customer reviews, consumers are savvy in ways they've never been before. Lies and slick manipulations won't cut it when all of the information about any given product is only a few clicks away. And that means the aggressive, slicked-back-hair, Alec-Baldwin-in-*Glengarry-Glen-Ross* vision of a sales professional has got to go.

In place of the infamous "Always Be Closing", Pink offers a new sales ABC: Attunement, Buoyancy, and Clarity.

Attunement

Pink argues that being a good salesperson is not just about output, but input as well. He defines attunement as "the ability to bring one's actions and outlook into harmony with the world around you." A champion persuader knows it's not just about hammering one's message, but reading the audience and tailoring your approach from there.

In fact, contrary to stereotypes, evidence suggests that the best sellers are not extroverts, but rather ambiverts—those people who sit at the middle of the introversion-to-extraversion scale. A careful blend of listening, while also staying firm enough to close a sale, seems to be the ticket.

Empathy can be helpful in this regard, but Pink champions what he calls "perspective-taking," which transcends feeling how your customer feels, to thinking how your customer thinks.

One simple way to bring yourself in tune with your audience? The next time you need to make a pitch, try subtly mimicking their body language and facial expressions. (More on this later in the book.)

Buoyancy/Mindset

Of course, all the attunement in the world won't protect you from setbacks. That's where buoyancy comes in. It's slightly more nuanced than simply maintaining a positive attitude; instead, the goal is optimism with a dash of realism thrown in as well.

In place of pumping yourself up with positive affirmations, Pink recommends preparing yourself with questions, like "Can I nail this presentation?" By challenging yourself ahead of time, you can discover weak spots in the presentation and work on improving rough patches prior to presenting. Like a great chess player, you dwell on the solutions to the moves you're likely to encounter from your opponent.

Positivity is important, and Pink notes that it certainly helps to believe in what you're selling, whether it's a Fuller Brush or a new way of video chatting online.

When rejections do come, the goal should be to frame them as a three-step process to minimize their effect.

1. Temporary ("Better luck next time"). This helps to take the sting out of rejection and sets your brain up not to think the setback is forever locked in stone. You recognize sales is in some ways a game of numbers, and persistence often wins the day.

2. Specific ("My problem was that I need to practice using more emotional connecting words in closing"). This moves the brain out of dwelling on the negative and increases the likelihood of incremental improvement towards a goal by becoming more solution focused.

3. External ("This is not a good time in the economy for _____"). This will help you not to see each "no" as a lasting personal judgment about you, but simply a condition of that particular situation. Maybe the vendor is already overstocked on the very product you desire to sell. That's an external issue unrelated to you or your product.

When you look at the Sales Geniuses out there, the people who make sales look effortless, are you encouraged? ("Maybe with hard work, that could be me.") Or does some part of you feel threatened? ("Terry's a natural at sales; I'll never be able to close a deal like that.")

The answer to that question is vitally important, because it's a key window into your selling mindset. In studying human achievement, Stanford professor Carol Dweck repeatedly found that one of the best predictors of success boiled down to the way people saw the world around them. She discovered people exhibited one of two mindsets: growth or fixed.

Are you a fixed mindset salesperson? In a fixed mindset framework, positive traits—in our case, the ability to sell—are seen as innate, or fixed. It suggests that we are all born destined to reach a certain level and then stop. The goal is to hope you turn out to be a member of that race of magic people.

If you approach sales with a fixed mindset, you are discouraged by setbacks—dry periods, difficult customers—because it makes you secretly doubt you've got that "special sauce." Challenges mean risking failure, and failure is devastating, since it seems to reveal an inner truth about just how talented you are—or aren't. When others sell better than you, this sparks jealousy and feelings of your own inadequacy, to the point where you might find yourself rooting for your peers to fail.

Fixed mindset salespeople are wary of change. They don't like learning new systems—after all, trying something different is a form of risk. They resent peers who sell more. Every pitch and every presentation feels do-or-die, and rejections are devastating. It can feel harder and harder to bounce back from each "no."

A growth mindset, on the other hand, suggests that talent, intelligence and so on can be increased with hard work and practice. People operating under a growth mindset are thus willing to try to learn and improve as much as possible, even if it means admitting what they don't yet know.

If you're a growth mindset seller, you're excited by challenges. A finicky customer is an opportunity to test a new persuasion technique. Challenges could mean failure, but failure is a learning opportunity, so the stakes of any one particular interaction might not feel as high. When others sell better than you, your takeaway is, "How can I get there, too?"

Growth mindset salespeople are always looking to expand their pool of knowledge. They might eagerly ask their peers for new tips and tricks. Every pitch and every presentation is a chance to get a little better at selling. Hearing "no's" isn't fun, but it is an opportunity to examine presentations for weak spots that could be improved. Growth mindset is a mixture of optimism and realism that keeps a good salesperson springing back after each rejection.

In a study published in *Proceedings of the National Academy of Sciences*, researchers examined mindset in subjects by asking these kinds of questions and having the subjects rate themselves on a scale of one (never) to five (always). Take a look at these questions and try rating yourself.

- When stuck on something, how frequently do you stop and ask yourself, "What can I do to help myself?"

- When you feel like you aren't progressing, how frequently do you ask yourself, "Is there a better strategy for doing this?"

- When facing difficulty, how frequently do you ask yourself, "What can I do to improve at this?"

Subjects with higher scores, indicating a growth mindset, tended to achieve better outcomes. In following studies, higher scores were also a predictor of greater success in a professional challenge.

These types of questions serve as both a reminder and a guide to adopting a growth mindset that will help propel you past your competition by honing your abilities through continuous challenge and incremental improvement.

Depending on any given situation, you might be more predisposed towards a growth or fixed mindset. It is not an all or nothing proposition. The human brain is complex; you are not always growing or always fixed in your mindset.

The important thing to remember is that although over the years you have habituated certain growth or fixed mindset behaviors, once examined, you have the power to alter your thinking. Mindset is, therefore, a choice. Understanding this allows you to actively cultivate a growth mindset towards, for instance, learning new selling techniques.

Growth mindset is not simply the more enjoyable way to engage with your sales career. In today's fast-paced, ever-shifting market, being willing to change, adapt, and learn is a necessity.

For a real-life example of someone who learned to go from a fixed mindset to a growth mindset, we can look to another arena equally competitive as sales. In her paper "The Mindset of a Champion", professor Dweck discusses the almost-professional baseball career of Billy Beane.

You might remember Billy Beane from Michael Lewis's book *Moneyball*. Beane was the famous Oakland A's general manager who enjoyed numerous successful seasons by combining competent scouting with a wonkish handle on baseball statistics.

Beane as a player is another story. In high school, he was a natural athlete who enjoyed interest from professional teams in baseball, basketball and football. He was considered to be the next big thing, and yet his chosen career in baseball came up short. After stints with several different teams, he eventually washed out of the major leagues.

Unfortunately, Billy Beane's natural talent combined with a history of being rewarded for skill over work ethic probably led him towards a fixed mindset. His reasoning went something like this: *superstars don't and shouldn't need to practice all that much. That's why they're a cut above, that's what defines them as superstars.*

The problem with this approach is that when adversity shows up, the "superstar" has developed absolutely no mechanism for overcoming it. The need for additional help or practice is seen as only highlighting one's personal flaws.

You may be another Billy Beane, born with exceptional talent. But as with the tortoise and the hare parable, it's the willingness to hang in there and keep plodding along on the road of self-improvement that eventually brings the win. Ultimately, becoming a Sales Genius is a never-ending quest for incremental growth.

The good news? Since mindset is just a state of mind, and since the plasticity of the brain means neural rewiring is an ongoing opportunity. Beane was ultimately able to pick up more of a growth mindset by recognizing his shortcomings as an opportunity instead of a detriment and then working diligently towards improvement. Dweck believes this contributed to Beane's eventual success as a GM with the A's.

Clarity

No matter what it is you're selling, a confused customer won't buy. Clarity is the ability to anticipate a customer's true needs—curating information and asking the right questions to get to the heart of the real solution.

For true clarity, it's important to examine the way your sales routines are framed.

For instance;

- If you can narrow down your customer's options to a handful of the most relevant choices, studies show they'll be more likely to bite.

- Assigning a positive label to a person or group can elevate their behavior.

- Experiential framing, that is, pitching not objects but experiences, is a good way to make your pitch more attractive.

- People are more likely to get excited about potential than actual performance, which is why it's great news for you if your idea could be "the next big thing."

Attunement, Buoyancy, and Clarity. It might not trip off the tongue like "Always Be Closing," but as advice goes, it's considerably more helpful.

For that reason, the rest of this book is dedicated to more than just guiding you through the cool cognitive science behind great selling. Instead, it will teach you how to adopt a growth mindset, and how to learn, practice, acquire, and master the techniques necessary to unleash your brain's true potential by moving you into that all-important *flow* experience towards becoming a Sales Genius.

Here is the million-dollar question: *Just how good are you at sales?*

Not too bad, pretty good, above average, amazing?

Research shows that "above average," or "pretty good," although not scientific quantifications, is essentially how most of us see ourselves. Not many of us would rate ourselves as horrible, lousy, mediocre, or even average when it comes to selling.

Some might suggest they have reached Sales Genius status, but that's a bold claim given that our experience has been that roughly only one out of every 25 salespeople operate at this level.

That's why "pretty good" might feel comfortable. Would you agree that like most things, there's always room for improvement? (After all, that's why you're probably reading this book.)

Next question: how did your brain arrive at "pretty good," or any of the evaluative words above for that matter? Chances are you didn't run a spreadsheet, or engage in some deep strengths, weaknesses, opportunities, and threats (SWOT) analysis, and yet intuitively you got there without much deliberation.

In a split second your perception kicked in and supplied you with your answer, whatever it was. We can debate the accuracy of that answer, but not its speed.

That decision speed is at the very foundation of how everyone—yourself and your customers—make decisions. This is very important: your decision wasn't grounded in empirical data, at least not the kind of number crunching we tend to think of when it comes to analysis. Your decision relied on the subconscious part of your brain to deliver an answer on the spot.

Old School Sales Formula

This is game-changing, and why old-school selling is starting to fall by the wayside. Old school salespeople say selling involves a careful, rational exploration of the features and benefits of a product or service, and those ideas, once clearly defined, allow your customer to make a rational purchasing decision in your favor—provided your product or service has good features and benefits.

Features are the "how" of a product–– *brand X paper towel cleans and disinfects by killing harmful bacteria!*—and the benefit is the "what,'–– *what your kids won't catch is a raging stomach virus thanks to the superior disinfecting quality of new and improved brand X!*

Seems straightforward; you've seen those kinds of commercials countless times. Explain the *how* and the *what* in thirty seconds and you're on the way to a sale. *Here are all my products' features, and here are all the products' benefits.* Sales was basically seen as a game of memorizing the feature/benefit list, plus the willingness to run enough commercials on TV to drive home the message, or knock on enough doors to make your rational pitch in person.

And that would be fantastic if that's how your customer's brain made purchasing decisions, following from a rational and logical list of features and benefits.

Spoiler alert: we now know your customer's brain doesn't usually decide that way, thanks to what we've discovered about the subconscious, emotionally-driven brain's amygdala. Sometimes you just sense the answer, in the same way "pretty good," might have felt like a natural description of your selling ability.

The Brain's Dual Decision Mechanisms

One of the evolutionary advantages of the human brain is its ability to operate two different decision-making mechanisms depending on the circumstances. This dual decision capacity allows for speed, accuracy, and efficient energy consumption.

Your subjective assessment of your selling skills just used the first system, which is part of the brain's evolutionarily older limbic system. The limbic system is emotionally driven, and comes to decisions very quickly. Nobel prize-winning psychologist Daniel Kahneman called the mechanism responsible for these lightning-fast, intuitive, unconscious "gut decisions" System 1.

System 2 on the other hand is newer (evolutionarily speaking), slower, and more rational. Rational decision-making is one of the keys to keeping you alive. It allows you to do things like book an airline flight, read and understand spreadsheets, do SWOT, and calculate a tip on a bill—all pretty important in the big scheme of things.

The catch is that System 2 runs about a half second slower than System 1, and consumes more mental energy. It is possible, and even not that difficult, to tire System 2 out.

Feature and Benefit selling is designed to appeal to your System 2, with its analytical process of comparing and contrasting in ever greater specificity. You narrow your options to arrive at a final decision through the process of elimination, and you are mentally aware that you're doing it.

When you're carefully reading the fine print of your company's health insurance policy and trying to decide on your best health selection option, you're engaging in a System 2 task. Choosing a health option is important, can be extremely time consuming, and there is nothing terribly interesting about it, but it still needs to get done. These kinds of tasks are where your System 2 shines.

The more you dig in and try to understand all the legal mumbo jumbo in the health plan's footnotes, the more mental energy you burn. You've probably been through this task before, but since you only do it once every year or so, your memory is a little vague on the particulars.

For the most part, you find yourself in re-education mode, pouring over the facts and trying to make sure you make the right healthcare choice for the upcoming year. And once you've made the decision, chances are you put it out of your mind until next year rolls around. Much like buying license plates or a metro card, it's one of those things that isn't exciting but has to get done.

Your System 2, acting like a buttoned-up accountant, does this kind of work for you without a lot of fanfare; but as stated, it requires a fair amount of mental effort in the process. In this regard, using System 2 is costly to the brain's operation system. As a result, deep analytical decision-making is not the mechanism most of us employ all that often. It's just too tiring.

Here's how the mental effort of System 2 works. You eat food, and that food is converted into glucose. Glucose is the fuel your body and brain run on. Your brain is the hungriest organ in the body, consuming up to 20-25% of the energy from all the food you eat. The problem is that your brain never knows how much glucose you are going to provide it at any given time. Some days you eat a big breakfast, and some days you skip breakfast altogether. You simply don't eat the same foods or quantity every day. And yet your brain, the all-important command and control center, has to run your system regardless of the quantity or quality of the fuel you supply it with.

If you fail to fill your car's gas tank with gasoline or charge its battery, it stops running and won't move again until you resupply it with fuel. What if you skipped breakfast, ran out of fuel mid-morning and crumpled to the ground, lying there still and helpless until somebody was kind enough to shove some food down your throat to bring your brain back online?

Imagine an office setting where all day long people were dropping like flies for lack of a constant glucose supply. Let's face it, there might be a few people at work that you let lay there until the end of the week, gingerly stepping over them, enjoying how much more pleasant the work day was without them.

But there are over 7.53 billion people on the planet and we would never have survived as a species if we operated this way. This is one of the reasons why your brain is so miraculous. It finds a way to keep you going even when you don't constantly regulate the quantity or quality of its fuel supply.

Still, you do pay a price in efficiency. Your brain, in order to save energy, switches over to your more primitive System 1 gut decision-making process. System 1 burns way less glucose and is your default setting when your brain is in fuel conservation mode. Interestingly, your brain follows a similar energy-saving conservation curve as your laptop computer. It saves energy whenever it can.

This means, depending on your diet and exercise regimen—if you exercise regularly your brain stores an additional glucose supply in its cell walls—your brain may not be using your System 2 decision making system all that often. For most people, the quicker but less qualitative System 1 is their go-to. System 1 is short on analytical processing and long on emotional impressions.

System 1 at Work

Emotions

Just how do these emotional impressions form?

In his book *Self Comes to Mind*, Antonio Damasio describes emotions as complex and largely automated neural programs. He writes that emotions can be triggered by real-time events, events of the past, or images related to events. This, in turn, sets off a chain of chemical reactions in the brain. In our case, those chemicals are shaping the customer's buying experience.

Certain kinds of emotions tend to activate specific brain regions, producing a kind of lock and key effect. While at the University of Wisconsin in Madison, psychologist Aaron Heller and his team, using MRI scanning technology, found a link between the emotion of happiness and the brain's ventral striatum. The ventral striatum is part of the brain's reward system and is associated with the "happy hormone" dopamine.

If dopamine was triggered the last time you bought a pair of new shoes, the next time you go shoe shopping that happy hormone is likely to be triggered again. Eventually, shoe buying and dopamine become linked and shoe buying creates emotionally rewarding feelings.

Situations involving fear unlock the brain's amygdala region and trigger additional chemicals associated with fear, like cortisol and adrenaline. Our perceptions of those internal changes are what we call feelings.

Feelings are the body's readout of what's happening internally, combined with your moment-by-moment state of mind. As Damasio says, "Feelings are the consequence of the ultimate emotional process; the composite perception of all that has gone on during emotions—the actions, the ideas, the style with which ideas flow—fast or slow, stuck on an image, or rapidly trading one for another."

During an emotional state, be it positive or negative, our rapid body readouts allow us to weigh the likelihood of reward and punishment, all in an attempt to predict what might happen next and what we'll do about it.

Basic negative emotions like fear, anger, sadness, and disgust can be understood as a more nuanced approach to the evolutionary choices of fight, flight, or freeze.

In primitive times, depending on the level of fear and the context of the situation, you might freeze in place, where you'd begin to breathe shallowly—important if you're trying to remain motionless in order to elude a predator.

On the other hand, you might make a run for it, resulting in an increased heart rate to drive blood into your legs. And your cognitive resources would be redistributed; interest in things like food or sex would temporarily fall by the wayside.

Your customer may no longer have fear of being chased by a lion, but the way their brain would have reacted to that lion in ancient times is still how they deal with troubling situations online, in a showroom, or in a direct sales situation.

Damasio adds that the brain's emotional process follows the same strategy as our body's immune system. When a swarm of outside invaders show up, our white blood cells dispatch a number of antibodies. These cells lock onto the surface shapes of the trespassers in an attempt to neutralize them.

Similarly, when your customer finds themselves in an alarming situation such as problems with performance, damage or delivery, their amygdala dispatches commands to the hypothalamus and the brain stem, increasing their heart rate, blood pressure, respiration pattern, gut contraction, blood vessel contraction and cortisol release, in addition to triggering a metabolic ramp down of digestion, culminating in a contraction of the facial muscles we would read as a frightened or angry expression.

As a salesperson, it's this very condition you should dread. Especially since once the stress hormone cortisol is released in your customer, it has to work its way through the body's system over a period of time. It's the same reason why a child that has been separated from their parent momentarily, when reunited, doesn't immediately stop crying once the parent picks the child up. The child's stress hormone takes time to break down in their bloodstream, and so the crying continues until the cortisol has largely dissipated.

From a customer standpoint, even though you might have apologized for a problem or offered a viable solution, in that moment of anxiety the customer might not immediately be on the same page with you. Multiple apologies and constant reassurance are frequently in order. Taking time to allow the customer to come up to speed on solutions to problems and allowing their cortisol to dissipate, along with a healthy dose of empathy, are some of the hallmarks of the Sales Genius.

Like a dimmer switch, the basic emotions give us graduated options. Thousands of years ago as we evolved, instead of entering full-on combat mode when an encounter went poorly, the aggrieved may have chosen to simply show their disgust towards the instigator, thereby saving precious glucose and decreasing the chance of getting knocked on the head. Or in today's world, the customer might choose not to argue with the salesperson, but simply walk out and shop online or work with a competitor.

In sales, it's essential to understand that emotions are at the core of your reflexive System 1 emotional decision-making. Because emotions evolved as part of a survival strategy for times long ago, the reliance on lightning fast impressions can quickly lead a modern-day customer astray. In a sales situation, human emotion will always be present, and understanding and accommodating for that natural tendency can only enhance the customer's experience.

If your analytical System 2 is like the low-key thoughtful accountant doing the dull, boring, but still important detailed decision work, System 1 is the slightly unpredictable emotional cousin, who can be the life of the party or the bummed-out friend in the corner after a long night of indulgence.

System 1 reacts to your emotions, doesn't express itself through language, burns lower amounts of mental energy, and runs faster than System 2, but frequently produces less accurate decision results.

For quick decisions, your emotional System 1 usually works just fine, and it's the default system that many of us use in our daily lives. It's actually the decision mechanism many of us use almost exclusively, regardless of the nature or magnitude of our decisions.

This is an interesting point. You'd think we would outsource super important decisions like getting married, having children, changing jobs, buying a house, or buying a car to our more rational and thoughtful System 2.

But falling in love, for instance, is an emotionally driven enterprise, and as such System 2 takes a backseat. It's doubtful that you built a detailed spreadsheet, then scrutinized and evaluated it ad nauseum, before you proposed or accepted the proposition of marriage. Have you ever seen a framed spreadsheet next to someone's wedding photos, points all tallied up, proudly exhorting their rational wedding decision?

This might help explain why so many marriages in the United States end in divorce, as love defies an analytical process, and we rely on System 1, our primitive decision mechanism, to call the shots for something as momentous as marriage. This is also why getting married a second, third, fourth, or fifth time is sometimes described as a "triumph of hope over reason.'

Your emotionally dependent System 1 often can be tipped towards a decision based on one or more of the following impressions:

Emotional Tipping Points

It feels easier — (time saving products like phone apps, dishwashers, etc.)

It feels safer — (insurance, home security, guns, etc.)

It feels good — (food, drugs, sex, rock and roll, vacations, etc.)

It makes me feel special — (fashion, name brands, cutting-edge products, etc.)

Notice all four tipping points are based on the subjective perception of how it makes me *feel*. It's important to note they don't pinpoint any kind of exactitude but reflect more of a perceived sensing.

For this reason, these points are not easily encapsulated in a System 2-friendly feature/benefit scenario. They are not objectively verifiable because they are based on emotions, which makes them exceedingly tough to measure. This also means System 1 gut decisions can feel right in the moment, but don't necessarily result in the best decision long-term—as in the high divorce rate in the U.S.

It's System 1 that reaches for the chocolate donut because it *feels good* to do so at that moment, vowing to start healthy eating tomorrow. It's System 2 that understands that the same chocolate donut is five hundred calories, and another pant size in your future.

It's not that System 2's penchant for the deep analysis of feature and benefit are totally overlooked in this scenario, but it takes a backseat to System 1's gut level, rapid fire, feels-right-in-the-moment decision. Again, it's important to point out that System 1's processing speed, although evolutionarily "older technology," runs almost a half second faster than System 2.

This means that System 2 is often late to the decision party. The lightning fast System 1 pushes the memory feedback button––gets a quick feel from past experience and then boom—ladies and gentlemen, we have our decision. It's chocolate donut time!

System 2 shows up after the decision was made and—not wanting to be left out of the loop—rationalizes and thereby legitimizes the decision. Please keep in mind that rationalization occurred after the decision was already done, *not* pre-decision.

How do we know this to be true?

In the 1950's and 1960's, a brain surgery technique was developed to help mitigate some forms of epilepsy. The brain is made up of two separate hemispheres connected by a neural bridge called the corpus callosum. This bridge allows the two hemispheres to communicate with each other. When epilepsy was present in only one hemisphere, surgeons discovered that they could cut the corpus callosum, severing the bridge between hemispheres and as a result keep the epilepsy confined to one hemisphere.

Cutting the corpus callosum is a big deal but not as consequential as you might think. For the most part, the patient goes on to lead a pretty normal life with the odd exception where once in a while, because the two hemispheres are no longer in lock step, the brain sends two separate messages at the same time.

For example, one hemisphere directs you to zip up your jacket, while the other hemisphere implores you simultaneously to unzip your jacket. This leaves the patient in a bit of a quandary.

The bottom line? This surgery pioneered by renowned neuroscientist Roger Sperry led to a series of experiments called the split-brain studies. These studies shattered our understanding of how decisions were actually made. Among the findings was that the left hemisphere interpreted language and the right didn't. Sperry went on to share the Nobel Prize for his split-brain research.

His team discovered that decisions could be coming out of one hemisphere, but the reasoning for the decision was arising in the other hemisphere. Since the corpus callosum had been severed, there was no bridge for the two hemispheres to be sharing information. In other words, the decision and the reason for the decision were not connected.

And to compound the problem, the reason for the decision was, in fact, showing up after the decision had already been made. This was totally backwards. It had always been assumed you came up with a reason to do something first and then decided. That makes sense, but because System 1 fires almost a half of second ahead of System 2, it was discovered that oftentimes people *feel* their way to a decision and then rationalize it afterwards. Decisions, it turns out, can be less about reason and more about feeling your way to an answer with your System 2 providing a neat alibi after the fact. This is one of ways the brain can generate false explanations that are so easily believed.

In the selling process, if the emotional System 1 jumps out first and calls the shots, then feature and benefit selling takes a back seat.

The following example represents your System 1 at work and how your System 2 covers for it:

Imagine you buy a pair of sunglasses you don't really need, and your friend asks you, "Why did you spend so much on those sunglasses?"

The truth, and what actually happened at the split second the decision was made: *"Theses sunglasses will make me _feel_ cool if I buy them."*

What you rationalize a half second later and actually say out loud is, *"The sun was in my eyes, and I was struggling to see, so it made sense to buy these sunglasses right now, even though I have a pair at home."*

In this example, System 1 made the decision based on *feeling* and System 2 rationalized that decision, creating the appearance of true and thoughtful intentionality. This one-two-punch happens over and over again in countless sales situations. Regardless of intelligence, it's not hard to hustle the rational brain.

This is why when questioned about a sunglasses purchase––even though the buyer might not really know why they decided to buy the sunglasses in the first place ––System 2 can frequently supply a plausible "reason" for an impulsive purchase thanks to the ability to generate ready-made answers after the fact.

Recognize in this scenario there wasn't any real analytical thought at play guiding the decision, but by then it's too late. System 1, like Elvis, had already done its thing and left the building.

Let's take a closer look at our sunglasses example. Imagine that the Sunny Sunglasses Company has plowed significant research and development money into their UV and polarization technology. In fact, this might be their entire marketing strategy: doubling down on quality, and promoting the best sunglasses in the marketplace from a vision safety standpoint.

The Sunny sales team has been drilled on selling the outstanding features and benefits of Sunny Sunglasses proprietary UV and polarization discoveries. And yet the real reason someone might be enticed to buy a pair of Sunny's glasses has far more to do with the perceived "cool factor" of the relatively inexpensive purple plastic frames.

The subconscious *feeling* that purple looks good on me—or doesn't look good on me—can easily swamp the more rational expensive technology the sunglasses company staked its sales future on.

When it comes to choosing a child's car seat, you'd think well-articulated features and benefits would be the consumer's number one differentiating factor. After all, what is the purpose of a car seat but to protect your child? Safety features, determined through product testing, should be easy to quantify and list out to a consumer, making car seats a System 2 driven decision.

But internal research at a prominent child's car seat manufacturing showed the reason for picking one car seat over another had more to do with looks and fashion. That's right, fashion. Safety played a role to the extent a consumer assumed the car seat had to be safe or it wouldn't be offered. Let that sink in and you begin to understand the power of System 1 to mess with the rational thinking process.

Clearly the rational reason for a child's car seat is to keep your child safe, but the emotional reason it actually sells might have a whole lot more to do with the trending colors that buying season, and a lot less to do with scrutinizing the safety features or safety record of a particular choice.

Hence, rational feature/benefit selling can often miss the mark. As we have seen, rationalizing is often what we do after the purchase, but subconscious emotional decision-making is frequently at the core of the actual decision. My former brother-in-law, a University professor, once described his car buying experience as carefully researching and weighing all the pertinent car data, and then going with his gut.

This is not to say that System 2 can't take control of the decision, but it generally works the best when it has time to work out the details and thought process ahead of time, and employs a little pre-purchase strategy.

Rational Logic vs Emotion

Most marketing experts know the story of the infamous New Coke rollout debacle—or at least, they might think they do.

April 23, 1985, the day New Coke was introduced, marks one of the most notorious corporate sales blunders of the last century. "What group of geniuses could look at a time-tested brand like Coca-Cola and decide to reconfigure the product's formula?" we ask rhetorically. "What were they thinking?" After all, what was—and still is—the most beloved cola on the planet?

If you're like most people, your answer would probably be "Coke." And you'd be right—and wrong.

As a Pepsi TV campaign once famously showed us, a blindfolded person tends to prefer Pepsi over Coke. And yet, culturally, Coke is the icon and Pepsi is the runner-up, the also-ran. Pepsi has never even come close to touching Coca Cola's sales numbers—1.8 billion bottles per day as of this printing.

"Culturally" is the keyword here. Over a century of marketing momentum has enmeshed Coke in our brains, building strong unconscious System 1-driven emotional associations with childhood, America, sports, nostalgia, and Christmas.

Even the modern red-suited version of Santa Claus came from a Coca Cola ad; before that, Santa had no official outfit. Years and years of past "feel good" experiences mean that when you pop open a can or bottle of

Coke, you're not just drinking any old brown carbonated liquid. You're drinking the distillation of a thousand images, ideas, and positive emotional memories.

And so, for a purely logical person focused on the benefit of superior taste, Pepsi would be the choice over Coke hands down. But in a contest of what feels good, and what makes me feel special, Coke reigns supreme thanks to our media-saturated world.

And in fact, it's possible to know exactly what those Coke execs were thinking back in the eighties. They'd done their homework, and time after time in blind taste tests, New Coke was found to be the clear favorite over existing Coke.

New Coke's lighter, sweeter flavor seemed to be the obvious winner. (This is generally true; with nothing else to go on, blind tasters tend towards an option that can supply more of a sugar rush, whether it be Pepsi or a sugar-hyped newer version of Coke.) Based on the research, switching the formula to a sweeter one seemed like a slam dunk, a no brainer, money in the bank.

The trouble is, life is not a blind taste test.

As we've noted, frequently, even the most rational among us do not employ System 2's logical, analytical decision process all day. Our emotional, instinctive System 1 rules the day, and so instead of rejoicing at the new—dare we say more Pepsi-like—formula, loss aversion kicked in and swamped the new Coke brand.

Loss Aversion

In addition to a penchant for sweet-tasting things, System 1 has a built-in cognitive bias: it hates the feeling of losing. For the emotional part of the brain, a loss is a big deal. The brain often weighs a loss as more than twice as powerful as a win. The trouble wasn't just the change—itself disconcerting—but the sudden unavailability of the Old Coke. Nothing could soothe the pain of no longer being able to access those built-in associations of warm, fuzzy memories just by pouring a tall, fizzy glass of familiar cola product.

And so, the Coca-Cola company learned its lesson, quickly pivoting back to what they now called "Coca-Cola Classic," a fitting term for this classic tale of image over substance, and one bubbly brown drink over another.

But in terms of sales and the big scheme of things, the real issue wasn't really about Coke vs. Pepsi. The real issue was which of the brain's two decision processes was going to make the final call, and on what basis: logic and taste or emotion and memory association?

Imagine the frustration of being a Pepsi executive and realizing that you produce a drink which, by empirically objective standards, a majority of people judge as tasting better. Yet, because of the brain's emotional decision process you suffer sales defeat again and again to the runner-up in taste.

The take-home message is simple. Sales Geniuses, the best of the best, generally make their pitch to the brain's System 1 whether they know it or not. It's capitalizing on stored memories and feelings. That's where the gold is. To increase your selling chances, you must appeal to your customer's emotional sense of feeling good, feeling safer, making something easier, or feeling special. Remember to keep in mind the power of loss aversion.

Loss aversion is one of the reasons the gambling haven Las Vegas exists. If rational thinking was the default for everyone, when someone lost money on a bet in Vegas, they would naturally stop betting. Yet, this is often not what happens. It is common for someone who loses on the first try to keep betting in order to recoup their initial loss. This is a perfect example of loss aversion in action. Since the feeling of losing is twice as strong as the feeling of winning, System 1 drives the emotional need to mitigate loss. The negative feeling of losing the bet makes a person double down on their next bet.

Ironically, the end result is typically more loss. This is one way your System 1 "feeling brain" is not always working in your best interest, both in gambling and certain buying scenarios.

Loss aversion is one of the reasons why a sale on a limited time offer is so effective. As the end of a sale deadline approaches, a potential customer's System 1 kicks in and the emotional sense of losing the discounted price beckons towards buying before it's too late. Timestamping a sale with specificity, like "The sale is over at 12 p.m. on Saturday, June 10th," creates even more urgency to buy.

One caveat: if a vendor is constantly repeating the time-dated sale, a customer's brain becomes conditioned and responds with less emotional chemicals, thereby lessening the effect. As a result, one of the keys to a good sales promotion is randomness, where the brain is surprised and thus treats the event as a unique occurrence.

Building Memory

Salespeople are in the memory business. The words in a conversation immediately disappear after they are spoken, and your customer must remember what was said in order to pick up the information you're trying to convey.

It's not just the sales process. In your everyday life, you have to remember what someone told you a minute ago, a day ago, a month ago or even years ago. Recalling past conversations stored in memory is a functional must.

The Homo sapiens brain can be described as a three-process approach to storing memory. Scientists refer to these processes as short-term memory, working memory, and long-term memory.

Working memory is sometimes spoken of as interchangeable with short-term memory, but they are slightly different. Short-term memory is older terminology and can simply be described as the retention of immediate information. Working memory is the real-time application of what you just retained.

For example, trying to remember an address would involve your short-term memory, and if simultaneously you were trying to take in directions someone was giving you to that address, that would be your working memory in action. Working memory is therefore the memory being applied for use.

When the brain is first introduced to new information, it goes into a temporary holding tank: your short-term memory. It functions much like a chalkboard; it generally gets overwritten after a brief period of time, depending on a whole host of factors like your stress level, your interest level at the time you acquired the information, and so on.

Your short-term memory holds information for roughly 20-30 seconds—just enough time to remember where you parked your car, for example.

Have you ever parked your car, and then come out of a grocery store fifteen minutes later unable to find it? That's an example of short-term memory failure. Think about that: a car is on average 15 feet long, five feet high, six feet wide, and weighs in at just under 3000 pounds. That's an enormous thing to lose in a parking lot, but it is a perfect illustration of how fickle your short-term memory can be.

As such, vast amounts of the world your senses perceive are no more than fleeting impressions, retained in an instant and then dumped out. This is why we can lose something as large as an automobile.

Short-term memory is like a video camera, constantly recording snippets of your life, and then recording over them almost immediately. Some of those snippets your brain, through a process not entirely understood, will decide to retain. Those retained snippets then get uploaded into your long-term memory storage for further consideration and practical application down the road.

We can—and do—talk about long-term memory as a storage facility, but it should be understood that there is no single storage area. In fact, memories are stored in bits and pieces of cells throughout the brain and when summoned, are reconstituted to recreate the original memory.

Depending on the circumstances of when you recall the memory, other information can be added or bits of the original memory can be deleted. Due to the changeability of memory, the more times you remember an event, the less accurate and stable the memory becomes. The first time you remember something will likely be the most accurate; after that the particular memory will degrade over time.

This is why you or your customer may recall an event with minor, or sometimes significant, detail changes. Memories are not exact replications of what has occurred in the past. And yet our information retention depends upon this faulty system. For better or worse, that system is vitally important. With lightning speed, your brain is able to access those memorable experiences and use them to help you make decisions.

Without memory, a person can't really function in the world. This is part of why dementia and Alzheimer's disease are so devastating.

Remembering what happened before allows you the possibility of modifying your next decision for improved results. If you became terribly ill the last time you had shellfish, then that bit of information is vital in deciding whether to sit down to a big plate of lobster.

Part of the brain's memory warehousing mechanism includes a coding system—not barcodes of course, but a system that's proven to be effective for hundreds of thousands of years. Through the use of chemical markers, your brain can attach emotional feelings to a past experience. And these emotional markers allow your brain to locate and access a past experience in the blink of an eye.

When you recall your fourth-grade birthday party, you replay what feels a little bit like a mind movie in your head, but it's not a sterile recollection because accompanying your mind movie are some of the feelings you experienced at the time. And depending on the memory, those feelings that have been coded to the event can be amazingly powerful in the replay. This serves three purposes.

First, the feelings that are glued to the memory give your brain an efficient sorting method to pull that memory back up to re-experience.

It's like a trail of chemical breadcrumbs for the brain to follow when accessing memories.

Second, the emotionally rich memory allows you to compare and contrast against a current impending decision. This gives you some valuable insight into possible outcomes, good or bad, and saves you from potentially repeating an unwanted result.

Lastly, attaching feelings to a memory helps to enhance the rich tapestry of your experience and serves to create meaning to your life.

Sometimes those remembered experiences can be less than desirable.

This is why a veteran returning from a war can suffer from PTSD, Post-traumatic Stress Disorder. In battle, the brain has linked chemical emotion markers to a frightening experience. In this kind of situation, the event can be so laden with chemical markers, in the form of terrible feelings, that the brain gets stuck on the battle memory and keeps re-looping the soldier's mind movie.

This is not relegated to war experiences. When it comes to picking a restaurant, our brains hold onto the memory of a poor food-related encounter. If you recall that the food was unappetizing the last time you dined out, that your server was surly, or that the restroom was dirty, those momentary reflections can doom an establishment in your mind for good.

Recently, scientists have come to understand that the brain's memory warehouse is much more robust than we ever thought. Subtracting for sleeping hours, your brain stores pretty much your entire waking life in its memory vault. But it tends to only access those memories that have been more powerfully coded with chemical emotion markers for recall.

In his book *Brain Rules*, John Medina writes that there is a shortcut into building more powerful memories: "Emotionally charged events are better remembered–for longer, and with more accuracy–than neutral events." Essentially, when your emotions get fired up, System 1—which we've seen helps form and power your emotions—releases dopamine, which creates the markers to enhance memory and information processing.

Sales promotions that involve bright colors, unique characters, and weird situations capitalize on this effect of dopamine release for emotionally charged events creating more sticking power. That's why an insurance company might choose an animated character like a gecko as its spokesperson, or more accurately its spokes-gecko. It fills the bill completely for remembrance, bright color, unique character and weirdness.

It's why you might not remember what you ate for dinner a week ago, but you can probably still conjure up some strong recollections of your favorite elementary school teacher—or conversely, your least-favorite teacher. When feelings are activated, memories stick.

This is why, although your brain has the information somewhere in its memory warehouse of what you had for dinner a week ago, the relatively non-remarkable event is not something your brain will position at the front of the warehouse for quick access.

This sorting of what the brain deems as vital and important information versus general and mundane information is critical for decision-making. Suppose you considered buying a new car, and to help out your brain opened its memory warehouse and accessed every car you have ever seen, and every bit of car data you've taken in. The sheer overload would swamp any attempt to make sense of a new car purchase against a lifetime of car-related information your brain had chronicled. Attaching emotional markers in a top-down hierarchical fashion is vital to the way people operate and make decisions.

Scientists understand the process of memory—the nuts and bolts—including the warehousing and stack ranking of memories, but how it all actually takes place inside the brain is still an unfolding mystery.

The Power of Recall

We are an almost alarmingly forgetful species. In his famous memory experiments, Psychologist Hermann Ebbinghaus found that within 30 days, most people forget 90% of what they've recently learned. Part of your job as a salesperson is to make you and your products or services stick in your customers' minds. Fortunately, there's an easy brain hack for this.

So, how can you connect your sales offerings with powerful emotions? Here's one trick top salespeople already know on some level, even if they can't put it into words: don't sell objects, sell experiences. "Several researchers have shown that people derive much greater satisfaction from purchasing experiences than they do from purchasing goods," notes Daniel Pink in *To Sell is Human*.

To underscore this idea, Pink cites a study by Leaf Van Boven and Thomas Gilovich which asked half the survey respondents to describe their feelings about their most recent purchase of an experience (say, tickets to a show), and the other half to do the same with their most recent material purchase.

The study found that experiential purchases made people happier, added more to their overall life happiness, and generated less regret after the fact.[4]

This may seem like bad news if you sell a material good, but it doesn't have to be. The same study also noted that the line between the two can be extremely blurry. Whether a customer sees a purchase as a physical good or an investment in an experience can come down to the way it's framed.

A good salesperson highlights the various features of their product. A Genius salesperson uses those features to tap into customer emotions by painting a vivid picture of how life will be with that product—the doors that will open for them.

High-end catalogues use these tricks all the time with blurbs that sometimes read more like short stories than product features.

A new kitchen is more than a collection of cabinets and appliances; it's a place where the family will gather to share meals, do homework, and entertain. A brand-new blender is an investment in a healthy, active lifestyle, as opposed to a machine that breaks and grinds fish up into small edible chunks ala the "Bass-o-matic" from the iconic Saturday Night Live sketch. New clothes or makeup will result in a more confident self-image, leading to new outings and a new attitude and potentially the person of your dreams.

Sales Geniuses use words to build mental movies, creating scenes that have the power to activate emotional memory markers and stick in the brain. Worried your product isn't "cinematic" enough? Don't be. These movies can be built around the most mundane products.

Imagine that you are tasked with selling a carpet stain remover. You could discuss the formulation of powerful chemicals, or highlight your product's recycled packaging. Maybe you would brag about the prominent people or agencies endorsing your product or the incredible number of spray bottles you've already sold. These feature/benefit pitches are familiar to you; the airwaves are full of them.

Now imagine evoking a scene for your customer:

So, you're hosting a dinner party in your recently remodeled living room, when your best friend half-trips over the coffee table, spilling red wine all over your brand-new white couch.

Essentially, it's a kind of horror story. The idea of pristine furniture being forever stained is a powerful scenario. That this accidental act of destruction could come from your best friend only adds to the mental discomfort and stress of the whole situation. Altogether, this picture fires the amygdala's fear response, delivering a healthy shot of the stress hormone cortisol. Increased cortisol levels boost memory formation, and these memory markers in turn drive the brain towards a viable solution.

In this format, the emotional decision-making System 1 comes online, and before System 2's analytics can offer any kind of debate the credit card is out and the purchase is being made. Offering an emotional solution that saves your best friend's dignity and your new couch to boot feels like giving the brain the superpower of a do-over. It doesn't get much better than that. No description of active chemicals or cool packaging has nearly the effect.

And this is all achieved by tying together your best friend, your expensive couch, the destructive powers of red wine, and finally the deal-closer, the power you'll possess to make everything all better again. When explained in this way, you can begin to see how your emotional System 1 brain falls prey to an experience-driven sales pitch. The Homo sapiens brain is built to seek comfort, be it physical or mental, and will go to great extremes to find it.

Of course, fear-based sales has been around a long time. The entire insurance industry was built on the back of the brain's System 1. Basically, in an insurance sale, you're fearful something bad might happen—say, your house burning down, or you becoming seriously ill—and the insurance company is assuaging those fears by taking your regular monthly payment in exchange for peace of mind. (We are not saying insurance is a bad thing, simply that the brain processes it through System 1, and therefore, that kind of sale is extremely potent.)

That's not to say that System 1 isn't also susceptible to the prospect of positive experiences. How many car commercials have you seen featuring beautiful people careening around a picturesque mountain, having the time of their lives, seemingly ignorant of the sheer drop-off and dangerously narrow road with its countless winding turns? That sense of freedom from the ho-hum capitalizes on the brain's production of dopamine, a chemical that rewards risk-taking.

If the music is just right, you might find yourself feeling something deep down that will trip memory and thereby initiate a buying response. Never mind that the new car does not come with the beautiful people, the mountain scenery, or the highly potent music ushering in each turn.

These mental movies have been a mainstay since the advent of television advertising, but now brain science is revealing just how much more powerful they are than the typical dry delivery of face-to-face feature/benefit sales. Sales Geniuses, through the use of colorful words and storytelling, summon the brain's memory response much like a well-crafted visual commercial.

Spaced Learning:
A Memory Hack for Learning Faster

How else can memory be heightened? How can you hack your own memory to remember all the new brain information and selling techniques?

When you hear the term "spaced learning", you might think it has to do with learning that takes place while you're "spaced out." But spaced repetition or spaced learning is the less-than-catchy phrase used to describe a scientific breakthrough in memory acquisition.

Pretty much everyone has something they wouldn't mind learning, whether it's a new language, a dance move, or just a way to memorize all their Internet passwords. Is there a way we can leverage what we know about how the brain works in order to more efficiently retain information?

In a word, yes. It turns out that if you space out your study sessions, you'll remember more, and it will even take fewer total hours of studying.

Spaced repetition, as it's called, takes advantage of a quirk of the memory: the spacing effect. Basically, we learn more if we allow time between study sessions so that the brain has room to develop new neural connections. In "How to Remember More of What You Learn with Spaced Repetition," Thomas Frank likens the phenomenon to building a brick wall: for the most solid construction, you need to allow time for each layer of mortar to dry.[5]

But if you space out your learning, won't you start to forget your lessons? Yes...but if you do it right, that's actually an asset.

In his book *How We Learn*, science reporter Benedict Carey outlines his "Forget to Learn" theory, in which memories have two strengths: storage strength and retrieval strength.

Storage strength doesn't actually deplete with time. Once the brain considers information important, that information resides somewhere in your head. You can train up your storage strength through repeated recall.

Retrieval strength, on the other hand, is your ability to actually dredge up the information. As you might know if you've ever had someone's name on the tip of your tongue, it can leave you quickly and without warning. Regular maintenance is required to keep it running smoothly. When you forget something you once knew, it's a matter of faulty retrieval strength.

Learning is fundamentally about sticking something into your memory for retrieval later. During a learning episode, information first moves into your short-term memory and creates a new neural pathway. If that pathway is repeatedly stimulated, that retrieval triggers the brain to transfer the information into your long-term memory. The neural pathway acts as both conduit and code for that information upload. Therefore, strengthening that pathway through repetition is key to long-term learning.

This process has been well known in the scientific community for some time. But what if there was a way to speed up learning, to absorb an entire history module that would normally take a month in about an hour? In his *Scientific American* article "Making Memories Stick", neuroscientist Douglas K. Fields says it's possible.[6]

Fields and his research team did experiments to determine how much time was optimal in terms of the brain's ability to absorb new information.

Due to the limitations of attention bandwidth, 15 to 20 minutes was assumed to be the gold standard for human focus and concentration. Much more than that and the brain begins to move into default mode—daydreaming or mind-wandering.

Knowing this, Field's team began to experiment with how much time was required between learning sessions. In other words, how long should you wait before engaging in a second learning module? They were surprised to discover the interval of time *between* learning sessions was even more critical than the actual time devoted to a learning module. So, what's the magic number? About 10 minutes.

It appears that 10 minutes is the optimal time the brain needs to upload information and translate it into long-term memory. Spaced learning is all about leaving the right amount of "space" between learning hunks of information.

If that sounds strange, this might sound even stranger. In order to facilitate the uptake of information, Fields suggests that you spend the 10-minute break portion doing some sort of physical activity, like playing catch with a ball or modeling with clay. This kind of rote motor activity allows the part of the brain involved in memory acquisition to tune up and operate without interference from competing thought processes.

In a teacher resource titled "Spaced Learning: Making Memories Stick," Angela Bradley and Alec Patten outline an ideal spaced learning protocol:

- Input of key facts/information, ideally 10-15 minutes
- 10-minute break doing an unrelated activity
- Recall of key facts/information
- 10-minute break doing an unrelated activity
- Application of key facts/information

This sequence of input, recall, and application, sandwiched with breaks of physical activity, leverages how the brain assimilates information and provides a shortcut for rapid learning. This is how a month's worth of lessons can be uploaded into the brain in about an hour.

So, what are the implications, and specifically how can you apply this information to gaining the most from this book? How can you use this to accelerate your path to sales mastery?

As you read through the book, you will come across bolded key concepts you'll need to commit to memory for later use during a selling experience. To do this, we need to follow the learning protocol above. For example, later in the book we introduce the concept of the Rule of Threes. The Rule of Threes is a technique that Sales Geniuses employ to reduce the time a customer spends in the selection process and at the same time improve their actual selection and likelihood of purchase.

Using the protocol, you would take ten to fifteen minutes to read the section on the Rule of Threes with the intention of absorbing as much information as possible. Then you would close your book or tablet, and do a physical activity that doesn't require a lot of thought like throwing a ball, a quick bout of dancing, or tic tac toe. The activity doesn't have to be terribly physical—modeling with clay works—it just needs to be an activity that doesn't require much System 2 analytical thinking. A physical activity, even a mild one, switches the neural wiring in your brain, allowing for an easier uptake into long term memory for the selling technique you are trying to learn.

After the ten-minute break, you would take out a sheet of paper and write down as much information as you could recall from the Rule of Threes section. After you've exhausted your recall, you would open your tablet or book back up and carefully review the Rule of Threes section again, comparing it to what you had written down to see if you missed any important points. Then you would take another ten-minute break. After that break, you would write down examples for how you could apply the Rule of Threes in your next selling session.

By following this spaced learning protocol of learn, break, review, break, and then mentally imagining how you can utilize the Rule of Threes concept in an everyday life scenario, you are engaging specific regions of your brain to maximize memory retention and create deeper concept understanding.

If you find yourself saying, "You've gotta be kidding me, this is how I'm supposed to read this book? It will take me forever," we understand. First, we aren't suggesting you read the entire book this way. You are already roughly 15% through the book and we are only introducing the spaced learning concept now.

You would employ this strategy when you get to a section that will require you to double down in order to absorb fundamental selling concepts, such as the buying patterns which will be coming up later. And it's not just our book; this is a great strategy to have in your back pocket when you have to absorb a lot of information, like when a manufacturer comes out with new specifications on a particular product or system.

The following graph shows a quick visual snapshot just how powerful this tool is when it comes to maximizing memory and learning.

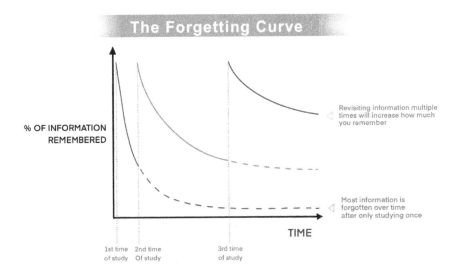

Are you worried that you'll forget key information in the ten-minute break between first reading about the concepts and reviewing them? Don't be. Here's the other half of Carey's theory: *the greater the dip in your retrieval strength (your ability to recall the information), the stronger that memory will be when accessed again.* It's the reason you might still remember an elementary school spelling bee word you tripped up once upon a time. All you have to do is be sure you access it again on a reasonable time table.

Carey found that if you want to remember something in a week, you should allow a one to two-day gap between your first and second study session. If you'll be tested in a month, that gap expands to a week. If three months, two weeks. If six months, three weeks. And if you want to remember something in a year, you should space out your learning sessions by a month. (That said, 27 days or 32 days is fine; these are all approximations.)

The next time you set out to really incorporate some new information, consider setting up reminders on your phone or other personal device at the appropriate spacing. You can use the protocol we've outlined for learning the key bolded concepts in this book, and then use Carey's method of following up periodically to make sure you've secured the key concepts in your long-term memory. Your brain, and your customers, will thank you.

Attention

Creating memory in your own brain to learn new sales techniques is essential. Creating memory in your customer's brain to understand and remember new products is one of the keys to selling. But before you can do that, you need their attention. Clearly if there is no attention, there will be no subsequent memory, or sale. And yet that's a tall order because we know that your customers' brains' default mechanism is to daydream in order to save energy.

We used to believe you were either awake or asleep, but now we know that parts of your brain can be shut down or on hold during your waking state depending on your brain's operating strategy. If you didn't get enough sleep the night before, if you're stressed out, if you're not exercising, if you're eating poorly—these are but a few of the conditions that will force your brain to change its operating strategy. Remember your brain's main goal is to keep you going, and it does what it has to in that effort, shifting resources and energy consumption to meet that goal. If this means shutting down certain functions during your waking state, then so be it.

Attention is one of the high energy-consuming properties your brain guards jealousy, and so once your brain determines you are probably not in danger in that moment, it tends to dial down attention and subsequent memory acquisition.

We are all aware of how easily our attention wanes. How many times have you found yourself struggling to pay attention, distracted by the littlest of things like the ticking of a clock, even though you know you should really be listening?

This is great news from an energy conservation standpoint, but if you're in sales and your customer begins to dial down attention, your chances of selling evaporate. Attention is not a commodity a Sales Genius can afford to squander.

Wouldn't it be cool if every human had a sensor on their forehead, which would glow bright green when customers were paying attention and glow bright red when their thoughts were elsewhere? What a tremendous advantage you would have in a sales situation knowing that your customer was totally focused or that they had completely tuned you out.

It would probably shock you how often your customer's brain sensor would be reading red. Many of us think we know when someone is listening by ticking through the following checklist:

1. Their eyes are directed towards me

2. They are smiling while I'm speaking

3. They are gently nodding their head along with my words

These are, after all, well established signs that someone is paying attention to you, right?

Yes, but with a caveat, sometimes those three behaviors can indicate attention but unfortunately, not necessarily. As you grow up, social customs dictate making eye contact is a matter of simple politeness. You learned this early: "Look them in the eyes when you're speaking." Unfortunately, you can be staring at someone or something and still completely zone out in the moment, barely even aware of what you are looking at. We all do that a lot.

Smiling and nodding your head are also pretty much hardwired into human interaction. If a complete stranger on the street makes eye contact with you, then smiles and nods at you, your System 1 will engage and you'll be smiling and nodding back at them often without even realizing you're doing it.

This leaves you as a salesperson in a bit of a dilemma. Your customer may be looking at you, smiling, and nodding along with your talking points; but if you could magically open their skull and peer inside their brain, you'd realize what they were actually thinking in that moment was, "Did I remember to turn off the coffee maker this morning before I left?"

How many times have you been on the other side of a sales interaction where the salesperson was prattling on about something that you really didn't care about and you found your own mind wandering? Keeping your focus in any interaction can be tough. **Attention, memory, and brain overload are three of the toughest conditions a salesperson must overcome.**

We currently don't have readout sensors on our foreheads indicating our level of attention, but you might be surprised to find that humans are walking around with another built-in brain mechanism that will give you a strong indication of attention level.

If I asked which part of the brain can you see with the naked eye, you'd most likely say you can't see any of the brain because it's encased in your skull. Spoiler alert: your eyes are actually part of the brain, linked through a cable called your optic nerve.

Your brain activity is registered through the pupils, the dark dot at the center of the eye. When someone is paying attention to you, their pupils tend to dilate. The pupil acts like a miniature rheostat, increasing in size when there is more neural firing and decreasing in size when there is less.

This means that by observing the relative size of a person's pupils at the start of a conversation and monitoring them as you speak, you can do a quick gauge on their level of attention. Enlarged pupils probably mean that someone is actually paying attention to what you are saying, but if the pupil size begins to decrease this may indicate that the person is beginning to mentally rest, lose focus, or even daydream.

Understanding the link between brain activity and pupil dilation is a relatively newer scientific phenomenon, but taking advantage of pupil dilation has been a mainstay in the upscale restaurant industry for a long time.

Upscale restaurants often dim their lights at night. This is the exact opposite of what you might expect logically. Wouldn't it make more sense to turn the lights up as nighttime sets in? Why the dimming of the light? It creates ambiance or atmosphere, of course, but how is it helpful to the restaurant when it's tougher to see? To understand that, we need to get in the wayback machine and take a quick trip back in time.

One theory about dimming light is that our ancient ancestors came to see the evening campfire as a pleasant and safe time, where predators were kept at bay due to the fire, and the clan could gather together for eating and sharing the day's events. Even today, humans are still hardwired in this way. We are very much social animals and the idea of an evening fire is still cherished by many people throughout the world.

It would be a bit of a problem if your favorite restaurant set about lighting fires near every table to recreate the mood and ambiance associated with the coming of dusk, so they do the next best thing.

Once the restaurant's lighting has dimmed is when brain science takes over. The dimming reduces the amount of light coming to the eye, and to compensate, the pupil automatically enlarges to take in more light. The System 1 emotional part of the brain keeps subconscious tabs on that sort of behavioral change and it registers in the observer's brain as heightened attention.

If I am sitting across from you and I subliminally pick up on your increased pupil dilation, I am likely to register this as you are starting to pay more attention. And since humans tend to be "me-driven," I'm likely to interpret that attention as directed towards me. In other words, it appears that you are suddenly more interested in me, and what I have to say.

This new-found interest tends to be reciprocated or mirrored back, and with all this attention exchange going on, we are likely to stay in the restaurant a little bit longer. This leads us to order more entrees, drinks and possibly dessert. And since our logical guard is now down, we succumb to our own brain's emotional trickery by ordering a piece of cheesecake and telling ourselves that since we are sharing it, the caloric intake is almost negligible.

As the bill mounts up, so does the tip. All of this has happened simply by making it a little harder for customers to see in the restaurant. And likely, unbeknownst to the restaurant staff, by dimming the lights they are taking advantage of the brain's visual and perceptual operating system to help pay the rent.

In the 1960's and 1970's, psychologist Eckhardt Hess studied the situations in which pupils dilate, beyond simply trying to let more light in. He found––and modern scientists have been able to replicate this–– that when test subjects are given increasingly difficult math problems, their pupils grow as they concentrate harder and focus more...up to the point where they can no longer solve the equations, when their pupils begin to shrink.

Bottom line: if a customer is paying attention to you, their pupils will either remain steady in size or increase from the onset of your conversation. However, if their pupils begin to shrink, then just like the test subjects, their focus is diminishing. Although humans don't have colored sensors on their foreheads to indicate attention level, pupil dilation turns out to be the next best thing. Paying attention to the eyes of your customer is really paying attention to their brain activity. Either way this subtle readout is the kind of activity that a Sales Genius is constantly monitoring.

If your customer's pupils are shrinking, you must react quickly to regain their attention. Lost attention equals a lost sales opportunity. If your customer stops paying attention, then they are no longer recording information in their memory, and if their memory is shut down or overloaded, then it's game over for you.

How Can I Keep My Customer's Attention?

There is a lot of conflicting information about the length of the average person's attention span. You might have heard the statistic that the modern human attention span has shrunk from 12 seconds in 2000 to 8 seconds by 2015. This is pretty alarming. It's also probably not true.

BBC writer Simon Maybin traced this figure back to the source and found an entry in a website called Statistic Brain but no attribution: no study, no person or institution to contact, and no proof.[7]

Instead, he quotes psychology lecturer Dr. Gemma Briggs, who notes that the very idea of a standard measure of average attention span doesn't hold any water. Simply put, it depends on who you are and what you're doing at a given moment. You may find your focus sliding away from you after five minutes of attempting to do your taxes, but at the same time, you could be riveted by a movie for a lengthy period.

What about paying attention to a demonstration or a talk? While there aren't many studies specifically for sales, research into student attentiveness during classroom lectures might provide the closest picture.

A 2010 study asked students to measure the timing and length of their lapses in attention during a lecture. The most common length of an attention lapse was a minute or less. As for the distribution, Saga Briggs (no relation to Gemma, we assume) reports,

"...the first "spike" in reported attention lapses occurred just 30 seconds into a lecture segment, reflecting the "settling-in" period; the next spike occurred at 4.5 to 5.5 minutes into the lecture; the next at 7 to 9 minutes; and the next at 9 to 10 minutes in."[8]

This "waxing and waning" pattern persisted throughout the lecture, the researchers said. By the end, disruptions in attention happened roughly every two minutes. All of which is to say, when you're estimating your customer's willingness to focus on you, it's best to be conservative. Don't assume you'll have their undivided attention forever. The longer you talk, it's likely the less they are listening.

Still, all is not lost. Briggs included some tips for better capturing focus, and many can easily be tweaked for sales. For instance, you'll keep your audience more engaged the more you involve multiple senses. Judicious use of humor allows for livening things up, and when possible, present your ideas in a narrative or story format with plenty of emotional substance.

Choice Overload

Have you ever found yourself getting overwhelmed in a Big Box store? Maybe you came in for one or two items but were quickly overloaded with the sheer magnitude of product offerings. You might even find yourself leaving without anything in hand.

One of the great misconceptions about selling is that the more product offerings you have, the more sales you'll make. After all, who doesn't like more choice?

The famed ice cream purveyor Baskin-Robbins made this a point in their unending marketing campaign by touting a whopping 31 flavors. Bresler's, a Baskin-Robbins competitor, advertised 33 flavors, hoping, I suppose, that the addition of two more flavors would be that watershed moment when people came to their senses and realized 31 flavors was simply not going to cut it anymore. And still it may come as no surprise to learn that the two most popular flavors are chocolate and vanilla.

Evolutionarily, the brain was not designed for endless choice opportunities, and as the pace of life and choice options have escalated, our poor brains simply can't keep up. Making choices burns a lot of brain glucose, and this leads to systematic overload, a condition that increases anxiety and doesn't, contrary to what marketers would have you believe, increase your likelihood of purchase—or happiness.

This was borne out by three clever experiments conducted by Sheena S. Iyengar of Columbia University and Mark R. Lepper of Stanford University. They summed up their findings in a paper entitled, *"When Choice is Demotivating: Can One Desire Too Much of a Good Thing?'*

To carry out their first experiment regarding choice overload, they used a popular boutique grocery store in California known for its exceptionally large product offering. In this store, they set up two tasting kiosks for gourmet jams. One kiosk offered a large array of 24 different jams for tasting, while another kiosk offered a pared down offering of just 6 gourmet jams. The study results showed that 60% of the consumers who passed the bigger jam display stopped and sampled the jams, as opposed to 40% of the consumers who passed the limited display and tried the jams.

So, at the outset it appeared that more people were attracted to the elaborate jam offerings. That doesn't seem like a huge surprise, but here is where the experiment started to get interesting: regardless of which kiosk consumers chose, when it came to actually sampling the jams people only sampled two choices on average.

Bottom line, more choices didn't lead to more jam taste sampling.

One might conclude from that result that even though people enjoy the idea of a lot of choice, when it comes to spending precious brain energy on decision-making, there is a limit to how far people will venture, even when it involves their taste buds.

Finally, the moment of truth: when it came time to purchase, the consumers who stopped and sampled jams at the smaller kiosk with just 6 choices purchased at the whopping rate of 30%. In contrast, those who stopped and sampled from the kiosk with 24 jam choices purchased at the rate of just 3%. This result is in direct opposition to how many salespeople believe the selling process actually works.

Manufacturers will tell you that the message they frequently get from their selling arm is "We need more options, we're getting killed by the competition because they are offering so much more than we are." That is such a common refrain that manufacturers typically respond with a big marketing push at least once a year rolling out, with trumpeted fanfare, their latest and greatest in an ever-escalating choice war on their competitors, and unintentionally their own customers.

Over my career, I've sat through countless marketing meetings involving manufacturers' ever-expanding product offerings. These invariably lead to a number of breakout sessions led by the sales team regarding the new gargantuan list of products they believe they still need to stay competitive. Or, put simply, "More equals Better, and Better is never enough." There are, of course, always a few exceptions to the norm. Proctor and Gamble once reduced their ever-popular Head and Shoulders Shampoo brand offering from 26 options to 15 and saw a 10% spike in sales.

In another study done to gauge motivation, the researchers did an experiment where university students were given the choice between a list of 30 writing assignment topics (large choice set) for extra credit, or choosing from a list of only 6 writing assignment topics (small choice set) for extra credit.

Again, the results showed that students who chose to work from the smaller topic set of six choices turned in more of their assignments and the overall quality of their work was judged to be superior to those who chose to work from the larger choice set. Even in this experiment that didn't involve any kind of purchase, overload played a disproportionate outcome, where an abundance of choice wasn't seen as an improvement.

Finally, the last of three experiments looked at customer satisfaction in the face of choice overload. In this experiment, subjects either chose from a set of 30 different Godiva chocolates or from a smaller subset of 6 Godiva chocolate flavors. By now, you might not be surprised by the results. Those who were exposed to the greater choice set of 30 different chocolates found the decision process both more enjoyable and more frustrating.

This makes sense if you think about the exhilaration of having all the chocolate choices available, but also the hard work of having to narrow it down and make a final decision from the vast array of options. What might surprise you was that those participants faced with the limited subset of 6 Godiva chocolate flavors were more likely to be satisfied with their final choice than those who had the 30 chocolates to choose from.

It seems that with the excitement of more choice comes the frustration of actually making that choice, and the reality that with that choice comes greater responsibility, which translates as risk, with more at stake for the chooser.

All three studies support the idea that overload in selection can have a detrimental effect on the outcome of final decisions, and limiting choice carries some real benefits for selection and the feeling of a positive outcome. We also note that in all three studies there was no distinction or difference in outcome based on ethnicity or gender.

The idea of "less is more" was also borne out in a nonscientific experiment that we once carried out in a series of kitchen and bath showrooms in the Midwest. The experiment was built around a prominent brand's solid surface countertop offerings. Understanding how confounding decisions can be in the face of numerous choices and given the many solid surface options, we decided to run a sale promotion we called "Lucky Seven."

We took the brands that were the two biggest sellers at the time, and randomly selected five more colors from their large stock of solid surface options. We heavily promoted these seven choices with a multilevel marketing campaign and tied that effort to a limited time sales promotion, feeding into customers' sense of loss aversion. To no one's surprise, the sales promotion proved to be effective and our solid surface countertop sales took off.

After the sale was over, we were interested to see what would happen if we continued to offer the "Lucky Seven" color choices as a grouping, but no longer connected them with any kind of sale or specific marketing promotion. We were delighted to find that this pared down grouping became exceedingly popular. The two best sellers continued to garner the most sales, but the five colors which were initially chosen at random sold well beyond the other choices in the brands much larger product offering.

One assumption was that like the experiments carried out by Iyengar and Lepper, a limited choice offering reduced cognitive overload and created more buyer momentum. Additionally, when the sales team conveyed to prospective buyers that the "Lucky Seven" group constituted our best-selling countertop selection, that third party endorsement seemed to have an enormous impact for those with a limited amount of domain knowledge about solid surface countertops. (Domain knowledge is knowledge of a specific, specialized area or discipline, as opposed to general knowledge.)

This latter idea seems to support the power associated with "groupthink," common among humans. Wanting to fit in and not wanting to make a decision that would fly in the face of perceived popularity can be a big driver of decisions, especially when the buyer doesn't have a lot of confidence in their own opinion. Paying close attention to the point where a customer is overwhelmed by choice and less likely to make a decision to buy is a fundamental operating principle for the Sales Genius and instrumental in providing a great customer experience.

I was once in a plumbing showroom, watching a customer stare like a deer in the headlights at an enormous wall of kitchen faucet samples. There were faucets of every make, size, and color combination, beyond what you might imagine is even possible.

As the customer, who was clearly experiencing mental overload, tried to wrap her mind around her faucet decision, the salesperson, completely misreading the customer, said, "Wow, you think this is a lot of faucets, I have more in the back room. I can bring them out if you'd like. They're a little dusty, but we've got tons." If this customer was drowning, the salesperson's answer was to throw her a boat anchor.

A customer drowning in choices experiences brain overload, and brain overload can lead to three less-than-desirable outcomes.

First, in the confusion of trying to decide, the customer may choose not to buy at all, leaving in frustration.

Second, the customer will decide, and then change their mind after the fact—sometimes over and over again—requiring additional time and energy from the salesperson in an attempt to rescue the sale.

By the way, if your customer is constantly changing their mind, it's likely that is more about the way you presented the buying experience and less about your customer being picky or someone who simply can't make up their mind.

(This is a hard truth when it comes to product selection: salespeople are frequently less part of the solution and more about adding to the problem. Sales Geniuses rarely overwhelm customers in their buying decision because Sales Geniuses understand and excel at choice presentation. In the coming pages, we'll see how they do it.)

The third outcome in choice overload might possibly be the worst: the customer decides under duress, buys the item, doesn't like it, and eventually wants to return it. This is known as buyer's remorse, a lose-lose proposition.

In psychologist Barry Schwartz's book *The Paradox of Choice*, he argues that reducing the number of available choices can greatly cut down on the dreaded buyer's remorse.

And indeed, grocery stores like Aldi and Trader Joe's seem to thrive in part by slimming their options, offering only one brand or one variety of each item. It's not just about reducing shelf space: the theory goes that curating the available options allows you to avoid overtaxing the customer's brain, and thus prevent decision paralysis.

On the other hand, superstores in the Unites States like Meijer aren't exactly struggling, despite their brain-blasting array of every conceivable product. What gives?

It seems that a larger array of offerings can lead to choice overload. But the truth is, as it turns out, a little more complicated than that. Researchers Alexander Chernev, Ulf Böckenholt, and Joseph Gordon analyzed a huge stack of choice overload studies, and found a number of factors that influence whether you'll prefer scanning an overflowing cereal aisle for your perfect breakfast, or if that broad expanse of boxes will make you just give up and opt for eggs instead.

Decision Task Difficulty

Decision task difficulty refers to the way that a choice is set up for you, and includes details like time constraints. If the customer needs to choose quickly, then an abundance of choices can overwhelm. This means a handful of offerings at or near the checkout counter can greatly benefit incidental quick sales. Grocery stores do this frequently where a smaller group of cereals will be pulled from the much larger selection elsewhere in the store and then prominently displayed right before you pay.

Then there is accountability. If a consumer doesn't need to justify a decision to someone else, they are more likely to be emotionally indulgent in their purchase and less concerned about details or how others will perceive them through their choices. Buying cereal with a high sugar content is much easier to do if there is no one looking over your shoulder judging you. Impulse purchasing is generally a solo affair.

To what extent can you do a one-to-one comparison of the traits of each cereal? The harder it is to do this, the more taxing it will be on the brain to sort through many options.

Stopping to compare traits like carbohydrate, protein, and sugar content can get you bogged down in your cereal buying decision, as opposed to the simplicity of choosing a cereal based on a single dimension like fiber content or its cost.

How many of the available choices meet your needs? Imagine you are comparing four different unknown cereals, and the nutritional content in all of them is relatively equal. The more choices that satisfy your parameters, the harder choosing will be without a clear differentiator. This is where name brands, by serving the role of differentiator, can play a disproportionate role in the buying decision.

How are the cereals presented? Is it easy for the customer to compare their options? Are the low sugar cereals shelved together, or non-GMO cereals in a special grouping, or are the gluten-free cereals displayed on the same shelf section?

Studies show products displayed at eye level and in logical groupings are much more likely to get scrutinized and purchased as opposed to cereals randomly displayed, or on a bottom shelf requiring bending down to access. This is why savvy vendors try to have a say in where their product will be placed, and why aisle end caps, which tend to get more visual interest, are always in high demand.

Choice Set Complexity

Here's where we evaluate the quality of the choices themselves. Is there one clear winner, a product that stands head and shoulders above the rest of the field? In that case, a large number of other options won't trouble you since those can be easily dismissed. Or is the field limited? Because you view all of your options as exceptional, your final choice might not be troubling, since in that scenario, you can't lose.

Preference Uncertainty

Do you already have strong preferences in place? If you already have a deep domain knowledge of cereal options, or if you already have the platonic ideal of what a cereal should be enshrined in your mind, you'll generally appreciate being able to choose from a broader spread of choices because you know precisely how to find what you want. On the other hand, if you have no idea where to begin, that same aisle can feel downright paralyzing.

Decision Goal

If you're just browsing with no intention of buying, the majestic expanse of cereal boxes can be an enjoyable experience. You can vicariously enjoy the rich opportunity that awaits a future purchase.

There's also decision focus to consider. It's easier to choose between one type and another than to narrow your choice down to a single item. Choosing between broad categories like wheat cereals or rice cereals is generally easier than choosing between the myriad of different brands and flavors of wheat or rice cereals.

Finally, there's what Chernev and his team call the "level of construal," which refers to how abstractly you conceptualize the entire cereal buying experience.

If it all feels very theoretical, you may prefer a wide variety of cereals to choose from because your final choice doesn't seem like it will be a big deal. You might tell yourself, "It's only cereal, after all."

On the other hand, if your cereal choice is paramount and you find yourself pausing to vividly imagine the "mouth feel" of each cereal as you move down the aisle, you'd probably prefer a smaller cereal selection.

While all of this might sound confusing, it's easy to remember, and research bears this out: consumers like the *idea* of choice a lot more when they're not actually in a buying situation. When customers are in a buying mode, an abundance of options can quickly lose its charm and turn into choice overload.

When it comes to choosing, overload is the unseen enemy, and Sales Geniuses avoid this dilemma when possible by carefully choreographing the buying experience. Their attention is laser focused on the most important buying needs for that individual customer and they present options in a way to avoid overload. This strategy is customer-specific based on buying patterns, and unfortunately rarely something the salesperson can predict ahead of time, unless they've used our strategies for determining their customer's buying pattern. (More on this later.)

A customer may say something like, "There are so many choices," or "How am I ever going to make up my mind?" For a Sales Genius, those are warning signs rather than a chance to take pride in your rich bevy of product offerings.

Voicing distress about options is a little like recognizing you're thirsty. By the time you realize you're thirsty, your body has already begun to shift towards a state of dehydration. A customer verbalizing decision difficulty has already tipped towards choice overload and away from a purchase. Unfortunately, this is a sign that even veteran salespeople often miss.

If you miss the signs of choice overload, there is a good chance you'll lose your sales opportunity or be caught in the trap of buyer's remorse in which the customer makes a poor decision, buys the wrong product, and then wants to return it. You can mitigate the chance of buyer's remorse by leading your customer through a better decision process.

WRAP

Buyer's remorse is but one flaw of the brain's decision-making powers as described in Chip and Dan Heath's book, *Decisive: How to Make Better Choices in Life and Work*. The brothers Heath have come up with the mnemonic device WRAP for their decision-making prescription:

Widen Your Options

When working with your customer, sometimes their momentary emotional excitement is so strong that they make a snap decision on the spot. This might seem beneficial, but if their choice is the wrong one the salesperson will, just like the customer, end up paying for it.

It's important to acknowledge your customer's enthusiasm while at the same time suggesting other options that might even better fit their needs. For example, "That's a great choice. Based on your needs you might also want to consider X, which seems like an excellent fit because _____." It's an excellent way to cover your bases, making sure the customer realizes all relevant options available and then later orchestrating the decision process through a binary choice scenario.

Reality-test Your Assumptions

Many of us make decisions that clearly had no chance of succeeding in retrospect. But once we lock down on an idea, confirmation bias kicks in and we tend to seek information that supports our theory and ignore valid contrary information. To get around confirmation bias, ask questions like, "What would be necessary for this idea to work?"

Case in point: in the kitchen and bath design business, a center island in a kitchen is a design element that is highly coveted. Unfortunately, the walkway needed around a center island means many kitchens are too small to accommodate one. Trying to explain necessary spacing to a customer, and shooting down their island dream is usually a recipe for disaster. It's not uncommon for an emotionally invested customer to suggest that the standard walkway parameters don't really apply to their situation, as if the laws of physics are somehow suspended in their kitchen. This is where the reality test of suggesting they go home and place something the size of the proposed island—such as a box—in the center of their kitchen and work around it for a week to get the feel of the space considerations.

A reality test like that provides a truth the emotional brain is forced to reckon with. It's not uncommon for a customer, having done the experiment, to come back and say, "Yeah, there's no way that island is going to work." They generally don't credit the salesperson with her or his initial insight; they are buoyed by the truth they have personally discovered. And that's okay, because in the end your goal is to make their experience the best it can be.

Attain Distance Before Deciding

Short-term emotion is powerful. In the heat of the moment, we sometimes make rash decisions that we would have avoided with the perspective of time. The Heath brothers suggest that in these instances, you invoke business writer Suzy Welch's 10/10/10 rule.

When you see the customer about to make an emotional decision which is likely not in their best interest, rather than simply pointing out it's a bad idea—which never goes well, explain how it's important to you that they are happy with the end result and recommend the following test. Ask the customer how they will feel about their decision 10 minutes from now, 10 months from now and 10 years from now.

This helps balance their short-term emotions with a longer time period perspective. Questioning in this format can propel a customer towards a much more realistic decision.

Prepare to be Wrong

Hubris is the mortal enemy of good decision-making, and it can lead us into deeply faulty predictions about the future. The Heaths say that when you plan for a future event, don't think of it as a single point to aim for—such as expecting a perfect moon shot—but rather as one of a host of possible outcomes. Preparing for what might go right as well as what might go wrong is a perspective trick they call bookending. By building in contingency planning, you can accommodate the unforeseen. NASA's planned redundancy saved the lives of the Apollo 13 crew members when the mission went dangerously awry.

Helping a customer recognize ahead of time that there are bound to be some hiccups in the process, and that you will be there every step of the way to problem-solve, is crucial. This is especially true in sales that involve some kind of design work where the look and feel of the finished product is likely to evolve as the process unfolds.

Learning how to present choice in a way that doesn't lead to overload is a key to good selling.

Many customers believe they are bringing some level of analytical intention to their decisions. That might make sense if our brains were more like Mr. Spock's, with thinking processes evolved beyond primitive emotion and the host of biases that plague us. But until the emotions driving phenomena like buyer's remorse are eradicated from the human genome, the WRAP strategy might be worth a try.

Brain Selling App

Apps for your computer and smartphone have become a necessity in a world driven by access to information. This has never been truer than in the arena of sales. And so, we are constantly seeking upgrades of both hardware and software to stay connected and stay informed.

But what about the most powerful computational hardware in the world: your brain? What can you do to maximize its efficiency, since a new brain transplant is currently out of the question?

Plasticity is one of the brain's most remarkable features: the ability to change its wiring through the process of learning. As information comes into the brain through the senses, the brain's internal malleability allows you to create what computer software engineers call new programming, or what neuroscientists call habits. It's basically a brain app.

This is where your electrical/chemical switches called neurons come into play. In the average adult, these 86 billion switches allow for an infinite number of connections and formations to be built, purposed, and repurposed over and over again.

Some neural code comes pre-programmed at birth, like breathing. Other habits are formed following your brain's strategy for survival. In a system that highly prizes the conservation of energy, your brain is frequently looking for efficiency shortcuts. Habits fit the bill, thanks to your basal ganglia.

The relationship between your basal ganglia and your working memory is a little like the one between Bat Man's Bruce Wayne and Alfred. The basal ganglia acts the role of faithful servant. How does it serve? It converts patterns into little bits of neural code—your brain's version of personal software programming—to ensure that a particular habit lives on in your subconscious. This frees up your working memory from having to remember and execute a particular task.

It is an incredible but powerful truth that as a sentient being your emotions, actions, and decisions all depend upon your brain's wiring and habituation. No matter which new selling technique we discuss, success depends upon changing the wiring in your brain to build those techniques into habit code.

What's interesting is that so much of what we habituate is unintentional. For example, there is a pretty high likelihood that tonight when you sit down for dinner—provided you eat at home—you will sit in the same chair you sat in the night before. Of course, there's probably no intrinsic value in that chair. It's likely there are at least three more nearby that look exactly the same. But over time, your habit-driven brain has programmed that little bit of neural code to free you from dithering each evening about chair choice. And now, with your habit firmly installed, if someone plops down into a certain one of those identical chairs you indignantly demand they surrender it with a, "Hey, that's *my* chair!"

These little automated preprogrammed chunks of information allow you to repeat thoughts, actions and emotions that are pertinent to your daily routines. It's estimated that more than half your day is composed of habituated processes: everything from turning on a light switch to driving your car down the highway. While your brain is running habit code, you can even engage in secondary activities. That's why you are capable of driving your car and listening to the radio at the same time.

Habits are formed out of repetitive actions. If you do something enough, the brain begins to recognize a pattern in your behavior and thus arranges neurons into what's called "neural code," a template that is accessible through subconscious memory and serves as a guide for that behavior. This is also known as wiring your brain for a habit. The more often you repeat an action, behavior, or thought, the more powerful the neural code becomes. This explains the famous neuroscience mantra "neurons that fire together wire together'.

When you are first learning, the neural code you're building is like a dirt path: uneven, tough going, and in terms of speed operating at about 3 mph. With enough repetitive behavior, your neurons respond with greater consistency of firing and wiring together, and the dirt path turns into a superhighway with speeds in excess of 250 mph.

Because neural code can be reused over and over again, it's an efficient use of the brain's energy, much like how it's much cheaper to use a highway once it's constructed instead of having to build a new highway every time you want to drive your car.

Since the actual process of wiring for a habit is an automated subconscious process, your brain's basal ganglia, or "habit central," is neutral and makes no judgment as to the quality or the affect the habit might have on you. It can wire a habit for substance abuse just as easy as wiring up a habit for your daily morning run. It's all about repetition of behavior.

Let's say you recognize the importance of staying hydrated and so you want to drink more water each day. Research shows that with enough repetition—in this case drinking more glasses of water—you can create the neural wiring in your brain to accomplish that task after roughly two weeks. On average, it takes the brain about two months to build enough neural code to create a habit. More complicated habits, like driving a car, can take many months to create.

And this is all done thanks to an area inside the basal ganglia called the striatum. If the basal ganglia is habit central, the striatum is responsible for coordinating habits and is directly linked to your brain's cortex where higher level thought takes place. The cortex is also, generally speaking, home to your System 2 analytical processing. Habits also rely on the midbrain, where brain cells rich in dopamine—a chemical related to excitement, rewards, and feelings of satisfaction—help to drive more habit formation and keep habits alive. Your infralimbic brain region initiates the habit when your senses pick up on certain environmental cues, feelings, or situations.

The great news for those who want to master the ability to sell is that this habit mechanism is available to be co-opted to your advantage. Although habits operate for the most part subconsciously, the beginning of habit formation can be initiated with conscious intention.

When we spoke with BJ Fogg—professor at Stanford and one of the foremost experts in the world on habit formation—for our book *Brain Apps*, he gave us some hacks on how to leverage your brain's habituation ability.

1.   Take advantage of neural programming you've already created by piggybacking on an existing habit. Your existing habit becomes the trigger for your new desired action.

2. Keep the motivation rolling by rewarding yourself after you've successfully completed the desired action.

3. Start small. Like, really small.

Here is one of Fogg's examples:

Suppose you recognize the value of flossing but seldom do it. Your basal ganglia has already built a habit for brushing your teeth each night, so use brushing as your trigger mechanism. Tonight, after you brush your teeth, floss. But here's the catch: start out flossing only *one* tooth. By making the initial hurdle so low, it's almost impossible not to do it. After you achieve your single tooth floss, treat yourself to some verbal praise like, "Aw yeah, check out that tooth! It is flossed so good! No plaque on either side of this sucker! I rock the flossing world!" This gives you a little squirt of motivational dopamine to reinforce your new behavior.

Each night after you brush, add more teeth to your flossing regimen. Eventually you'll find yourself flossing all your pearly whites. Following this simple process allows you to cultivate a tiny habit, motivate through verbal reward, and, after about 60 days, nurture a tiny habit into a fully programmed one.

As silly as this might sound, keeping your effort small and rewarding yourself for that effort triggers the release of the reward chemical dopamine. Since momentum is built on the back of tiny wins and your brain is far more likely to undertake a task if the amount of effort required seems minimal, this *slow and steady wins the race* approach works really well for building new neural wiring.

By keeping the initial goal small and ensuring that you can overcome your brain's reluctance to change, you increase your chance for success. Before you set out to consciously initiate a new habit, Fogg says there are five factors to consider for optimizing habituation. He calls these five factors your "Simplicity Profile." These are the five factors on the checklist to consider:

Time: How much time will you need to devote to the new habit?

You can think about this in two ways. First, to build the average habit, you will need at least two months for your brain to assemble significant neural wiring. Second, what will your time commitment have to be on a daily basis in order to get enough repetitions? This is where taking advantage of time blocking, and setting up a specific time to follow through on your reps, allows the brain time to build all of the new neural wiring.

Non-routine: How will the new habit affect the other areas and routines already in your life?

Changing behavior can be a hardship because it requires a redistribution of energy—something the brain doesn't undertake easily—and because you are probably adding a new habit in order to thwart an existing habit. This means that the change will impact your current routine. You'll most likely have to make some kind of sacrifice and give up something else in order to create room for the new habit. This decision should not be taken lightly because the sense of loss aversion can kick in and doom your new habit from the start.

Physical effort: How much physical exertion will the new habit require?

The first time salespeople work in a brick and mortar retail environment they are often surprised at the toll it takes on their feet and legs. Outside salespeople can be surprised by the sheer amount of product and sales literature they often lug around from customer to customer. Aside from the need for a good pair of shoes, are you prepared for the strain on your body of constantly moving to meet customer demands?

Brain cycles: How much mental effort will the new habit require?

Mental energy is finite and since your brain puts a premium on it, figuring out the best time of the day to engage in habit reps towards your new goal can aid your success. Waiting until the end of the day to engage in habit formation, when we're exhausted, tends not to serve most of us very well.

Money and/or resources: How much will the new habit cost?

Will you have to invest in any equipment, computers, smartphones, software, transportation, classes, books, or additional products to get rolling on your new habit? If so, have you budgeted appropriately for the added expense?

Here's a question. Why is it hard to kick an old habit?

Scientists have a name for this. It's called an "extinction burst." Sometimes when you try to subdue a current behavior in favor of a new one, the brain, sensing the loss, will double down on the old behavior and make a last-ditch effort to hold on to the old behavior. Dieters have numerous horror stories where they were proudly vigilant on giving up sweets for several weeks, only to succumb to an entire quart of rocky road ice cream during a midnight food binge.

Once you understand that your rational brain is up against an internal conspirator, you might not be surprised to discover the nemesis is your emotional brain, sometimes known as your reptilian brain, which has some habit maintenance shenanigans up its metaphorical sleeve.

Your reptilian brain cleverly waits to spring the extinction burst trap only after you've essentially overcome your bad habit and you are in the final stage of habit change, with your old habit all but shunned in favor of your new habit.

An extinction burst is much like a Hail Mary play in football, where desperation drives an all-or-nothing strategy for success. Your reptilian brain makes a final push to reestablish your old habit.

It's that quart of rocky road ice cream, which up until now you've been able to void, that seems to reach out and call to you like the sirens in the Odyssey. You can thank your reptilian brain for ramping up the ice cream craving to an almost unbearable level.

One theory for why your emotional brain might initiate a final extinction burst is that the wiring for a longtime habit is so deeply ingrained that the habit could be misidentified by part of your brain as something vital to survival. It works in much the same way that your body's immune system can misidentify a healthy food source as an unwanted allergen.

Extinction bursts are extremely dangerous to new habit formation, largely because they are part of a process that originates from inside your brain.

Odysseus solved his problem and fear of succumbing to the siren song of temptation by having his shipmates lash him to the mast of his ship. That might have worked for the famous Greek hero, but ship masts aren't always easy to find—especially in the dessert aisle of your grocery store.

There is no well-established playbook for fending off an extinction burst. However, knowing they can happen allows you to be vigilant and prepare for them by either removing perceived temptations ahead of time, or planning what you'll do should an extinction burst crop up.

The approach to keeping a new habit vital, and therefore the behavior you're more likely to engage in versus the old habit, is much like gardening. Sustaining a habit requires that you spend some time feeding and nurturing it. You can keep your habit thriving by stopping from time to time to review the benefits that the habit affords you and by reinforcing the habit by adding new rewards for your efforts.

When you choose to engage the new habit, you are undergoing a conscious effort which eventually drives the habit deeper into your subconscious brain and becomes automatic. What we are suggesting is that from time to time, you bring your habit behavior back into the light of your consciousness and review the positive attributes it affords you. This bit of maintenance, something that many of us don't ordinarily do, reinforces the habit's value in the brain. With this positive reinforcement you are essentially leveraging the "hold on at all costs" extinction burst on your behalf, in the event that your good habit find itself in jeopardy.

Investing time in pre-habit preparation is a must for success. It's also important to recognize that once the brain builds a habit, the neural wiring is permanent for the most part. This means that a new habit doesn't wipe out an old habit, destroying the old neural wiring with it. Rather, a new habit, if it's robust enough, can offer a behavioral alternative to the old habit. The old habit is still there waiting to be reactivated if needed. This is why it is possible to embark on a new habit, and then under certain circumstances, find yourself right back to repeating your old behavior.

Habits have three components: a trigger, routine, and reward. Once understood, you have a brain altering tool at your command. You can literally rewire your brain for better habits of any kind—but for our purposes, we're focusing on selling habits.

In an existing habit, a trigger—or cue—is the stimulus that alerts you through your brain's primary senses (taste, touch, smell, sight or hearing) or memory markers (associated feelings) to undertake an action. For example, a smoker's trigger might be just seeing a pack of cigarettes, or smelling the smoke from a random cigarette, or the fond memory of smoking with their friends in high school.

Once the switch is triggered in the striatum, the brain moves to the next step to initiate the routine associated with that trigger or cue. Remember the routine already exists because of the number of repetitions you have completed to create the superhighway of neural wiring associated with that routine after about 2 months of repetition.

In our smoking example, the routine would include the act of lighting a cigarette and then smoking it, all of which has taken place countless times (repetitions) in the past.

Lastly, there is the reward, a necessary habit component whereby you experience some sort of pleasure from doing the routine. This is where the "happy" neural chemical dopamine comes into play; the brain releases dopamine during and or at the conclusion of the routine to guarantee you'll repeat the routine in the future. This simple loop is what keeps habits thriving in the brain.

In the case of smoking, the nicotine you inhale triggers the brain's dopamine receptors directly, which is one of the reasons why a smoking habit is easy to start and tough to quit. However, the trigger, routine, and reward are like three legs of a stool: if you remove any one of these components, the habit falls apart, at least temporarily.

Now let's turn to a more positive habit than smoking. Let's assume that you want to build the habit of incorporating midpoint summation into your selling routine.

Midpoint summation is the action of taking notes and then verifying your written information halfway through the selling experience when the customer's memory tends to wane. This has the dual benefit of both ensuring accuracy and prodding your customer's memory for maximum information retention.

To wire the brain for this new habit, we need to build the appropriate trigger, routine, and reward associated with it. To maximize our chance of habit success, we first need to run it through BJ Fogg's 5-step "simplicity profile" of time, non-routine, physical effort, brain cycles, and resources.

For midpoint summation, there are two chunks of time to consider: the time it will take you to write down and record your notes, and the time to run through the informational review at midpoint with your customer.

Neither action requires an inordinate amount of *time*, but the willingness to do it requires significant motivation and accepting that this change will likely slow you down at first from what you are used to doing.

This brings us to *non-routine*. The change from what you are used to doing means you are adding a new behavior that will likely feel less comfortable in the beginning. For the best chance of success, you'll need to confirm your commitment to making this change ahead of time, and remind yourself to give the new process a fair chance.

The *physical effort* of writing notes and reviewing them is not all that taxing in the scheme of things, but as the brain tends to wear down by the end of the day, building *brain cycle* (repetitions) through practice is often more effective earlier in the day.

From a **resource** standpoint, obtaining a handheld device or a simple notepad and pen for taking notes seems possible for any salesperson.

In the case of midpoint summation, we've seen that by running it through Fogg's Simplicity Profile, there aren't giant barriers to implementation. It does drive home the need to accept some level of discomfort during the changeover. It also reminds us to be careful of extinction bursts, especially at the end of the day when you're tired and you find yourself abandoning note-taking to rely on your memory instead.

In my own experience of habituating midpoint summation, taking notes at first felt like just one more burden to endure—a great example of the unseen power of fixed mindset at work. If you feel some resistance too, it might help to actively engage your System 2 analytical thought process. Review the long-term benefits of making fewer mistakes, reducing overall stress, increasing your bottom line, freeing up your brain's working memory for more important tasks, and creating a great experience for your customers.

If that's not enough, consider the fact that you will be generating more positive word of mouth on your behalf. All of those positives versus the perceived hassle of taking a few minutes to record your customer's information seems like more than a fair trade-off.

This is where forcing your outlook through the lens of growth mindset by engaging your analytical System 2 can make the difference between average performance and Genius-level performance. It is a subtle but powerful internal view into how your brain processes change, and how you can leverage outcomes to your advantage.

With those caveats in mind, let's take a look at how we can wire up your brain for a new midpoint summation habit.

This is where habit building requires a bit of creativity. Remember, Fogg says one hack for building habits faster is to piggyback on an existing habit. For our example, we will start with the premise that you are a sales rep in a brick and mortar showroom. When you are summoned on the floor by the store's receptionist, your current routine includes popping a breath mint in your mouth before you hit the showroom floor. (A pretty wise move, given what you'll learn about your customer's olfactory sense.)

This is a great piggyback opportunity; since the breath mint is already built into the start of your present routine, you can now practice setting the roll of breath mints on top of your notepad, creating an instant reminder to take your notepad on the floor with you.

We've just set up the trigger for your new routine: breath mint = notepad = midpoint summation trigger. Because you aren't used to carrying the notepad out onto the selling floor with you, in the beginning this serves as an additional reminder to explain to your customer why you have it.

This brings us to the second phase of habit construction. We create the all-important *routine*, which for midpoint summation includes the following 5 steps:

1. You get permission from the customer to take notes (**commitment**)

2. You jot down important information, with a focus on detail, i.e. brands, model numbers, colors, options, prices, and all sales critical information (**detail**)

3. Halfway through the session, you stop and review the customer's selections and/or concerns that have transpired thus far, fixing and or adjusting as needed (**accuracy**)

4. You are careful not to move forward again until your customer has demonstrated that they are good with the proceedings at that point (**patience**)

5. At session's end, you offer to supply the customer with a copy of your notes to show good faith and further reinforce their own selections (**transparency**)

The brain loves soundbites because they conserve energy and are easily stored in the memory. The five steps of midpoint summation can be summoned up by learning this simple soundbite phrase;

Commitment to *detail* demonstrates **accuracy**, which proves my **patience** and **transparency**.

Writing the above sentence and reciting it until it becomes second nature is an easy way to put the five midpoint summation steps in order and remember them for future use. This soundbite is probably shorter than a chorus in your favorite song. It might not be all that catchy as a musical "earworm," but for our purposes it serves as a fast hack to the routine.

We are now at phase three in our habit build, the *reward* stage. We can think about reward in two categories: immediate gratification (short-term), or postponed gratification (long-term). The postponed gratification of all the previously listed positive effects of midpoint summation—fewer mistakes, re-engaging your customer's memory, etc.—is likely reward enough to keep the habit alive once it has become entrenched in your brain's striatum.

The problem is that during the "neural wiring" phase of practicing the routine over and over again, you will likely need some other kind of short-term reward to sustain you through the process. The drudgery of building a routine is precisely why more people don't do it, even though intellectually they understand the benefit.

This is where you need to take a few moments and ponder what has worked for you in the past when you set out to master some skill, large or small. Coming up with some small but important short-term reward might be exactly what is needed to guarantee new habit success. Self- and group-competition works well for many individuals.

When I first began doing seminars, it was important for me to get a feedback loop going with the audience, because more participation means livelier and more rewarding events. Simply asking people to participate didn't prove to be all that effective. I shared an experiment idea with a colleague in which I would toss out a reward of dark chocolate to people who asked relevant questions during the seminar to see if it would ramp up participation.

My colleague, frankly, was appalled. They said, "You can't do that, people aren't dogs responding to a treat on command." I knew that food bribes as a habit-building reward can be a slippery slope.

But I rationalized my own surgical use of a limited healthy food bribe—especially since dark chocolate is high in antioxidants, low in sugar, and an excellent clinically proven brain boost. I decided, despite my colleagues' misgivings, to run the experiment anyway. To my delight, it went fantastically well. People seemed to get a kick out of it, and the amount of feedback radically increased. Now I'm not suggesting you throw chocolates out to your customers. A seminar situation is a controlled setting with a certain amount of entertainment value, and I explain my use of chocolate treats ahead of time.

The take-away lesson from the chocolate experiment is that humans are highly motivated when they are in some form of competition, whether it be against themselves or a group. Even people who weren't huge dark chocolate fans would join in enthusiastically and hand off their chocolate winning to a coworker in the seminar. The experiment proved to be less about the actual treat and more about the recognition/competition. It worked in fourth grade when your teacher gave out gold stars for spelling, and it unsurprisingly has the same effect on adults.

Consider setting up a chart or calendar and keeping track of your wins: the number of times you managed to deploy midpoint summation during your first two month run of building out the habit. It has proven to be incredibly powerful and fun for many who have tried.

Especially if after each win you stop and verbally give yourself credit for it per BJ Fogg's suggestion. Does it all seem a bit ridiculous or maybe even a little foolish? It does. But does it work? Absolutely. It's not all that hard to trick your brain. As humans, we manage to do it all day long—often not to our benefit. But, in this case, you are intentionally leveraging your brain for positive long-term results.

Each star or check mark releases a small bit of the brain's dopamine. Over time, the cumulative effect slowly sustains and builds momentum. After about two months' worth of practice you've proudly turned the habit dirt road into a super highway.

At that point, it's the gift that keeps on giving. Once the brain automates the behavior, you're freed up from thinking about it as your subconscious brain takes over and runs the programming on autopilot. It just becomes something you do automatically.

This is by no means the only way to sustain your brain's momentum during habit formation. You know best what will most likely to work for you personally. Often, finding someone with whom you can share the experience creates enough of a support network to keep you focused on your joint habit goals, when the early stages of habit build-out (the practice phase) seems dull and unrewarding.

15 Minute Goal

One habit you might consider formalizing is your time commitment to your customer's attention span. As we have seen, locking in on your customer's exact attention span for information delivery, let alone choice, is scientifically impossible to predict. That said, the folks at TED Talks say that their research indicates that eighteen minutes is an excellent marker for creating interesting informational lectures that will both hold attention and stick in the brain.[9]

Our approach is to hedge our bets between Saga Briggs's memory research and TED Talks, coming in at about 15 minutes. We are taking the Goldilocks approach here: not too little and not too much.

The truth is, in a real-life selling situation, you won't be running a stopwatch. Still, it is important to realize that while "not enough" information can turn a customer off, overloading a customer with unnecessary detail is frequently the kiss of death.

This is a particularly acute problem among veteran salespeople who, over time, have acquired a tremendous amount of knowledge. Some of them come to believe that selling simply involves "offloading," or, more politely, teaching their customer about their product or service. It's as if their customer is a giant bucket and their job is to bring their firehose of knowledge, filling the bucket until it is full and their customer is ready to make a purchase.

But you can't assume your customer comes to your showroom or their online experience with an abundance of energy and an unlimited amount of time to spend. Like you and me, they are more likely balancing a whole host of endeavors and, as such, their unspoken goal is to get through as quickly as possible. They don't come to you with a giant bucket waiting to be filled; it's more like a thimble, and surgical information delivery on your part carries the day.

Sales Geniuses tend to follow the simple rule, "The more you tell, the less you sell." This isn't to say their goal is to hide information or be coy. They're simply selective in what they present to the customer. A less-is-more strategy makes sense.

It's key to keep your customer's attention level in mind and set goals to maximize your opportunities while your customer is most likely in a listening mode. But capitalizing on small hunks of time can pay dividends in other ways.

Why is it tough to do your expense account, start a jogging regimen, or complete just about any other new task you desire to do? We tend to have a bevy of items on our to-do list, many of them important, and yet day after day, little progress is being made. You just can't seem to summon the willpower. One answer for why things don't get done is again based on your brain's tendency to put energy conservation at the top of *its* hierarchical to-do list.

When faced with a task, your brain does a quick risk/reward benefit analysis and tends to come down strongly on the side of waiting until the future. One way to trick your brain into doing a task: instead of thinking in terms of the entire task, which the brain sees as a big energy expenditure, break the goal down into smaller time chunks. Tell yourself, "I'm going to set a timer and work on my expense account for 5 minutes, or jog for 5 minutes, or clean out the storage room for 5 minutes."

Whether it's a 5- or 15-minute strategy, you are giving yourself permission to ease into a task, establishing a simple deadline that's truly doable—who doesn't have 5 minutes to spare—and in essence, downgrading your brain's concern about saving energy.

Making the task less daunting means it's much more likely you'll begin, because the energy cost to entry is so small, and because just getting started is usually the biggest battle. Once you begin, you have the option to stick with the limited time you've dedicated. You may also keep going after you get over the "initial lack of momentum" hump, and that jog turns into a half hour. This is another example of using your System 2 analytical abilities to override your System 1's more primitive operating strategy.

Time Blocking

I learned about time blocking when I was the manager of a large showroom and my goal was to lessen the stress on a very busy sales team while at the same time wringing as much efficiency as possible out of our selling process. Time blocking is a simple idea based on setting aside a given amount of time to ensure a particular task gets done.

If I worked in a restaurant, I might time block the first 15 minutes each day before we open to make sure all the ketchup bottles and salt and pepper shakers were refilled. If I worked in customer service, I might set aside 15 minutes at 7:30 am each morning to review the call log from the night before.

In evaluating your own workday, it isn't hard to determine what tasks require time blocking. Basically, what you're trying to do is catch important tasks that tend to fall through the cracks during a jam-packed day, putting you in a stressful scramble mode.

There are two fundamental rules to time blocking.

First, to ensure that you build the task into a habit, it's important that you block the same time each day and you do it consistently. Remember: it takes the brain approximately 63 days to wire up for a habit.

The second rule is that during time blocking, you only work on the designated task; this means ignoring texts, emails, and so on. Depending on the task, 15 minutes is the perfect amount of time to set aside, especially in the beginning. Strive to block in the area of 15 or 30 minutes, and never more than an hour. Most people can't maintain productive focus for that long.

In a showroom setting, time blocking allows you to deploy your sales force strategically if you have individuals stagger their time blocks. If your business is one where customers might show up randomly looking for a particular salesperson who is quarterbacking a project for them, having set time blocks allows the salesperson to give the customer a heads up about their schedule at the first meeting.

The salesperson might say, for example:

"I'm really excited about working with you on this project. Just as a heads up, every day from 9 to 9:30 am I won't be available. It's important to me that you aren't inconvenienced and can plan accordingly, because I know how valuable your time is too."

This goes a long way to help ensure that you won't be interrupted during your block time by a customer who has the misimpression you're available 24/7 because you sleep on a cot in the backroom.

Your brain operates more efficiently with time blocking and you make far fewer mistakes when your concentration is not in jeopardy of being waylaid by a host of constant distractions.

Your stress level goes down because you eliminate the needless fretting that occurs when there is a task that must be done but for which you feel like you lack the time. Given the fact that at some point you're going to have to do it anyway, doesn't it make more sense to engage your System 2 analytical process and plan for it?

This is why it's important you actively engage your System 2, both to optimize your customer's focus and attention during a sales presentation and to manage a modicum of time each day to accomplish recurring critical tasks. Time blocking is one of the surest ways to nudge you and or your team towards incremental improvement.

PART 2

Brain-Driven Selling Techniques

part

3

The Primacy/Recency effect

As we have seen, the brain has a set of operating rules, and understanding those can boost your ability to translate a positive experience into a sale. There are two memory-driven rules that Sales Geniuses live by, whether they know it or not: the primacy and recency effect.

As a way to simplify these concepts and ensure that you will remember them, we have taken the liberty of combining them into a single concept we call *"the ghost curve."*

The Ghost Curve

The ghost curve says that people will tend to remember information delivered early in a conversation (primacy) and likewise remember information that comes at the end of the conversation (recency). So, if we remember the beginning and the end of a sequence, what about the middle? And therein lies the rub: in the middle of information delivery, the brain tends to relax and let go, generally storing very little new data.

So, what's going on? Remember that your brain is constantly on the lookout to conserve energy via resting, daydreaming or mind wandering. This guarantees that there will be reserve fuel for situations that the brain, running its survival algorithm, deems necessary.

At the beginning of any new situation, the brain is on high alert scanning and listening for danger cues. Once it determines that everything is okay, it tends to relax, dropping into energy-saving mode. The brain begins to daydream, but it subconsciously maintains a degree of vigilance, scanning sensory cues for change. Just the modulation in pitch of a salesperson's voice as they are wrapping up their presentation can be enough to bring the brain back online fully.

That means information from the middle of a conversation tends to get short shrift, and frequently does not get recorded in memory at all. Take a moment and let that sink in. In the middle of a conversation, your customer's memory tends to go on vacation. This has a profound effect on learning and, in our case, selling.

In conjunction with the ghost curve comes another memory phenomenon: short-term memory limitation. When you're only working off your short-term memory, your brain can hold onto between 4 and 7 chunks at a time. A chunk can be a word, a collection of familiar numbers like a famous date, and so on. A phone number—sans area code—is a perfect 7 chunks in length.

To drive this point home, during my speaking engagements I often run the following experiment with the audience. I ask everyone to put their pens and pencils down, sit up and take a couple of deep breaths to refresh their brain's oxygen supply. Then I read the following list of words slowly: *you, love, new, discover, guarantee, proven, save, results, health, safety*. The order of the word list is not important, neither is the word list itself.

Notice that the list consists of ten chunks (words), several more than the 7-chunk limit of the short-term memory cache. After the audience has had a chance to hear the words, I ask them to write down as many as they can remember.

I have done this experiment literally thousands of times in the US and abroad and no one has ever been able to remember all 10 words on the first try. People in the audience are always shocked at how poorly they do.

The average person gets about four words, with a smaller number remembering in the 5-6 range. Generally, in a room of about five hundred, five to seven people will remember 7 words. On the rarest occasion, someone will be able to recall 8 or 9 words, but this occurs about 1 time per 5000 people. Again, no one has ever, in the history of ten years of this experiment, remembered all 10 words on the first try.

After we verify the audience results, we plot out the words that people were able to recall—how many got the first word, the second, and so on. And in what looks like a crazy magic trick, this always creates an inverted bell curve, with most people getting the early words, few if any recalling the middle words, and most people remembering the final few words. Thus, we call this the ghost curve, where the ghosting happens in the middle of information delivery.

The ghost curve, along with the seven-chunk memory rule, is rewriting what we thought we knew about how sales and marketing work. Sales Geniuses take note of these important lessons and structure their selling information to avoid the pitfalls associated with the brain's limited short-term memory and general disposition of glucose conservation.

When you're teaching yourself new sales information, you can use the ghost curve to your advantage. When you sit down to study, divide your learning time into shorter mini-sessions, 15 minutes or less, to periodically restart the curve. Start by focusing on the newest or the most important points to maximize when your attention is the highest. Close out by reviewing these points again.

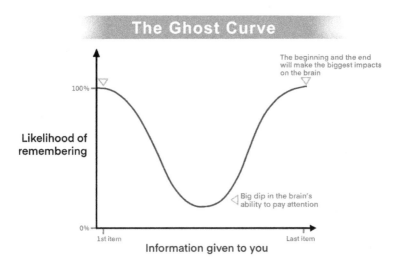

Midpoint Summation

Studying the ghost curve makes two things very clear. First, you need powerful opening and closing statements. Second, in the middle phase of a typical sales information delivery, very little gets stored in the customer's memory. This is a huge problem and a huge opportunity.

Obviously, it's impossible to just have a beginning and ending in a sales situation; you need a viable middle too. Sales Geniuses have an answer for the middle dilemma. It's called midpoint summation, the idea we introduced during the section on building brain apps or habits. It's a recap that focuses the customer's attention back on the information at hand. This reengages your customer's memory, which means all is not lost in the middle.

This is why taking notes—after getting permission—is critical to your selling process. By writing down the key aspects of your customers' wants, you have both a record that you can refer to later and a means by which to bring the customer's wandering brain back to focus.

It's not critical that you actually write the information down—as opposed to typing on a handheld device—but be aware that research shows the act of physical writing allows your brain to retain more information. This is because, as in sales, the more senses you engage the more powerful the memory acquisition. Writing involves a deeper degree of cognitive processing than typing[10].

To review midpoint summation: roughly halfway into your sales meeting with your customer, when their pupils and/or body language suggests they are zoning out, you stop and say something like, "Let me make sure I've written down exactly what you want."

This conveys two signals: that you're calling their attention to something important that's about to happen, and that they have a chance to review and change anything that's incorrect.

As you review your notes with your customer, don't be surprised to find errors—either in what you mistakenly wrote down, or what your customer said to you. Remember that mind wandering is a very human disposition.

A common complaint among salespeople is the stress brought on by mistakes in the ordering process. Our own internal data suggests that during midpoint summation, you are likely to catch at least one mistake 50% of the time. That is a giant opportunity. When would you rather catch a mistake, after the sale is made and the wrong product has shipped, or pre-order before it's a problem?

This is one of the hallmarks of a Sales Genius. It's not that they don't make mistakes. "To err is human," after all. It's that Sales Geniuses take a belt and suspenders approach to the sale by incorporating a double check to root out the possibility of error.

I suspect, like many salespeople, I learned the belt and suspenders method the hard way. I had just switched careers from school teacher to kitchen designer and I was working on 100% commission, where you only get paid when you sell something. In sales parlance, it's sometimes known as "eat what you kill'.

I was working out of a store in a rough section of town, picking up the broken wine bottles around the store before we opened each morning. Sales were poor and to say I was discouraged would be an understatement. There were days when only one or two people would come in the store—and some days none—so when an older woman came through the door she had my full attention. She explained she'd been to kitchen and bath stores all over town and no one could solve her problem. She had inherited a three-foot-wide antique heirloom cupboard from her ancestral home in Ireland and was determined to put it in her kitchen.

That didn't sound like that big of a deal to me, and I was confident we could make it work...until she showed me a carefully drawn layout of a tiny kitchen, with a special emphasis on the word "tiny." Not only was this kitchen more "postage stamp" than room, but it was in an old farmhouse and as such there were doorways everywhere leaving little in the way of free wall space.

I tried not to show my concern and asked her to give me 48 hours to work on her design. This was before commuter design software, and so I literally spent the next two days drawing revision after revision by hand, trying to squeeze her three-foot heirloom into her kitchen. I had all but given up, but the day before her follow up appointment, I woke in the middle of the night with an epiphany. I rushed to the showroom, kicked the wine bottles away from the front door, hustled inside, and completed the final design with only minutes to spare.

I proudly revealed my new design, complete with a three-foot heirloom cupboard. She was delighted, nodded approvingly and then furrowed her brow.

I said, "Is there a problem?"

She said, "What happened to my refrigerator?" It was at that moment I discovered where I had found the "extra" three feet in her kitchen.

By the way, leaving out a refrigerator in a kitchen design is difficult to recover from. It's not like you can eschew refrigerators in place of root cellars, or admonish the customer for not being emphatic about how important her refrigerator was to her before embarking on her design.

Bottom line: I didn't make the sale. I did learn the value of checking my work and rechecking it. You might argue about my design prowess but I never again designed a kitchen that lacked major appliances. Double checking and taking good notes will not solve every problem, but they will greatly lessen your chance of failure.

As you work your way through your notes, make sure you are getting buy-in on your informational accuracy. For example, if you sell furniture, there is an enormous difference between the wood species cherry, and some other lower grade of wood that's had cherry stain applied to it. This is the perfect application of midpoint summation, where you make that kind of distinction clear to your customer. You can see why we suggest this is one of the key selling techniques you'll want to wire into your brain's habit code.

Having a written account of what has transpired with your customer can prove to be invaluable after a week of busy sales interactions, when your memory of one transaction starts to bleed into another one.

Human memory is just not good enough to bank on recalling all the vital information that passed between you and your customers. This is the essence of the Ghost Curve. Trying to hold key information in your brain's working memory is both tiring and stress producing. Offloading content onto paper or a digital device is a must, especially as your customer base increases along with your newfound selling abilities.

Rule of Threes

You have an idea of the general shape of a successful sales pitch. Now, what's the most effective way to present your company's offerings?

It's time to brush up on a simple foolproof methodology called the "Rule of Threes." The idea is to break down a product or service into a hierarchical stack of the three most important emotional selling points, starting with the most important of the three, and then attaching an emotional marker to each. This caters perfectly to a customer's limited attention, and information expressed so succinctly is more likely to stick in a customer's memory.

Why focus on just three key selling points, when my product or service has so much more to talk about?

We've already seen that the vast majority of people can recall only four to seven chunks in their short-term memory, so focusing on three is a way of hedging our bets. This ensures we will stick vital selling points in the vast majority of our customers' brains by working off the lowest common denominator. Also, in this case, the chunks are more complicated––ideas and phrases, rather than single words or numbers. We want to be concise and precise.

Here is often what happens: when a customer asks the salesperson a question about a service or product, the salesperson's brain immediately starts searching for relevant information in memory retrieval mode. Unfortunately, the brain isn't designed to judiciously grab the most important information. Instead it tends to simply access the category, like the game show *Jeopardy!*, and pull out related information.

For example, if you worked in a furniture showroom and the customer asked you about a particular sofa, your brain might access the "sofa" category, pulling up brand, styling, color, price, and a myriad of other relevant information. The longer you've been selling sofas, the more information you've warehoused in your brain and the more you can wax on in detail.

This is one of the fastest ways to overwhelm and overload your customer's working memory. The customer doesn't generally have the bandwidth for your brain dump of information, and although they are likely to retain some of what you share, it might not be the most important information they seek.

Quantity of information is not the same as quality of information when it comes to selling. Surgical precision has an amazing sales effect. Sales Geniuses pay careful attention to exactly what the customer is asking for. Then they deliver their answer in the form of roughly three key selling points about a product or service.

How can they do this? It's a combination of trial and error, and doing their strategic homework.

To get started with this strategy, ask yourself, "If I could only tell my customer three things about this particular product or service, what would they be?"

Sit down and make a list of every selling point you can think of regarding a particular stock keeping unit (SKU). Once you have the list, you can go through and examine the points, refining and editing until you are satisfied that you've teased out the three most powerful selling points about that individual SKU.

Start with just a handful of SKUs, carefully building your curated list of key selling points. Then make yourself a cheat sheet of said points so that you can begin the memorization process. After enough practice, your System 1 process will eventually kick in automatically deliver the points immediately on demand without having to engage System 2. In other words, you won't have to think about it anymore.

The final step is to make sure that each key selling fact reaches beyond the simple notion of feature/benefit and creates an emotional connection. This connection should be something memorable that a customer is likely to relate to.

For example, if your job was to sell furniture, I should be able to point at any given SKU and ask you the following question:

"Tell me about this sofa."

You, the salesperson, should be able to immediately share three key emotional connected selling points without deliberation, along the lines of:

"Here are three things people love about this sofa. The fabric will stand up to caustic spills like red wine and nail polish remover. The backrest has been ergonomically designed to ease lower back pain. Lastly, this sofa was given the highest rating in *Consumer Reports* for best overall quality and price."

The formula above is three simple facts, each linked with an emotional connector. In this case we used *fear* of damage, *physical* lower back pain, and the *safety* of buying from a highly regarded consumer protection group's recommendation. This pre-planned blurb delivers key information with ready-made emotional markers that the customer's brain will earmark in memory for later access, likely tipping the customer towards a future purchase decision.

Practical Application

Let's assume you've done your homework. You've identified three key emotional selling points for each individual SKU you plan on selling, and you've created a cheat sheet so you can practice and memorize your points—the perfect opportunity to use Spaced Learning protocol!

Regardless of how you engage with the customer—via website, in a showroom, through a phone chat or as a road warrior making in-person calls—we've found this selling strategy to be highly effective.

Body Language

When you think of communicating, you probably consider speech an essential tool. Word-based language is a pretty cool evolutionary development, but it's not the preferred mode of expression in the subconscious brain. It instead speaks through body language: the playground of physical touch, gesture and nuance. Even in an area as talk-dominated as sales, body language can speak volumes.

A study done by the Cornell University School of Hotel Administration shows that a server who touched patrons on the shoulder for two seconds on average earned a tip of 14.9%, as opposed to 11.5% without the touch.[11]

So, what was going on? Keeping in mind that we don't endorse inappropriate touching, what does the shoulder touch mean?

One theory is that our brains still follow the primitive instinct to sort between *us* and *them*. The shoulder touch may game that system, creating a false sense of in-group intimacy.

Whatever the cause, there is no doubt that body language plays a far larger role in our everyday communication than what many of us might expect.

Sales Geniuses know that customers who lean in towards them when discussing pricing are far more likely to buy. And conversely, customers leaning back and away are less likely to buy, regardless of what they may be verbalizing.

Since so many gestures are controlled by the subconscious, it's difficult to detect all the informational cues you might be displaying at any given time. This is one of the reasons FBI interrogation sessions pay so much more attention to gestures than to words. *Telling* a lie is not all that difficult. However, getting your heart rate, facial tics, palms, posture, and eye movements in on the game is another matter entirely.

The next time you want to establish some in-group trust and camaraderie, pay attention to the things you're communicating before you ever open your mouth. But before you do that, you might consider the role that greetings and handshakes play when you have that all-important first-time interaction with your customer.

Peripersonal Space

In sales, we all know you first greet the customer in a friendly manner and determine exactly how you might be able to help them. Greeting seems like an obvious beginning in any selling situation––after all, there has to be the initial contact––but when that contact is face-to-face, neuroscience research has a lot to say about best practices.

Consider a story told by mother-and-son science writers Sandra and Matthew Blakeslee in their book, *The Body has a Mind of its Own*.

Team Blakeslee begins their story in an unlikely place: the region of your brain behind your right ear. It's known as your Right Angular Gyrus (RAG).

Before an epilepsy operation, a surgeon's standard procedure is to open up the skull and poke around a little to identify the various functional brain areas. Even though human brains share the same essential architecture, each brain is wired slightly differently. A quick round of poking and prodding is the best way to get a sense of the layout, and thus to know what not to cut.

Since the brain doesn't feel pain, this recon mission is done with the patient awake. The surgeon probes a given area, and the patient reports back what they are feeling. For example, a gentle touch on one area of your brain might register as if someone is tickling the big toe on your left foot.

One day, a neurosurgeon enacting this procedure happened to probe the patient's right angular gyrus. Much to the surgeon's surprise, the patient excitedly explained that they had the sensation of hovering above the operating table and looking down on their own body. The same thing has since happened to others as well. It turns out that at least some of the time, the classic out-of-body experience is as simple as knowing where to poke.

So, what's going on? In trying to predict and understand its environment, the brain constructs maps of the real world. This is how we can remember the floor plan in our house or apartment, or find our way back to the grocery store again and again. In a very literal way, your sense of self reaches beyond your own skin.

In fact, your brain annexes and maps the area around you as if it were an extension of your body, albeit a virtual one. Scientists call this zone "peripersonal space." The out-of-body experience, from the brain's point of view is not so "out of body," it's just working from a different definition of where your body begins and ends.

This makes the use of tools in our lives much more meaningful. When a baseball player picks up a bat, their brain treats the bat as a logical extension of their own arm and hand. In the same way, an experienced backhoe operator's command of the machine's controls turns the machine's bucket into their own giant robot arm, thus extending their reach in an almost literal way.

The Blakeslee's also point out that your peripersonal space is not static, but "morphs" based on your movement and intentions. This is why a sight-impaired person can learn to navigate so well with a cane.

And as they make their way down the street, even though they are simply maneuvering with a stick, their extended brain mapping allows them to feel the texture of the pavement, and extract a very real sense of the ground they are traversing.

However, unless you're holding on to something like a broom or your body is contained in something like a car, your peripersonal space tends to extend only as far as the length of your arm.

In Western culture, your arm's length usually signifies your comfort zone. As long as a stranger maintains that amount of distance, your brain feels at ease. But as soon as that person moves further towards you, passing through your peripersonal bubble, your brain's amygdala sounds the alarm and produces the stress hormone cortisol.

It's not uncommon for an exuberant salesperson to move through a potential customer's peripersonal space during the initial greeting or handshake. It may seem like a trivial matter, but once your customer's peripersonal space has been encroached on, their cortisol-flooded system ramps up their sense of fear and trepidation.

Clearly, this is not the way that you want to begin your selling experience. When cortisol levels are high in your customer's brain, they will not be in any kind of buying mood.

We've all experienced this kind of spatial encroachment in the extreme in the form of a "*close talker*," as in someone who gets uncomfortably near to your face during conversation. Your natural instinct is to back up away from them. This is a preprogrammed response your brain initiates; it's not the kind of thing your parents had to teach you as a child. It's something your brain enacts for safety reasons.

You'll notice that when someone gets on an elevator that's already occupied, everybody tends to shift a bit to create a little more distance between themselves and the new rider. As more and more people board an elevator, maintaining personal space becomes increasingly difficult. I suspect it would be rare to find someone who, as the elevator fills up, feels a sense of joy and thinks to themselves, "Oh this is so comforting, I wish more people would join us."

Stepping into a handshake—which many of us do unwittingly—may be ramping up a customer's stress level, predisposing them to being initially unreceptive to your sales information. Sales Geniuses are careful to always keep their feet planted during an initial customer contact, and avoid invading their customer's peripersonal space.

Handshake

Your peripersonal space is only one aspect of the way your body subconsciously navigates its way through space. It is important to allow that space to act as a buffer, giving your customer's brain time to interpret your intentions towards them. As a result, it's a good idea to avoid stepping into the handshake. But what is the best strategy for shaking hands, if there even is one?

People have been clasping hands with each other as a way of sealing an agreement or declaring peace since ancient Greece, but the history of the grab-and-shake greeting maneuver remains shrouded in mystery.

There's some thought it was used in its modern meaning as far back as medieval Europe, possibly to prove neither party was concealing a weapon in their right hand. The gesture was preserved in some Dutch communities, where the equality-loving Quakers picked it up as an alternative to more hierarchical greetings like bowing. As open social hierarchies fell slightly out of fashion in the nineteenth century, handshaking was there to fill the gap.[12]

While a longtime mainstay in the Western world, handshakes may be going through a revision or possibly even extinction as we more vividly understand how disease and viruses are transmitted. During the height of the Covid crisis handshaking all but disappeared. Still, for many, the handshake is a deeply ingrained habit, and so it is important to understand how its message can be subconsciously sent and interpreted.

You are no doubt familiar with a variety of handshakes.

The normal handshake, where both parties apply a reasonable amount of pressure, seems to communicate that the customer is open to discussion.

Then there is the limp handshake, sometimes referred to as "the dead fish" which feels a bit disconcerting on the receiving end. It's generally interpreted as a lack of commitment in which the customer is telling you that they have not decided one way or the other about you, your product, or service. It is a way of conveying to you that it's your job to win them over.

There's also the overly exuberant handshake, "the crusher," where it seems like your customer is trying to rearrange your metacarpals. This move is letting you know that no matter what, they need to be seen as in charge of their own fate in the transaction.

There is another phenomenon that can occur in a handshake, one that you may or may not be familiar with: the wrist turn over, or what is sometimes referred to as a "power move." This is where the customer exerts just enough side pressure to turn your wrist over, leaving your palm facing upwards at the end of the shake. Psychologists interpret this as the shaker's need to maintain control. They are often subconsciously trying to send a message to you that you are subordinate to them during a transaction.

This is generally more subtle than "the crusher," but the meaning is pretty much the same. It is like an opening move in a chess game, where the intention of your competitor can be gauged as the need to dominate.

Recognizing a power move gives you several options. One, you can ignore it, knowing that you can cater to the customers' needs during the sales transaction and help them feel like they are more in control.

Another option is to neutralize their effort. To neutralize a power move, you can counter with a double clasp. The double clasp is where you bring your other hand into the handshake and use it to help square the hand back to the normal vertical position. In effect you are now shaking hands with both your hands, palms facing each other.

Your customer might attempt to start the transaction on a stronger footing by engaging in the shoulder shake. This is where your customer is not only shaking your hand, but at the same time their free hand has moved up and grabbed your shoulder, in effect controlling your entire arm movement. This is not so subtle, and unlike a handshake power move, the recipient is often aware of the aggression.

This ultimate shoulder power move has become a mainstay in the political arena. You can frequently observe this behavior on YouTube during the opening exchange in political debates. This is something political coaches teach their clients. Watch both parties' participants purposely seeking the upper hand with shoulder power moves.

Is this just the penultimate power move before we adopt the head-butt? Let's hope not. Regardless of what physical gesture your customer might use to open a sales negotiation, it's important for you to be observant and use that informational clue to create a more rewarding customer experience.

The Hug

We've seen the effect of the stress hormone cortisol for those who step into the handshake or greeting, but what about the hug?

Hugging is a common part of established friendships and relationships. When you are good enough friends where a hug might be part of your greeting, your brains are delivering a fairly positive chemical experience.

A parent's brain produces a brain hormone called oxytocin—sometimes called "the love drug"—as that parent cares for their child. It is a chemical that helps establish a sense of closeness or bonding to another individual. From an evolutionary standpoint, the release of oxytocin helps guarantee that a child is more likely to be cared for as opposed to abandoned. That's a pretty important step for ensuring the human race continues to thrive.

Oxytocin is not strictly reserved for parent/child relationships. When you have a close relationship with someone else, the act of hugging produces oxytocin as well. Scientists have determined that giving out eight hugs a day can release enough oxytocin to raise their own mood an entire level, creating the same effect as some antidepressants.

We are not suggesting that hugs should replace antidepressants, or that you should start your day seeking eight hugs from whoever randomly crosses your path. What we are saying is that oxytocin and cortisol both serve valuable roles in making someone feel either bonded or uncomfortable.

In sales, knowing where you stand with your customer should give you insight into the appropriate greeting. Keeping your feet planted firmly and respecting the customer's peripersonal space during the handshake phase is by far the safest course of action.

Knowing when you've established the level of friendliness with your customer that a hug is in order is less clear. Salespeople who like to call themselves "huggers" should take note: it's not a given that your hug will be received as it was intended, nor does it follow that a hug will automatically convey a message of trust or friendship.

For all parties involved, it's probably best to follow your customer's lead, but staying outside their peripersonal space will generally serve you well.

The Passenger Seat

With your new knowledge of personal space boundaries and the effect of handshakes and hugs, there is one additional caveat that's important to understand. Like all rules, there is bound to be an exception or two. The brain pays acute attention to certain approaches, with your stress hormone delivery system at the ready during a frontal approach.

This is *not* true when someone is standing or seated next to you as in the passenger seat of a car. This "passenger seat" position, as far as your brain is concerned, is less of a threat and so feels far more comfortable. An evolutionary explanation suggests it's much easier to strike someone from the front then the side, so a stranger confronting you from the front appears to be potentially more dangerous. Thus, your brain plans accordingly

Pickpockets figured this out a long time ago. One of their standard operating procedures is to approach their intended victim or "mark" from behind or from the left or right of the person, carefully avoiding the mark's frontal peripersonal space area. To see this in action, check out YouTube videos of pickpocketing expert and professional entertainer Apollo Robbins. In his stage shows, Robbins frequently performs his magic-like feats of pickpocketing to the side of his "mark."

Some psychologists are also aware of the passenger seat phenomenon. They'll suggest that when you are trying to have a meaningful conversation with your junior high child, you'll often get more direct and honest information if you go for a ride together in the car as they ride shotgun. There is something about not looking directly at a person that can create a more relaxed conversation.

Sales Geniuses often make it a habit—particularly when discussing money—to stand or seat themselves next to their customer in the passenger seat position, avoiding bringing up delicate information from a frontal position.

Even when walking a potential customer through a showroom setting, it's advantageous to position yourself to the side of a customer when you stop to admire a display. Avoid any perception of confrontation and you're more likely to foster feelings of working together as a team.

This is also why it's not necessarily to your advantage to sit directly across from your customer while you sit behind an office desk. It's true that the setup of having a desk between you and the customer gives you some additional comfort, but for that same reason it works just the opposite for your customer.

This, in sales, is sometimes referred to as the "banker position," reminiscent of going to a bank in the often-uncomfortable position of asking for a loan. Trying to close a sale from behind a desk is something Sales Geniuses tend to avoid. Instead they are more likely to move out in the open to a round table where they can take full advantage of the passenger seat position.

One way of putting this learning together: after the initial greeting—and potentially handshake—your next move is to take a slight step to the side. This is sort of a "mini-passenger seat" move.

This move will be virtually imperceptible to your customer but their subconscious brain is likely to feel some small measure of relief as the amygdala's constant guard relaxes. This is one of those incremental moves that helps tip a customer towards comfort, thereby improving their chance of remembering your products and key selling points.

Increased Oxygen and Blood Flow

Oxygen and blood flow are incredibly important to brain function, both for gaining nutrients and metabolizing them. In a brain-driven approach to selling, we look to maximize these factors.

Studies show that simply standing up increases blood flow and oxygen levels. A 2017 study divided its participants into a sitting group and a standing group, and then administered a test which asked the brain to quickly deal with mild contradictions—such as printing the word "blue" in red font and asking you to pick the word in red. It's a reliable measure of our brain's processing ability, and the standing group consistently performed better.[13]

For even greater benefits, your brain tends to operate at its best when you're moving. Exercise has long been linked with greater brain oxygenation and blood flow. Many studies demonstrate that during or immediately after physical activity, even a simple walk, people perform better on tests of memory or attention. A 2014 study by Stanford researchers found that a person's creative output goes up by an average of 60% when walking.[14]

There are several implications to consider. First, walking your customer through a showroom means they have the best chance of absorbing information. It also means that your cognition will be higher as well, increasing the likelihood that your selling strategies will be more cogent.

Getting your customer to stand up and take a quick walk across the room is a great way to reboot their brain after they've been seated for a while and their natural disposition for mind-wandering has kicked in.

If you sell out of a showroom, think about the space as more than a repository of cool selling SKUs. It's the stage upon which you can choreograph a selling experience.

This means that you need to use the information you glean from body language and pupil observation to know when it's time to get your customer moving and maximize your time together.

You can combine this new information with what you've learned about the passenger seat and peripersonal space. Since humans are more comfortable with a lot of space around them, it stands to reason that you can enhance your chances by delivering your sales quote out in the openness of a showroom rather than behind a desk. Consider a center island, where you and your customer are standing on the same side of the island looking at the quote together. You're in the passenger seat, of course.

In the customer's mind, standing next to each other creates the sense associated with partnership and working together, and reduces the anxiety and sense of confrontation that a face-to-face interaction might have. This allows you to present the information more as a team member than the adversarial "banker's position." And because you're both on your feet, you'll have greater cognitive firepower.

Smile Power

We've seen how body position and various forms of greeting play into the customer experience, but what about smiling? How beneficial is that?

Have you ever passed time in a crowded space just people-watching? If you have, you've probably encountered the weird phenomena of seeing faces that look like they belong to people you know—doppelgangers of friends and family. You've seen the mind's trickery played out on stranger's faces.

Faces are important. It's estimated that a third of the brain is dedicated to reading and interpreting faces. If that area—specifically the fusiform gyrus—gets damaged, you walk around without the ability to recognize anyone by sight. People with prosopagnosia, or "face blindness," are unable to pick out the faces of their mother or best friend out of a lineup.

How good is your "face vision?" Try this experiment. Think of someone you know really well and then try to describe their features. After several minutes when you've exhausted all the basics—notes, mouth, eyes, ears, forehead, cheekbones, hair, scars and maybe a spare mole or two—you'll find that your description would still fit a large percentage of the population. Despite your best attempt, your ability to describe faces in a meaningful way is still shockingly inadequate. It makes you wonder how you're able to pick *anyone* out of a crowd.

Lately, neuroscientists have begun to crack the face code. One theory is that we don't actually store faces per se in our neural wiring. Rather, we store a set of data points. Think of a grid with a north/south and east/west axis. Now imagine that your facial recognition software begins with a perfectly balanced idea of a face, a kind of generic "every person."

When you encounter someone, your mental software kicks into gear and searches for key data points against this generic face. The further their features move away from these axes in any given direction, the more recognizable they become.[15]

The beauty of this system is that it conserves a ton of space. Instead of cramming a bunch of whole faces into the deep basement of our mental repository, we only need to store the point variations along the axes. When artists draw caricatures, they're just accentuating a handful of unique data points that stray from the central axes of John or Jane Doe. Amazingly, with this limited number of clues we can tell exactly who they've drawn. A couple of curvy lines later and you've got Abraham Lincoln.

These facial data points stored in your fusiform gyrus allow your customer to recognize you, as well as most people they encounter from their past.

Some people have extraordinary facial recognition. Scotland Yard in the UK retains a handful of these "super-recognizers" in their employment, and they use them to screen hours and hours of video in search of those who are wanted for questioning or crimes they've committed.[16]

What does all this face talk have to do with selling? Frankly, a lot. What goes into your facial recognition database are emotional markers to help make recall easier. This means that whether you're smiling or not when you meet a customer for the first time is likely to positively or negatively affect the feeling that gets attached to your face pattern.

Humans also fire neurons any time they observe another human doing something. For instance, if I see you slip on a banana peel, my own brain is probably simulating that activity and giving me both a sense of empathy and a general understanding of what you are feeling.

Scientists believe that consciously and subconsciously reading body language is essential for how humans learn and communicate. This is why kids who receive "the look" from their parents stop dead in their tracks. This is also why a single glance from a friend can speak volumes. With faces, a picture really is worth a thousand words.

Bottom line: if you're not smiling the first time you meet a customer, you might inadvertently be predisposing your customer towards a bad impression of you, which will continue to be reinforced with each subsequent meeting.

That first smile impression is key. It happens whether the customer sees you in person or a photograph of you. Realtors frequently attach a pleasant picture of themselves to their business cards. They might not have known the neuroscience behind a positive smiling impression, but intuitively they figured out the value.

But smiling is more than just a good sales strategy. When you smile, your brain releases an uplifting dose of dopamine, actually fostering a happier feeling. Studies show that marathon runners can boost their efficiency and lower their perception of difficulty by adopting a smile in the final tough stretch of a race, even if it doesn't reflect their mood in the moment[17]. So, smiling is really a two-way street: you can smile because you feel good, or you can feel good by smiling. Either way, smiling is often the gateway to a sale.

That said, smiling is only one aspect of communication. Body language in general is capable of telling us much more than speech. Where it is relatively easy to tell a verbal lie, scientists recognize it's actually pretty difficult to alter your body's physical cues to hide when you're lying. This is why the FBI is so keen on reading body language during an interrogation.

When I work with a customer, I slowly match their body position—for example the way they are standing or where their arms are placed. This is called "mirroring." Research shows that mirroring has a calming effect and makes me seem more trustworthy from my customer's brain's point of view. Like understanding and using the passenger seat position, mirroring is a tool that allows for a smoother salesperson/customer interaction.

Taking Notes

Starting with a smile is a good strategy, but it's also important that you begin by demonstrating a recognition of your customer's importance. The human brain is designed for survival and as such it places extreme importance on the self. Altruism and empathy are coveted qualities, but humans are "me-driven" at the emotional System 1 level. Because System 1 is usually what comes online during a sales situation, it's vital to recognize your customer's "me-driven" needs.

This is where taking notes comes in to play and why we continue to drive this point home. Of course, you don't technically need permission to take notes. It's unlikely a customer will decline, unless they are in the Witness Protection program—and that opens up a whole other can of worms. But by asking, you are calling the customer's attention to how important their words and thoughts are to you.

The divorce rate in the United States has been dropping since the 1980's but still hovers just below fifty percent.[18] Research suggests one of the main reasons the rate is so high is because one or both parties in the marriage feel that they aren't listened to. Interestingly, this is also one of the main reasons why an employee is likely to quit their current job.

We've already covered the benefits of midpoint summation, but by calling the customer's attention to your note-taking, you're also giving a clear indication that the customer must really matter to you, because you're willing to go to the hassle of writing down what they say.

As we mentioned earlier, the second benefit of taking notes is that your own working memory won't be heavily taxed to remember everything that happens during the sales transaction. Not only will your recall be better, but you'll be able to devote more attention to what they're saying and less to sifting through which details to remember. And later you can review your notes to make sure you are on the right track, and what the next steps should be.

Taking notes is therefore a twofer. You get the chance to show the customer they matter, while creating an invaluable supplement to your brain, helping to offset its bias for daydreaming.

We can't overestimate this vital note-taking strategy. Have you ever been to a restaurant with a large group of people and the server proceeds to take your table order without writing down your order? Maybe there are eight people in your party, and you marvel at the server's ability to remember the fine details of everyone's individual order.

But after a few seconds, your marvel wears off. On some level, you know from experience about the brain's very limited short-term memory, and you start to estimate the odds that the order will be correct. And lastly, because humans are me-driven, you begin to worry that it will be your order that gets screwed up. It's a pretty common scenario where wonder turns to concern and concern turns to worry.

Juxtapose this against the waiter or waitress who diligently writes down your order and then reads it back to you, ensuring that it will be correct. Clearly this process is far more mundane and certainly not as flamboyant as a demonstration of an advanced memory system. But let's face it: you'd rather have your correct order than risk being a casualty of someone else's faulty memory showcase.

Assuming you've done your homework, you are ready to deliver your three key emotional selling points when your customer asks you about your product. With that done, you must do something that is uncomfortable to many salespeople: you must wait for a response. You need to keep yourself from filling the silence if your customer doesn't respond immediately. This waiting is important because your next move is entirely dependent upon what your customer says and does.

You should be prepared to go deeper into your product or service description if your customer asks questions, but know our own internal data suggests that around 80% of the time people will not follow up beyond the three key selling points you've laid out. As we've pointed out, the brain is pretty happy with concise, easy soundbites, and the simplicity of that sort of response tends to create a comfort level.

Personality Testing and Sales

Is there a way to figure out the personality type of you customer and use that information to help product selection?

If you've been hired for a job in the last thirty years, chances are you've heard of Myers-Briggs, more formally known as the Myers-Briggs Type Indicator (MBTI) survey. It's a personality diagnostic tool used by everyone from self-searching college kids to Fortune 500 companies.

According to *Business Insider*, it was used by at least 89 of the Fortune 100 companies as of 2014.[19]

The Myers-Briggs purports to divide people into 16 "types" by placing respondents on four different continuums: are you more extroverted or more introverted (E or I); more likely to intuit subtleties or focus on sensing objective information (N or S); driven more by thinking or by feeling (T or F); and do you prefer to come to solid conclusions or continue to keep your options open (J or P)?

Each possible four-letter combination is associated with an archetype, and each archetype is said to approach the world in a certain way—with certain skills, shortcomings, wants, and needs. For instance, a type more adept at reading people might be better suited to a job with a lot of face-to-face communication.

People embrace their Myers-Briggs designation, labeling themselves ENFJ or ISTP with the same certainty as height or blood type.

There's just one problem with this. Actually, a couple of problems.

Okay, more than a couple.

Given its prominence, you might think it's surely been all proven out through multiple studies. We're talking the kind of careful, thorough science necessary when people's egos, and personal livelihoods, are balanced on a handful of test answers.

The problem is that science has the same relationship with Myers-Briggs that it had with alchemy back in the Dark Ages. It's true that Myers Briggs has turned into gold, but a different kind of gold to be sure.

Isabel Myers, daughter of Katharine Briggs, conjured up the personality test at her kitchen table in the forties, shortly after World War Two. She had no formal training in psychology or testing. She based her system on her reading of Carl Jung, who had in turn been a student of the famed Sigmund Freud. Jung suggested in one of his writings, *Psychological Types*, that human behavior seemed to break down into categories.

Myers, believing that Jung was on to something, went on to build her personality test. Jung himself considered the MBTI to be an oversimplification of his ideas, noting that each and every individual is "an exception to the rule."

Undeterred, Myers made the rounds of academia, hoping to drum up support for her newly minted system. She was repeatedly turned away due to an utter lack of scientific bona fides.

But in true entrepreneurial spirit, Myers soldiered on. She eventually found a buyer in Henry Chauncey, who had just started up a company called Educational Testing Service. You might know it better as the developer of the Scholastic Aptitude Test, or SAT.

Back in the late fifties, Chauncey decided that a personality test would be a nice addition to his fledgling college entry exam. According to Annie Murphy Paul in her book, *The Cult of Personality*, Myers was then able to leverage her Chauncey connection into some measure of respectability.

While some successful businesses may use the MBTI, we should be careful not to attribute correlation to causation. If 89 of the Fortune 100 companies also use the same brand of water cooler or coffee bean, do we assume that coffee brand is helping their business prosper, or simply that it's broadly popular?

In "Goodbye to Myers Briggs, the Fad That Won't Die," Adam Grant quotes management researchers William Gardener and Mark Martinko, who developed a comprehensive study of the MBTI and noted that, "Few consistent relationships between type and managerial effectiveness have been found."[20] Interestingly, this study was published in 1996; the information has been available for a while.

Criticizing the Myers Briggs has enjoyed a bit of a resurgence over the past couple of years, in pieces like Vox.com's video "Why the Myers Briggs test is totally meaningless," an episode of the myth-debunking series *Adam Ruins Everything*, and Vice.com's bluntly titled "The Myers-Briggs Personality Test is Bullshit."

It's been argued that measuring people on these four particular axes creates a number of false dichotomies. A person can avidly gather both facts and interpretations of those facts, weighing them a roughly equal amount. A person could also not feel very driven by either type of analysis. A person could selectively, in some areas of their life, seek hard data, while taking a more emotional, subjective approach when it comes to other issues. And all three people could find themselves placed at the midpoint between S and N, without much commonality to their experiences.

And as comprehensive as that four-letter profile can sound, even two people who consistently test as Extroverted, iNtuitive, Feeling, and Judging might behave in wildly different ways depending on their personal values. For instance, a group-oriented ENFJ might use their assertiveness and people-reading to advocate for fairness and harmony in a workplace, while a more individually-driven ENFJ might seek to influence a team in order to advance their own ideas.

It can certainly feel good to read about your "type," and if you've never stopped to consider whether you're more extroverted or introverted, you might even feel like you've gained some additional understanding of yourself. On the other hand, the same could be said for horoscopes. Maybe the real magic of your average personality test is just giving people an excuse to open up and describe themselves. As team-building exercises go, it beats "trust falls."

Unfortunately for Myers, one group never fully bought in: psychologists. They have their reasons, including studies where people's answers on the Myers-Briggs can differ significantly depending on the time of day it's administered. One study showed that up to 40% of the people who are given the test a second time end up with a different personality profile. It's also been suggested that because of the way the test was constructed, with little emphasis on negative traits, most people tend to accept their results without examining it too closely.

So, what's the bottom line? Is Myers-Briggs a bunch of baloney? At least on an anecdotal level, there certainly appears to be some connection between people and distinct communication styles.

However, it seems like an overreach to suggest Myers-Briggs, or any test for that matter, could ever capture one's personality as neatly as trapping a firefly in a glass jar. We've witnessed this oversimplification before, with the idea that a single number can represent the breadth and width of one's IQ.

Myers-Briggs, like IQ tests, do tell us something about ourselves, and it probably makes sense to consider them as one interesting set of data points on an incredibly complicated spectrum of human behavior. But in the end, putting too much emphasis on a personality test appears to be less about science and more about alchemy.

Since the invention of Myers Briggs, there always seems to be a new personality test popping up out there with avid believers and supporters. Like Myers-Briggs, they are unfortunately not grounded in any real science.

So, is there any scientifically-based personality testing that can be used for sales purposes—a test that can easily give you an absolute breakdown of an entire personality with all its intricacies, its highs and lows, and attribution for a myriad of behaviors? Bad news: that kind of test still doesn't exist, and might never be available.

The Beginning of Buying Patterns

Still, there is hope for sales. To really understand what's going on, we can travel back in time to 370 BCE. The great Greek physician/philosopher Hippocrates was chilling out in the local public square and doing a little scientific inquiry. In modern jargon we'd call this "people watching." As he hung out and observed, he realized people fell into roughly four groups: the pushy ones, the ones that talk too much, the anal-retentive ones who get bogged down in detail, and the doom and gloomers who think the sky is falling. Of course, he called them by different names because he spoke Greek. But you get the idea.

Fast forward to circa 2008 CE. Dr. Helen Fisher, a biological anthropologist and Senior Research Fellow at The Kinsey Institute, was chilling out in her research lab doing a little scientific inquiry with the folks at Chemistry.com. Dr. Fisher was collecting information regarding decision-making in dating.

Along with some neuroscientists, she discovered that people fall into roughly four groups: the pushy ones, the ones that talk too much, the anal retentive, and the doom and gloomers who think the sky is falling. Sound familiar? Of course, she called them by different names because scientific terminology always pretties things up, but you get the idea.

Not to be outdone by an ancient Greek who never owned a smartphone—or a single pair of pants––Fischer and the neuroscientists, with the help of fMRI technology, tied the four groups to four brain chemicals: Dopamine, estrogen, testosterone and serotonin.

Top dating sites have taken the Fischer study (initially about 40,000 people strong), and built their business model around her neural algorithm. They are busy matching people up based on "compatibility."

For a species that can boast space travel, our derivative wants and needs are shockingly predictable, falling into very few select decision-making buckets. The pushy people have been making morning traffic unbearable since the invention of the chariot; the anal retentive among us are still a giant pain when you find them on your core team at work; the noisy people, who are guaranteed to be sitting in the row behind you next time you go to the movies; and the worriers started fretting about the collapse of society about an hour after society began.

I wonder what Hippocrates would think if you could plunk him down in the middle of Twitter for a half hour or so. Assuming he could get past all those smartphones, would he really be surprised by what he would discover?

We can put people in fMRI's, chart their brain activity, predict their next epiphany and discern the neural chemical mix that dictates personality. But in the end, for all our technical prowess, modern society is largely a continuation of the ancients. A quick trip online confirms this. Sadly, as a social species we've made very little progress in a formula for deep-dive personality dissection, and Myers-Briggs, like so many other personality diagnostics, has proven to be a giant overreach not based in science. So where does that leave us in using personality testing and sales?

Maybe there's another way to frame that question. What if we don't really need to dig in deep enough for an intricate analysis of personality? What if we could simply tap into some actual hard science and glean just enough information to understand the brain's chemicals and decision-making patterns—or for our purposes, what we call "buy/sell patterns?"

This is where we can learn from the research that Helen Fisher has done, the actual neuroscience powering dating sites like Chemistry.com. We don't need a deep dive into understanding personality. We simply need to understand the relationship between people and their tendencies towards decision-making in a buying experience—their buying patterns. For this we can capitalize on the four patterns Hippocrates observed and what Dr. Fisher has gone on to prove scientifically using cutting edge brain tools.

Four Buying Patterns

There are four basic patterns that Homo sapiens express when it comes to what drives their decision-making in general, and in our case, buying products or services. These patterns are not specific to age, gender, intelligence, or cultural background. The patterns seem to be, in part, a neat piece of neural hardwiring that you are born with. To what extent the patterns are nature versus nurture is the old chicken and the egg question, which for our purposes doesn't really matter.

What matters is if you can identify which of the four buying patterns your customer displays. If you can, then it's likely you can better cater to their preferred method of purchase, increase the likelihood of a better customer experience, and come away with a sale. It's a basic win-win proposition. The good news is that customers tend to display clear signs of their buying patterns. With practice, you can learn to read these signs and react to them effectively, significantly increasing the odds of making a sale.

The fact that decision-making revolves around four patterns is one of the prime reasons why, as we stated at the start of this book, most selling systems don't universally get the job done. These systems tend to focus on only one pattern type—usually the same pattern as the creator of the system—and as a result of that internal bias, tend not to be wholly effective for the other three patterns.

It would be a bit of an overstatement to suggest that a given customer will always display the same buying pattern. Many customers are able to drop into one of the other three patterns depending on the situation. It's just that due to neural wiring and the power of habit, they tend to have their go-to buying pattern—the one that represents the bulk of their serious purchase decisions.

This is the key to maximizing your customer's buying pattern.

You need the ability to step out of your own pattern long enough to register your customer's pattern, and then mirror their communication style.

This last demand, the ability to temporarily suspend your own pattern, is oftentimes the toughest part of the learning curve as your habits and biases tend to favor your own pattern. In other words, salespeople tend to *sell* the way they like to be *sold*.

When a salesperson's buy/sell pattern matches up with their customer's pattern, the likelihood of closing the sale goes way up. Essentially, the salesperson and customer are speaking the same language. They have "compatibility." However, when a salesperson encounters a customer's pattern that doesn't match with their own, the incompatibility decreases the likelihood of selling to that particular customer. They are in essence no longer speaking the same language.

It's not that you're dating your customer. But on some level, what makes for a great match in a dating relationship is also true in sales: we seem to get along, we understand each other, and there is an element of trust shared between us. And as every psychologist will tell you, one of the essentials to a good relationship is the ability to actively *listen*. Sales Geniuses are all about listening to their customers and interpreting their customers' desires into the right product and services. This in turn creates the feeling that the salesperson really cares about them, and that sense of empathy is one of the cornerstones of compatibility.

If you are already in sales, imagine the following experiment. We video record you over a several-month period during all your selling encounters. At the end of the time period, we play you back the highlight reel of your selling experiences.

For most, we'd see that your selling approach—your buy/sell pattern— is extremely obvious, and it generally would not change regardless of who you were attempting to sell. It makes perfect sense. Because of habit and experience we find that we repeat what we believe is tried and true, which is usually also what we would want to hear if we were the buyer.

After years of experience, our approach to sales is for the most part fairly rote and standardized. This is especially true if you've experienced some level of selling success. That success tends to bias your brain towards your own buy/sell pattern. At that point it's simply the way you roll; it just *feels* right. Why would you change your approach if it's working?

It's a good question.

Think of it this way: if there are four buying patterns, and you are amazing with the one that represents you, you sell a great many customers with a compatible pattern to yours. But what about the other three customer buying patterns out there to whom you aren't currently specifically catering?

In our scenario, you are essentially batting one for four, or roughly 25% in sales opportunities.

Dan McDade at Prospect-Experience Insights writes, "A well-known industry analyst firm reports that best-in-class companies close 30% of sales qualified leads while average companies close 20%."[21] That statistic says it all. Salespeople might be effectively walking right past 70-80% missed opportunities by taking a one-size-fits-all approach.

Don't be embarrassed by this. In the heat of the battle, it's often difficult to focus on improvement and experiment with different selling strategies when your energy and time are being fully consumed just trying to keep your head above water. We tend to stick with what seems to have worked before. Your brain is even designed to operate in this mode as a means to save energy.

Your brain's energy-saving strategy and some level of success can therefore work against you by clouding your perception and keeping you from reaching the next level. This is one of the prime reasons why, in our estimation, only 4% of salespeople reach Genius level status, in which their selling success is in the exceptional range and their relative stress level is on balance. Many salespeople find their selling comfort through personal trial and error, and then hunker down in that groove, grinding away with some level of success and a whole lot of stress. Frazzle becomes par for the course.

To seriously boost your selling performance and balance stress—to operate in flow at the Genius level—you need to show mastery in all four buying patterns and demonstrate the ability to be a selling chameleon, dropping into the pattern of your customer. In other words, how you sell your customer is not about your own pattern but rather about your ability to be compatible with your customer's buying pattern. In this sense, the customer—not you—determines how they will be sold. This is at the essence of creating a truly exceptional customer experience and unending word-of-mouth referrals.

The good news is, you are probably already pretty good at speaking to one of the buying patterns: your own. As a result, chances are that you'll need the least help with that one. Still, you'll want to learn all four patterns. In any event, consider this work as essential, the blocking and tackling required to reach the highest mountain of sales.

In order to make it as easy as possible to learn the four patterns, we have given them names and suitable corresponding visual icons. This is our own invention. As we identify the four patterns, keep in mind that one pattern is no better or worse than another. Each pattern has its pluses and minuses depending on the situation.

Again, these decision patterns have been observed since the time of the ancient Greeks, and are not specific personality types. They are simply hunks of habits our brains employ as a way of navigating the world, and have proven to be incredibly useful when it comes to buying and selling.

We are including a diagnostic tool to determine your own buy/sell pattern. We suggest you take the time to run the experiment and see where you fall in regards to the four patterns.

Buy/Sell Pattern Diagnostic

You can use the form provided below to diagnose your Buy/Sell Pattern. The Buy/Sell Pattern Diagnostic is also available at www. BestMindframe.com using the password "diagnostic".

To use the tool below, read each statement. If it is generally true about you, mark an X in the corresponding blank under Column A in the grid. If the statement is generally not true about you, leave it blank. Note it's important to respond with an X or leave the box blank quickly and without deliberation. The faster you complete this step the better.

When you finish, you may have a lot of boxes checked, some boxes checked, or you may have only checked a few boxes. Any of those results are perfectly okay and to be expected.

Buy/Sell Pattern Diagnostic

Put an X in Column A next to statements that describe you.

Column A

1	I like to be unpredictable
2	I am consistent in my routines
3	I always read the owner's manual
4	I'm good at reading my friends feelings
1	I frequently act on the spur of the moment
2	I respect authority
3	I pride myself on getting every detail right
4	I care about what others think of me
1	I get bored with the same old
2	I like to explore my options thoroughly
3	I like clear choices; I'm not good with shades of grey
4	I often make decisions on gut feelings
1	In a discussion I'm usually right
2	I follow each step in a process
3	I am analytical and logical
4	I can be a chameleon depending on the group
1	I am at my best when I'm in charge
2	Rules are important to follow
3	I always double check my work
4	I often change my mind
1	I come up with stellar ideas

2	I take scrupulous care of what I own
3	I solve problems without emotion
4	Emotional experiences can move me
1	I seek out new experiences
2	My key people say I am traditional
3	I like figuring out how things work
4	I have a great imagination
1	I am always trying and doing new things
2	I am a meticulous person
3	I can be tough-minded
4	I am not afraid to show empathy
1	I feed on enthusiasm
2	I tend to be cautious in nature
3	I like a detail driven debate
4	I often get lost in my own thoughts
1	I am not afraid to take risks
2	More people should behave by the rules
3	I often have a hard time making choices
4	I am a real people person

Notice in each box you marked, there is a corresponding number: 1,2 3, or 4. Now go back and total all the statements you checked that are marked #1. Enter that total number in the Grand Total table below. Individually do the same for all #2, #3 and #4 statements and enter those totals. When you are finished you should have a final number above the word Driver, a final number above the word Manager, a final number above the word Engineer and a final number above the word Actor.

(Note: This tool should not be used in any other capacity then as a gauge for determining buy/sell patterns, and is not by any means meant to represent a personality assessment.)

Grand Totals

Total #1	Total #2	Total #3	Total #4
Driver	Manager	Engineer	Actor

Assuming you've taken the time to complete the diagnostic and come away with your results, you're probably thinking, *what does it all mean*? And why take the assessment before the buying patterns are fully explained?

It's important to run the diagnostic before we explain the buy/sell patterns in depth because research shows that telling you about the meaning of the patterns first might unconsciously bias you towards answering the statements differently.

The reason we suggested you answer as quickly as possible was so that we could engage your System 1 emotional brain systems, which is at the heart of buying and selling, and not your more analytical System 2 brain systems. In other words, if you think too much about the statements, your answers might reflect a conscious or unconscious attempt to "game the system," defeating the purpose and effectiveness of the diagnostic.

If you followed the directions carefully and worked quickly and honestly, this tool should be extremely valuable to use in your selling future.

We have had excellent results using this tool in the field of sales. That said, because it is only one diagnostic, it will only be as accurate as your answers to the statements. What we mean by that is that your level of honesty, anxiety, sleep, hunger, and so on can affect your end results. If you feel like your results won't really represent your behavior, we suggest you take the diagnostic again at a better time, prior to reading this next section where we describe the patterns in detail. It's important to have an accurate assessment of your pattern.

Your Own Pattern Breakdown

Look back to the diagnostic exercise. You should have four numbers on the bottom side of the page, each a compilation of your answers, each total tallied under one of the four icons. It might look something like this:

Example 1

Total #1	Total #2	Total #3	Total #4
10	3	1	8
Driver	Manager	Engineer	Actor

What example 1 tells us is that when it comes to selling, you are most likely to lead with a Driver approach. It's probably what feels the most natural, since it is the highest score on the diagnostic. Based on this data, you find it easiest to sell other Drivers. Because the Actor score is 8—close to your Driver number—you either find Actors easy to sell to *or* learning how to sell in the Actor pattern won't be as tough as learning to sell to the relatively unknown Engineer pattern.

Let's take a look at another example. Suppose your numbers came out more like this:

Example 2

Total #1	Total #2	Total #3	Total #4
3	8	8	5
Driver	Manager	Engineer	Actor

The first thing you probably notice in example 2 is that your Manager and Engineer scores are both the highest and tied. This suggests that depending on the circumstances, you might find either of these selling patterns as your normal go-to response. When selling to Managers and Engineers, you have the highest comfort level, and based on the numbers, Driver customers likely prove the most challenging to you. To significantly up your game, you would concentrate on learning the Actor pattern and putting additional time in on the Driver pattern.

Let's look at another example. Suppose your numbers look more like this:

Example 3

Total #1	Total #2	Total #3	Total #4
7	5	9	4
Driver	Manager	Engineer	Actor

Here we see that Engineer is the highest, with the Driver pattern close behind. You will likely find the Manager a bit of a challenge and the Actor is probably your toughest sale. In terms of improving your ability to connect with customers and increase your sales, you will need to put more energy towards learning the Manager and Actor patterns.

Let's look at one more example. Suppose your numbers look more like this:

Example 4

Total #1	Total #2	Total #3	Total #4
1	7	3	9
Driver	Manager	Engineer	Actor

What example 4 tells us is that when it comes to selling, you are most likely to lead with an Actor approach. It's probably what feels the most natural, since 9 is the highest score on the diagnostic. Because the Manager score is 7, you likely either find Managers easy to sell to or will more easily learn how to sell in the Manager pattern. Your low "Drivers" score suggests learning to sell in this pattern will be more challenging.

When we look at this assessment, we usually focus on the two highest scores. They most likely reflect your current selling strategy—your go-to selling patterns. If there is a tie, you might effectively have dual capabilities as your go-to option.

What Does it Mean?

Now, we'll explain the buy/sell patterns in detail. You will be able to begin working on your domain knowledge as it relates to each pattern. Studying the buying patterns as a part of your daily regimen will allow you to create a systematic approach towards a comprehensive selling strategy.

All your customers have a buying pattern, as do you. If you are in sales, it turns out that your *buying* pattern also happens to be your *selling* pattern. Keeping that in mind, let's take a look at how this all works.

The four buying pattern icons:

Driver

Actor

Manager

Engineer

Driver Pattern

We begin with the Driver pattern. Just like the name implies, a Driver is someone who has definite ideas about where they're going and how the sale should transpire. They like to take charge early and feel like they are in control. The brain chemical dopamine is prominent in the Driver pattern and dopamine creates a tendency to seek novelty.

Positive attributes: Drivers can be fun and generous. They are willing to take risks to enjoy new products and features, intense and exhilarating adventures, and can be impulsive and uninhibited. They are comfortable to be the first on the block with the new thing. Drivers enjoy being trendsetters, and going against the grain.

Look out for: Their desire for adventure and devil-may-care attitude means loyalty is not necessarily at the top of the Driver's list. They are energized by conflict, which can cause them to come off as contrarian and combative.

Notes: Drivers like to feel like they've gamed the system, and feel especially good about getting in on the ground floor of a deal. Winning is all-important.

For Driver Salespeople: If you are a Driver pattern as a salesperson, one of your challenges to overcome will be putting extra energy in listening to the customer and not simply telling the customer what they should buy.

When selling to an Actor, use your charm and go out of your way to win them over, remembering that a compliment to an Actor is like a picnic basket to a cartoon bear.

When selling to a Manager, be patient and keep in mind that they don't respond well to pressure or assertive behavior. They don't see the world as a competition of win/loss as much as a chance for everyone, when treated as equals, to share in the winning.

When selling to an Engineer, remember the role that detail plays in decision-making. The more you slow down and provide them with an adequate data set, the more likely they will reward you with a sale.

When selling to another Driver, revel in the excitement of finding a true and worthy competitor, and the good chance that the end result will be a sale, but only after you've both established your alpha credentials.

Dealing With a Driver Pattern

General Behavior

- The Driver wants to be in charge, and sees your role largely as one of service.

- The Driver doesn't enjoy small talk when they are on a mission, so get right to the point.

- Remember, the Driver is assertive and wants to be in control.

- The Driver never wants to be wrong and considers themselves an expert; be sure to acknowledge their insights when possible.

- Be totally organized in your presentation with everything thought out and ready to go for your meeting ahead of time.

- The Driver will want to set the timetable, so make sure the timetable reflects their personal need.

- Drivers don't like to spend a lot of time listening (because they lose control) so keep information short and efficient—for example, bullet points in presentation mode.

- Drivers like one-page summaries.

- Making any idea feel like the Driver's own idea will increase selling opportunities with them.

- Drivers are time oriented and don't like to wait for anything.

- Drivers don't want to know the process or the steps; that will turn them off. Be super-efficient with your Justification process, move quickly and with certainty.

- Drivers like to get the big things out of the way immediately, and then solve small problems on the fly.

- Drivers in their need to win will often frame situations in terms of competition.

- Driver have a strong need to be recognized for their expertise

- Drivers are driven to be seen as the best and relentlessly push themselves, seldom satisfied with the end results.

Results Mode

- Move quickly to close the deal; impatient Drivers will seek out another vender quickly if they sense a lull in the action.

- Drivers like results and getting immediately to the bottom line. ("What is my price?")

- Drivers are opportunistic, so loyalty or relationship does not drive purchasing decisions.

- Avoid meeting with a Driver at the end of the day. You need to be fresh and on your game, as their mode of operation involves testing you, your thoughts, ideas and concepts.

- Never give the Driver a single option; give them a clear binary choice.

- The Driver will test your competence by a couple of quick questions; if you can't answer them, it's game over.

- Drivers like a structured work space and like to be busy based on their own agenda.

- Drivers are task driven and like to constantly be measuring for results.

- Drivers can show a warm side, but when the chips are down, they will tend to assert themselves often moving into a dictatorial mode.

- Drivers pride themselves on their ability to make timely decisions and have little time for those that are not decisive.

- Drivers put a lot of emphasis on someone's prior track record and verifiable results.

- In a team setting Drivers are only satisfied with winning, even a second-place finish will be written off as a loss.

- Drivers assess others quickly and will discount people, and avoid working with those that appear to be weak in any one of a variety of categories.

- The motto for a Driver might be summed up as "Win at all cost."

An Encounter with a Driver

A Driver may show up a little late, barely make the appointment time, or repeatedly reschedule. They might come confidently striding into your showroom while talking on their cell phone, and begin the conversation while still on the phone. This might appear rude, but from a Driver perspective, it is just being efficient with time.

The Driver will get to the point quickly and ask bold and direct questions like, "How much will this cost?" or "What is your best price?" These questions can often occur even before there has been any explanation about products or services on your part.

I once worked with a veteran salesperson who would respond to a Driver question like "How much is this new landscape design going to cost me?" with the line:

"How much is a bag of groceries?"

This very direct and Driver-like response would catch the Driver customer off guard, and they would ponder for a second, and then respond with something like,

"Well it obviously depends on what you put in the grocery bag."

The salesperson would smile, and say, "That's exactly the right answer, so let's see exactly what you'd like to see in your new landscape plan and then we can determine the price." This bold response to a bold question is something that makes perfect sense to a Driver.

Drivers love to begin early in the conversion with a challenge: "I've been to your competitor already, so am I wasting my time with you or can you be competitive?"

The Driver may begin by playing what they perceive as the expertise card on you with a line like, "I've remodeled and flipped a ton of houses, so let's just cut to the chase about features and price...."

The driver style can come off as strident, but they actually learn through challenge, and this is critical to understand. The speed of your immediate and knowledgeable comeback, your readiness to engage, and what seems like your delight in taking on the challenge has a profoundly positive buying effect on the Driver.

Here is a Driver in action: "I've never heard of this brand you're talking about. What makes it so great?"

A good response? "Great question. For someone like you, who obviously knows what you're talking about, you'll understand why *Consumer Reports* rated this the best air conditioning unit on the market for both price and efficiency." And then you proceed with the Rule of Threes and emotional underpinning bullet points bolstering your claim.

In this short response, you acknowledge the Driver as smart, give a nod to their expertise—both highly important to the Driver's image—then use brain science to make your case. For example, let's say you were in HVAC sales and working with a Driver customer. At some point in the dialog, you might drop in a line like this: "Because this particular air conditioner is selling so well, we fully anticipate the vendor to be raising prices very soon on this unit."

For a Driver who loves getting in on the deal—not to mention the near-universal desire to avoid feelings of loss aversion—the idea of buying at a lower price before it spikes is attractive. Drivers pride themselves on their deal-making and love regaling their friends and family with the deals they get, especially when the deal is the result of their negotiating skills. Undoubtedly, you've been at some social function trapped by a relative or friend who happens to be a Driver, and heard them tell the story about the time they negotiated the most amazing deal on X. In fact, if you know that person well enough, it's likely you've heard that story multiple times.

If you are new to sales, or your own pattern is primarily that of an Actor or Manager, the onslaught from a Driver right out of the gate can seem daunting and immediately put you on the defensive. Keep in mind that boldness is one of the Driver's key operating tools, and to succumb to feelings of inadequacy or write the Driver off as rude or arrogant will make you look weak in the Driver's eyes and put the sale in jeopardy.

It's important to understand that a Driver's abrupt manner isn't meant as a personal affront. In other words, it's not really about you; it's more about the habit they've adopted and how they see their must-win role in the competitive battle of getting a good deal. Knowing this and showing yourself as a worthy match will yield surprising results with a Driver.

If you take on the Driver with the spirit of game strategy, proving your knowledge and that you're not immediately intimidated, Drivers will often abruptly soften their approach. It's as if they become highly receptive to the possibility of a sale only after you have been proven "worthy." Sometimes this occurs simply by acknowledging the legitimacy of their point of view.

It's not uncommon at the beginning of a seminar I'm leading on selling techniques to have a Driver in the audience push back and challenge a concept I've introduced. By recognizing the Driver and giving them a chance to express themselves, I've found at the end of the seminar the

Driver will be enthusiastically buying into new ideas, staying after the seminar to further the conversation.

Drivers, unlike an Engineer, will often make a buying decision right on the spot. This is because Drivers operate from the gut, and tend not to second-guess their decisions. Drivers, when confronted strategically, are among the easiest patterns to sell. It seems counterintuitive, but Drivers, for all their aggressive approach, are often quick to decide and fast to buy.

Because Drivers' decisions are often transactional in nature, they may show loyalty as long as the relationship is perceived by them to be in their favor. This is how it is possible to forge a recurring buying relationship that is years long, only to find one day the Driver has moved on with your competitor. Loyalty as such is conditional, and although the Driver still might hold you in high regard, that won't necessarily preclude them from purchasing elsewhere. In that sense, quid pro quo isn't generally an important concept for the Driver. It's more, "What have you done for me lately?"

For the Driver, you earn each sale as you go without any cumulative sense of obligation on their part, no matter how many times you've come to their rescue. Drivers, because of their competitive nature, were the kind of kids in school who might have gotten the highest score on the test in the class, but they still weren't satisfied because they didn't get 100% of the answers right. Drivers can be easy to sell, but sometimes tough to service because they challenge from the start and continue that strategy all the way to the sale's logical conclusion, always prepared to renegotiate in order to better their situation.

If you are not a Driver pattern, as a salesperson, you will need to mentally prepare yourself when you encounter a Driver in a selling experience. Because of their belief in self, their dogged determination, and their competitive nature, Drivers often find themselves in leadership roles in the business world. One of the not-so-secret secrets to selling a Driver is to make them feel like they are directing and orchestrating the sale at all times. Avoid the game of one-upmanship with the Driver; they don't respond well to being proven wrong or bested in competition.

Actor Pattern

The Actor pattern puts a lot of importance in how they are perceived, and how things look and feel. They tend to operate in a form-over-function mode. They also enjoy the back-and-forth of human interaction. The brain chemical estrogen is prominent in the Actor pattern. (Estrogen, and for that matter, testosterone, are not solely female/male hormones, but are present in all human brains regardless of gender.)

Positive attributes: Actors can be the life of the party and, because of their spontaneous and people-pleasing nature, they can be great company. They are excellent at reading other people and adjusting how they express an idea to best connect with their audience. Because of this, Actors are natural communicators.

Look out for: Actors need to be liked and their reliance on compliments can sometimes make them seem superficial. Actors are quick to show friendship, often giving the appearance in new situations that you are their new best friend. Because Actors are more "big picture" and less about the details, this can sometimes lead them to eschew responsibility when problems arise.

Notes: When Actors go shopping, they seek selling experiences that are personally rewarding, even life-altering. They are looking for the big "wow." In this regard, Actors tend to bias towards new and unique product features, and will upgrade a purchasing decision to achieve the feeling of a specialized personal experience.

For Actor Salespeople: An Actor salesperson has to be careful that they are not perceived as simply sucking up in order to make a sale, especially when working with non-Actor customers.

When selling to a Driver, you will be challenged—so don't take it personally. Play the part of a worthy competitor and be willing to challenge back a little to establish your worth in their eyes.

When selling to a Manager, bonding with them should be no problem. Keep in mind that superficiality won't impress them, so be careful with overdoing compliments.

When selling to an Engineer, remember they require a lot of data, so gear up for that. Don't push features and benefits until you're sure they have the detailed information they request, and you've provided them with answers to the deeper dive questions with which they're likely to confront you.

When selling to another Actor, enjoy the experience but remember: it is still on you to get all your i's dotted and t's crossed. As the salesperson, it's your job to be the adult in the room and keep the meeting on track. The chances of an Actor salesperson selling an Actor customer lean strongly in your favor, especially after the "friendly fest" that's likely to occur.

Dealing with an Actor Pattern

General Behavior

- An actor's workspace is often chaotic and unorganized, which they attribute to a creative approach to problem solving.

- Actors enjoy a fast pace and relish spontaneity, which means it's important to adopt tools like binary choice and Good-Better-Best—more on those later—in order to bring some level of order to the process.

- Actors, when uncomfortable, can be sarcastic and attacking, and can be quick to blame the salesperson when things go awry.

- Actors are irritated and stymied by inflexibility and will seek a selling environment that feels less controlled.

- The actor pattern is generally warm, friendly and loves engaging in conversation, which makes it imperative that a salesperson with an Actor customer conducts an orchestrated Justification session

- You must establish a relationship with an Actor, even if the relationship is slightly superficial. They enjoy flattery; recognizing them and using their name is important.

- Actors tend to dress fashionably and stylishly when they want to impress, and they will invest in cutting-edge products and services.

- Actors like relationship over task and will move through the tasks quickly to get back to conversation.

- For actors, personal worth is measured by recognition and compliments

- Actors look to their salesperson for inspiration and see that as one of your vital roles

- An actor seeks support of their ideas and needs constant reassurance that they are making the right choice throughout the selection process.

- Status is important to an Actor, and they like the feeling of being treated as special.

- Actors are dreamers and love experience so engage as many senses as you can in their product selection.

- Understand their concept of a dream purchase and you will sell the job.

- Actors like to be out in front with new trends and ideas: "What's the hottest stuff, what is cutting edge?" Make sure you show them "the latest and greatest in product and design."

Results Mode

- Help actors imagine their buying dreams by painting a picture with evocative words that heighten the experience beyond simply making a purchase.

- Actors are not driven by time and will take as long as they need to complete a sale. This means *your* time.

- Actors make decisions based on how they feel rather than a step-by-step approach or process; if it feels right, they will buy with little hesitation.

- Actors generally prefer form over function.

- Actors value the visual over the mechanical working of a product so the overall look is key to creating their dream experience, which means dwelling on detail can sometimes turn off the Actor profile.

- The Actor processes ideas by talking about them, so they need plenty of time to talk through their purchasing vision.

- Actors don't always read the small print so make sure you get important sign offs.

- Actors change their minds easily so it is critical to achieve Justification and lock them down.

- The Actor is open and often thrives on changes in design, so be specific about what is included in your services ahead of time.

- Name brands can be an important factor for Actors and they tend to gravitate towards them.

- The Actor is among the easiest buying patterns to sell, because the sale is often built on the back of excitement as opposed to a deep dive into details.

- It will be up to you to set the timetable as Actors aren't often deadline-driven.

An Encounter with an Actor

An Actor may show up a little late, barely make the appointment time, or repeatedly reschedule. But unlike the Driver pattern, they will express remorse and spend time detailing how their schedule got away from them.

The Actor generally won't ask bold and direct questions like, "How much will this cost?" or "What is your best price?" Instead, their questions will center around themes like, "What is hot right now?" or "I saw X on TV or the Internet, do you carry that brand?"

Also, it's not uncommon to have an Actor enter a showroom not having really spent any time prior to the meeting honing in on exactly what they want. Like a kid in a candy store, Actors frequently ask to see everything.

Because the Actor places relationships at the pinnacle of how they operate, they might spend some time attempting to ingratiate themselves with the salesperson. This might seem counterintuitive; after all, who is selling whom? But the Actor's need to be liked can make this relationship a precursor for them to fully enjoy the buying experience.

This strategy of wanting to be your new best friend is also one of the signature moves of an Actor salesperson pattern, and as such, they will often employ liberal use of compliments towards the customer in order to win them over.

The Actor style can come off as disorganized, but they actually learn through the back-and-forth of conversation. This is critical to understand. The Actor customer is much more likely to have a positive response if you can engage them by listening intently to their ideas, and then showing excitement and delight in taking on the challenge.

Here is an Actor in action: "I've heard great things about X brand of air conditioner, can you tell me more?"

Here's a good response. "Great question. For someone like you, who obviously knows what you're talking about, you'll appreciate coming in from one of those 100-degree wilting days in the unforgiving sun to enjoy what feels like that cool and refreshing breeze coming off the ocean."

Notice for the Actor, your leadoff goes right to the emotional impact of physical feeling, as opposed to the Driver where we immediately emphasized the *value* afforded by a good review from *Consumer Reports*. And then as in the case of all buying patterns you encounter, you proceed with the rule of threes and emotional underpinning bullet points bolstering your claim.

In this short response, you acknowledge the Actor as smart, giving a nod to their self-importance and what they deserve (the cool breeze), which is vital to the Actor's image. Then you proceed, using brain science to make your case. For example, let's say you were in HVAC sales and working with an Actor customer. At some point in the dialog, you might drop in a line like this: "Because this particular air conditioner is so incredibly popular right now, we'll be lucky to keep these units in stock."

For an Actor who wants to be part of cutting-edge trends—not to mention the near-universal desire to avoid feelings of loss aversion— the idea of buying what currently is in vogue tips them towards the sale, even on something as seemingly mundane as a cooling appliance. Actors pride themselves on their cutting-edge discerning savvy for the latest and greatest, and love regaling their friends and family with the unique purchases they make.

Note that this may sound somewhat similar to the Driver pattern. There is some overlap between the two, but again, Drivers orient towards value while Actors orient towards novelty.

If you are new to sales, or your own pattern is primarily that of a Driver or Engineer, the onslaught of an Actor's ideas and their openness to any and all products can seem daunting, and immediately put you on the defensive. Keep in mind that hands-on experience is one of the Actor's key operating tools, and to try to force the Sisyphean task of keeping an Actor on track will only prolong and worsen the experience for everyone involved.

It's important to understand that, for the Actor, their possible lack of organization or direction isn't meant as a personal affront. In other words, again, it's not really about you; it's more about the habit they've adopted and the need to ensure an exciting buying and post-buying experience. Actors are endlessly in search of those bigger-than-life "wow" moments.

It's not uncommon during a break period of a seminar I'm leading on selling techniques to have an Actor come up and tell me how exciting the seminar is, and how they can hardly wait to get back to the sales floor to try out all the new things that they have learned. Interestingly, our research shows that for all their excitement, the Actors aren't necessarily any better on follow-through than any of the other patterns after a seminar. It's actually likely that as much as Actors mean to employ the new techniques they have learned, for some, their lack of time management makes it tough to work the new techniques into their daily routine.

Actors, unlike an Engineer or Manager, will often make a buying decision right on the spot. This is because Actors, like Drivers, operate from the gut and tend not to second-guess their decisions during the initial purchase. Actors, as discussed, are among the easiest patterns to sell. Actors, for their disorganized approach, are just like Drivers: quick to decide and fast to buy. That said, unlike Drivers, if the Actor's decisions weren't run through the Justification process properly, it's also not uncommon for actors to change their minds, often repeatedly.

Actors are particularly susceptible to overload, and when overloaded will often simply decide in the moment, not necessarily weighing the consequences because they assume there is some level of flexibility in the buying experience. It is easy to make mistakes when selling an Actor because they aren't driven to pay attention to the details, and assume you are there to mop up after them if problems should arise. For all the fun you can have during the sales process with an Actor, be forewarned that you need to be on your toes paying special attention to the details to which they aren't paying attention.

For Actors, like Drivers, decisions can be transactional in nature. They may show loyalty as long as the relationship is perceived by them to be in their favor. Loyalty as such is conditional on the salesperson's ability to continually demonstrate they are meeting the emotional needs of the

Actor customer. The Actor's motto is similar to the Driver's but with one added twist on the end: "What have you done for me lately, and do you still like me?"

Provided the salesperson is vigilant about keeping all the details in order, the salesperson will be rewarded with a steady stream of word of mouth referrals.

If you are not an Actor pattern, as a salesperson, you will need to mentally prepare yourself when you encounter an Actor in a selling experience. Because of their need to truly get the most out of the buying experience, Actors are likely to burn up a lot of the salesperson's time. Selling and buying for an Actor salesperson and customer revolve around one concept: the perception of a relationship. That sense of bonding, even in a superficial way, can tip an Actor customer towards a sale.

Driver Pattern

A Manager is someone who puts a lot of importance in fairness and empathy towards others. They tend to operate in a function-over-form mode. The brain chemical serotonin is prominent in the Manager pattern. Serotonin is associated with a sense of well-being.

Positive attributes: Managers aren't necessarily the life of the party, but because of their warm and people-pleasing nature, they can make good lifelong friends. They often seem reserved, and don't necessarily speak out or command the stage like the Actor pattern. They tend to be considerate and avoid making quick judgements, especially when multiple people are involved in a situation. Because of this, Managers tend to excel in team dynamics.

Look out for: Managers need a lot of time to make decisions and will often require some alone time to come to a conclusion. They seek meaningful relationships and dislike conflict. Because Managers are more detailed, and less about the 60,000 foot view, this can sometimes lead to a prolonged sale.

Notes: When Managers go shopping, they seek selling experiences that are logical and strategic, avoiding as much chaos as possible. They are looking for proof of reliability and an efficient, low-key buying experience. In this regard, Managers tend to bias towards new and unique product features, but only when those features serve a specific purpose and are not simply a fad, or eye candy.

For Manager Salespeople: A Manager salesperson, in their desire to cover all the bases, must make sure that they don't dampen the emotional excitement of the Actor or Driver pattern.

When selling to a Driver, you will be challenged, so don't take it personally. Play the part of a worthy competitor, scoring points along the way by demonstrating your efficiency of process.

When selling to an Actor, bonding with them should be no problem. Keep in mind that superficiality is part of their strategy for becoming your new BFF, and compliments are like currency for this pattern.

When selling to an Engineer, remember they require a lot of data, and during the Justification process you have a chance to really shine by demonstrating your command of domain knowledge and your finely-honed process.

When selling to another Manager, enjoy the experience. Your similar bent for an honest and fair encounter will serve you well and likely produce a sale.

Dealing with a Manager Pattern

General Behavior

- Managers are friendly, outgoing, and informal.

- Managers' dress is frequently casual; their goal isn't necessarily to impress

- Managers are slow to act on a purchase and don't like taking risks or feeling pressured to buy.

- Managers will stick to the timetable that is established. Don't expect to deviate from it.

- Managers don't like surprises. Make sure everything is explained up front, especially the steps if something goes wrong (for instance, damage and return policies).

- Process is important to Managers and they will not buy unless they thoroughly understand all the steps. "How does this whole thing work?" is a typical question.

- Managers are relationship-driven and will not purchase until they are completely comfortable with your relationship and you prove that you follow a system or process

- Trust is important to Managers so whatever you commit to, make sure you follow through in a timely fashion.

- Loyalty is important to Managers. A Manager that's had a good buying experience will often be your best advocate for referral business.

- Take your time in the Justification process, because it speaks to the heart of how the Manager thinks.

- Unlike Actors, Managers' relationships tend to be less superficial and more about bonding.

- Managers want to be seen as likable, in a way that is less about dishing compliments and more about a genuine sense of compatibility.

Results Mode

- If there are multiple decision-makers, the Manager will want everyone present for the meeting.

- Managers don't usually enjoy change so any alterations must be carefully explained in terms of why. "Why?" is a common question from Managers

- Managers need time to make decisions, so they will want to go home and think about any major purchase before they commit. Suggesting that they go home and sleep on their decision will give comfort and increase your chances of selling a Manager.

- Managers think in terms of team and consensus approval. If there arc multiple decision-makers involved in a purchase, you must get approval from the whole team. Even if the manager is ready to purchase, they will walk if the whole team doesn't buy in.

- When it comes to sales, Managers practice the "slow and steady wins the race" approach.

- Managers are turned off by aggressive selling behavior.

- Managers are not looking for the upper hand in a selling situation; their sense of fairness precludes a winner-take-all strategy.

- Under tension, Managers will often give in, but maintain a long-term slight if they feel that they have been taken advantage of.

- Managers go to great lengths to avoid confrontation and will forego a purchase where the salesperson or environment makes them feel uncomfortable, even if the product is of a superior nature.

- Managers pay attention to details and will make decisions about a salesperson by watching how much empathy they afford other people they work with or come in contact with.

- Managers look for all the steps in a process to be complete and done in an orderly sequence

An Encounter with a Manager

A Manager is likely to show up on time or a little before the appointment, having done some homework on products or services associated with the buying experience.

The Manager generally won't ask bold and direct questions like, "How much will this cost?" or "What is your best price?" They won't ask questions centering around themes like, "What is hot right now?" or "I saw X on TV or the Internet, do you carry that brand?" Instead they will ask process questions like, "How long will this take?" or, "What happens in the event that something comes damaged?"

Also, it's uncommon to have a Manager enter a showroom not having spent any time prior to the meeting honing in on exactly what they want. But if they do enter your showroom having not already prepped, they will take as much time as necessary to understand the products and your company's processes, asking specific questions regarding the "How and Why" of your particular enterprise.

Because the Manager, like the Actor, places relationships at the pinnacle of how they operate, they might spend some time attempting to understand the salesperson's background and level of expertise. The Manager, unlike the Driver pattern, sees the buying experience as far more than just a product review and a decision to be made; they also need the experience to be hassle free, where they are not subject to a high-pressure selling tactic, or a salesperson who seems quota driven.

Their strategy doesn't involve wanting to be your new best friend, but they do want to feel that you, the salesperson, are displaying a level of honesty. If things should go awry, the Manager wants to count on you to quickly remedy the situation without additional prodding or threat on their behalf. They may go out of their way to avoid a situation of confrontation as their motto might be "fair and hassle free.'

The Manager style can come off as being proactive and buttoned up, and they learn through thoughtful and deliberate discourse. This is critical to understand. The Manager customer is much more likely to have a positive response if you can engage them by listening intently to their ideas, showing excitement and then detailing how your process has been designed to lessen mistakes, but how, should they occur, your solutions have proven effective.

Here is a Manager in action: "I've heard great things about X brand of air conditioner, can you tell me more about the warranty?"

A good response? "Great question. You'll appreciate that our warranty is X and designed for your safety, so that no matter what happens we'll make sure you'll never be left in the lurch, and we'll supply you with a temporary unit at no charge. Of course, we don't anticipate that, but we pride ourselves on being prepared for the worst possibility."

Notice for the Manager, your leadoff goes right to the emotional impact of feeling "safe," as opposed to the Driver where we immediately emphasized the value afforded by a good review from Consumer Reports. And then as in the case of all buying patterns you encounter, you proceed with the Rule of Threes and emotional underpinning bullet points bolstering your claim.

In this short response, you give a nod to the Manager's diligence and that they can rest assured should a problem arise, which is vital to the Manager's peace of mind. Then you proceed, using brain science to make your case. For example, let's say you were in HVAC sales and working with a Manager. At some point in the dialog, you might drop in a line like this: "Because this particular air conditioner is so incredibly trouble-free, positive word of mouth from past customers on these units means we're lucky to keep them in stock."

For a Manager who wants to have a long-term hassle-free experience and avoid loss aversion, the idea of buying what has currently been proven to be safe and maintenance-free tips them towards the sale. Managers pride themselves on their logical assessment capabilities and the verification that they are making a wise buying decision.

If you are new to sales, or your own pattern is primarily that of a Driver or Actor, the Manager's onslaught of how, why and what-if questions and their need to have a thorough understanding of the products and services can seem tedious and immediately put you on the defensive. Keep in mind that hands-on experience and the need for proof is one of the Manager's key operating tools, and to try to force the Manager towards brevity or speed up the information or selection phase of the sale will often cost you the sale.

It's important to understand that the Manager's need for a deeper level of explanation or detail isn't meant as a personal affront. It's really not about you; it's more about the habit they've adopted and their need to ensure they haven't made a mistake or entered into a buying or post-buying experience that will cause them stress. Managers are endlessly in search of those well-orchestrated experiences where everything fits neatly together. Should problems arise, they want to know there is a viable solution waiting right around the corner.

It's not uncommon during a break period of a seminar I'm leading on selling techniques to have a Manager come up and tell me they are enjoying the seminar, and then proceed with a real-life sales experience and solicit a more nuanced response they might be able to use in the future to guarantee a better outcome for their customer.

Our research shows that for all the excitement the Drivers and Actors demonstrate in the moment, they aren't necessarily any better on follow-through than any of the other patterns after a seminar. However, it's a slightly different story for the Manager pattern, since what we are offering in a selling techniques seminar is a brain-driven process approach. Since managers are process driven, laying out a series of steps they can follow to enhance their customer experience is right up their alley and they tend to gravitate towards clearly defined non-confrontational problem-solving.

Managers, unlike Drivers and Actors, generally don't operate from the gut. They tend to second-guess their decisions until they've had enough time to thoroughly analyze their buying choice, at least during the initial purchase. For this reason, Managers, as discussed, can be a much tougher sale.

A Manager's process strategy is perfectly set up for Justification. This will be your greatest opportunity to sell a Manager by explaining the specifics of the product, service, or design that you are offering and thereby assuaging their fear that they could be making the wrong decision to purchase.

Managers are particularly susceptible to overload, and when overloaded occurs, will often simply decide to postpone their buying decision to another time. The more they are pushed for a decision, the further likelihood that the decision will require additional time or that the purchase will be jettisoned altogether.

Managers in a non-routine setting—such as making a major purchase—will rely on strategy, using a series of steps they have developed as a guideline. Should the salesperson gain their trust and offer a well-defined process, Managers will adopt that for arriving at their final decision. Such is the power of a well-executed Justification meeting. The Manager can be super focused on attention to detail and won't necessarily respond well to a glitzy marketing pitch highlighting the bells and whistles. Selling a Manager, nevertheless, can be a highly rewarding experience because there is very little game-playing and they generally recognize their role in making a buying experience rewarding by doing their research.

Unlike Drivers and Actors, Managers tend not to be transactional in their decision-making. Managers often make decisions based on a genuine feeling that the product or service, along with the salesperson, is above-board and won't require any kind of intervention to guarantee a satisfactory outcome. If treated fairly, Managers show incredible loyalty to a salesperson and are frequently one of the best advocates for you, creating the essential word of mouth that keeps your business viable.

Provided Manager customers feel you've properly demonstrated a level of fairness and your product or service is of high quality, they will reward you with years of purchasing, eschewing competitors in favor of maintaining a long-term relationship. Acquiring Manager customers takes work, but by the same token, they tend to be easy to do business with.

If you are a Manager pattern as a salesperson, you will need to mentally prepare yourself when you encounter a Driver and Actor in a selling experience. It's important not to overestimate the need for detail and lose the excitement and chance for the immediate gratification that can be at the art of non-process patterns, like Drivers and Actors. Justification is still a must but it must be done with an eye towards the customer's buying pattern and their immediate level of attention. Selling and buying for both an Actor or Manager salesperson and their subsequent customers revolve around one concept: the perception of a relationship. That sense of connection, in a superficial way for the Actor or a more permanent way for the Manager, can tip either customer towards a sale.

Engineer Pattern

Engineers put a lot of importance in specificity, detail, and being correct. They tend to operate in a function-over-form mode. The brain chemical testosterone is prominent in the Engineer pattern. Testosterone is associated with self-esteem and competitiveness.

Positive attributes: Engineers think before they speak and are analytical in their deliberations. They tend to be organized and work diligently in an effort to avoid making mistakes. They are fact-based and find importance in gathering information. Engineers often seem reserved, and don't necessarily speak out or command the stage like the Actor pattern. They tend to be considerate and avoid making quick judgements, especially when multiple people are involved in a situation. Because of this, like Managers, Engineers tend to excel in team dynamics.

Look out for: Also, like Managers, Engineers need a lot of time to make decisions and will often require some alone time to conclude. They are not conflict-driven but will stand their ground when they are confronted, often to the point of stubbornness. Because Engineers are even more detail-oriented than Managers, this can sometimes lead to a prolonged sale.

Notes: When Engineers go shopping, like Managers, they seek selling experiences that are logical and strategic, avoiding as much chaos as possible. They are looking for proof of reliability and an efficient, low-key buying experience.

For Engineer Salespeople: An Engineer salesperson can easily overload the other patterns by their insistence on exploring the minutia of product. Just like the Manager pattern, it is a must that the Engineer make sure that they don't dampen the emotional excitement of the Actor or Driver pattern in their zeal to explain and prove.

When selling to Drivers, recognize you will be challenged. Be strategic in confronting them with information that might stand in contrast to what they have expressed. It is not in your best interest to do battle over small incidentals.

When selling to Managers, bonding should be no problem. Keep in mind that they too enjoy a defined process and highly level data set. Just remember that a really deep dive into detail should be carefully managed based on the interest level of the Manager.

When selling to Actors, they can sometimes feel like your Achilles heel, both for their need of constant reassurance and a less-than buttoned up approach to the selling process. The Actor pattern will require you to dig deep and bring as much flexibility to the experience as possible.

When selling to another Engineer pattern, your chances of selling escalate compared to the other patterns. Just remember not to lose the forest for the trees in your effort to support the experience with detail. Keep in mind that part of your task is to create a fun and rewarding customer experience.

Dealing with an Engineer Pattern

General Behavior

- Engineers love to know the nitty gritty about the detail and inner workings of a product. Their questions include: "What is this made of?" "What is the life expectancy?" "Do you have specification for this?"

- For Engineers, the mechanical aspects of the product are often more important than the visual.

- Engineers thrive on data, so website information, spec books, and meaningful handouts are essential.

- Engineers want concrete proof of product reliability and workmanship.

- Engineers will choose to work with an expert with deep domain knowledge, and don't like being handed off to subordinates.

- Talk to Engineers in terms of pros and cons, but don't give an Engineer multiple options. They expect that you've already figured out the best option, which is the one backed up with factual information.

- Engineers respond exceptionally well to binary selection. More on that later.

- Engineers will ask a lot of questions, many of them technical, and expect the salesperson to have access to the answers.

- Engineers require a lot of time, both to satisfy their need for information and to make a rational choice.

- Engineers will expect you to know your competition's product in addition to your own in order to give them the most accurate and complete purchase picture.

- Engineers often come to you having done their homework ahead of time, so you need to acknowledge this and prove you are up to speed as the salesperson.

- Engineers don't like to make mistakes or be wrong, so written guarantees help confirm they've made the best choice.

- Engineers can be stubborn about their opinion, and need to be won over with data.

- Engineers sometimes struggle with seeing the big picture as they can get bogged down in the minutiae.

- Engineers are keen on process documents that provide the kind of deeper dive into information that brings them greater comfort when deciding.

Results Mode

- Engineers are slow to make purchase decisions and can sometimes find themselves in analysis paralysis, so bringing information in a concise and clear format is important.

- Although Engineers are often data-driven, creating too many decision points and the demand for immediate answers on the part of the salesperson can swamp the Engineer's ability to decide.

- Engineers will insist that every last detail has been hammered out before they will sign on the dotted line.

- Engineers attempt to come to a buying decision from a rational viewpoint.

- Engineers are more likely to enjoy a buying experience when there is a clearly defined process and they have plenty of time to ask questions and experience products for first-hand comparison.

- Engineers need to feel like they are setting the timetable in the sales process, which will likely require showing flexibility to accommodate them on the part of the salesperson.

- Generally speaking, Engineers can be one of the toughest pattern to close because their personal bar for both attaining enough information and thoroughly exploring their options tends to be higher than the other patterns.

- Once an Engineer makes a selection choice, they generally stick to that choice and don't second guess themselves, be careful not to oversell.

- Engineers often see the bells and whistles of a particular product as relatively inconsequential in the buying experience as opposed to the structural integrity or efficiency.

- Engineers look for symmetry, balance in design, and if the product lacks these qualities they are likely to avoid the purchase

An Encounter with an Engineer

An Engineer, much like a Manager, is likely to show up on time or a little before the appointment, having done some homework on products or services associated with the buying experience.

The Engineer generally won't ask bold and direct questions like, "How much will this cost?" or "What is your best price?" They won't ask questions centering on themes like, "What is hot right now?" or "I saw X on TV or the Internet, do you carry that brand?" While Managers generally ask process questions like, "How long will this take?" or, "What happens in the event that something comes damaged?", the Engineer customer will ask even deeper questions with a great deal more specificity like, "What was the annealing process used to harden the metal in this air conditioner fan?" or "How many layers and what type of glue were used to make this sheet of plywood?"

Also, like Managers, an Engineer will usually enter a showroom having already honed in on exactly what they want. But if they do enter your showroom having not already prepped, they will take as much time as necessary to understand the products and your company's processes, asking specific questions regarding the how and why and physical makeup of your products.

Unlike the Manager or Actor, Engineers do not place relationships at the pinnacle of how they operate. They might spend some time attempting to understand the salesperson's background and level of expertise, but only to verify that the information they are receiving is accurate. The

Engineer, much like the Driver pattern, sees the buying experience as far more like a product review and a decision to be made. In this regard, the salesperson's bedside manner, as long as it falls in the acceptable range, will be sufficient to do business. This tends to be a challenge for the Actor's approach when attempting to sell an Engineer.

The Engineer's strategy doesn't involve wanting to be your new best friend, but they do want to feel that you, are displaying a level of honesty. If things should go awry, they want to count on you to quickly remedy the situation without additional prodding or threat on their behalf. Engineers do not seek, or necessarily enjoy, a confrontational approach. But should problems arise, they are steadfast in their belief and will take steps necessary to guarantee a fair resolution. The Engineer's stubborn defense is sometimes confused as the Driver pattern, but the essential difference is that they are not so much about taking a "never compromise, win at all costs," approach as they are, "hold your ground unless *proven* otherwise."

The Engineer style can come off as being proactive and buttoned up, and they learn through thoughtful and deliberate discourse. Like the Driver, they will often challenge and demand proof. This is critical to understand. The Engineer customer is much more likely to have a positive response if you can engage them by listening intently to their ideas, showing excitement, and then detailing how your process has been designed to lessen mistakes. But also be prepared to back up your claim with a variety of facts that the Engineer customer can access and review on their own.

Here is an Engineer in action: "Tell me about the airflow data on X brand of air conditioner, and can you tell me more about what is specifically included in the warranty?"

A good response? "You'll appreciate that our warranty is X and the critical internal patented design elements include Y. Let me get you a spec book (or the specs on the website) for this unit and you can see for yourself the high rating this unit has proven through extensive testing."

Notice for the Engineer, unlike the other patterns, your leadoff doesn't go right to the emotional impact of feeling the value, the safety, or the cool bells and whistles of the product. Rather, you appeal directly to the analytics and detailed decision-making process. And then, as in the case of all buying patterns you encounter, you proceed with the Rule of Threes and emotional underpinning bullet points bolstering your claim.

In this short response, you give a nod to the Engineer's diligence and assure them their decision will be one of fact-based proof, which is vital to the Engineer's peace of mind. Then you proceed, using brain science to make your case. For example, let's say you were in HVAC sales and working with an Engineer customer. At some point in the dialog, you might drop in a line like this: "Because this particular air conditioner has tested so well, its high efficiency rating, and its trouble-free operation, I can't imagine why anybody would consider buying anything else."

For an Engineer who wants to have a long-term hassle-free experience, the idea of buying what has been thoroughly tested and maintenance-free tips them towards the sale, especially on something like a cooling appliance. Engineers pride themselves on their logical assessment capabilities, knowing more than the average person due to their diligence and research, and the verification that they are making a wise buying decision.

If you are new to sales, or your own pattern is primarily that of a Driver or Actor, the Engineer's onslaught of "how, why and what if" questions and their need to have a thorough understanding of the products and services can seem tedious, and immediately put you on the defensive. The Engineer pattern places a greater emphasis on construction, making the Engineer function over form to the extreme. Keep in mind, like the Manager pattern, that hands-on experience and the need for proof is one of the Engineer's key operating tools, and to try to force the Manager or Engineer towards brevity or to try to speed up the information or selection phase of the sale will often cost you the sale.

It's important to remember that an Engineer's demand for detail isn't meant as a personal affront. In other words—you guessed it—it's not really about you. It's more about the habit they've adopted and their need to ensure they haven't made a mistake or entered into a buying or post-buying experience that will cause them stress.

It's not uncommon during a break period of a seminar I'm leading on selling techniques to have an Engineer approach and question in greater detail something I've said, or even challenge a fact. They learn through a robust experience of inquiry and are not afraid of the back-andoforth necessary to resolve an issue or come to a more nuanced conclusion.

Engineers don't operate from the gut, and tend not to second-guess their decisions, having thoroughly analyzed their buying choice. For this reason, Engineers, as discussed, can require a fair amount of effort to make the sale.

An Engineer is perfectly set up for Justification and this will be your greatest opportunity to sell the Engineer by explaining the specifics of the product, service, or design that you are offering. This assuages their fear that they could be making the wrong decision to purchase.

Engineers are particularly susceptible to overload. When overload occurs, they will often simply decide to postpone their buying decision to another time. The more they are pushed for a decision, the more likely the decision will require additional time or that the purchase will be jettisoned altogether.

Engineers will rely on strategy, using a series of steps they have developed as a guideline. As with Managers, should the salesperson gain an Engineer's trust through demonstrating product knowledge and offering a well-defined process, they will adopt that for arriving at their final decision—but with the Engineer it often requires a fair amount of deliberation. A well-executed Justification meeting is highly important to the Engineer pattern. Both the Engineer and Manager can be super focused on attention to detail, and won't necessarily respond well to a glitzy marketing pitch highlighting the bells and whistles.

Unlike Drivers and Actors, Engineers tend not to be transactional in their decision-making. Engineers and Managers often make decisions based on a genuine feeling that the product or service, along with the salesperson, is above-board and won't require any kind of intervention to guarantee a satisfactory outcome. Engineers, unlike Actors or the Manager pattern, will require truly exceptional experiences for them to invest in word-of-mouth on behalf of the salesperson.

Links Between Buying Patterns

When we look at the four buying patterns, one way to break them down is to consider the patterns as connecting either through a warmer, relationship-driven emotional connection with the salesperson, or a cooler emotional connection with a stronger emphasis on the product specifications and service.

Warm Emotional Connection

Actors and Managers are more relationship-driven. Who they buy from matters to them. Trust of the seller is important in their purchase.

Cooler Emotional Connection

Drivers and Engineers are less relationship-driven. They buy based on the cost/value/quality opportunity. Trust in the salesperson's knowledge of a product's attributes are most important in their purchase.

One of the most common patterns that we see in salespeople engaged in general sales is either their highest score in Driver followed by Actor, or vice versa. We call this "charm in a briefcase." These patterns suggest that the salesperson tends to lead with a little Actor level friendliness and flattery, but should things get tough, the salesperson is quick to play the more aggressive Driver card in order to steer the sale in a particular direction.

In a common pattern for sales areas that are more data-driven or technical, we often see salespeople with the highest number in the Engineer category followed by Manager, or vice versa. We call this "the salmon effect." These patterns suggest that the salesperson tends to be deliberate, steadfast, and persistent in their approach, like a salmon working hard to swim upstream against the current of snap judgments and shallow analysis.

Lastly, one more common selling pattern is a high score in Actor followed by Manager, or vice versa. We call this the "mac and cheese effect." These patterns both have warm drives as the highest combination and indicate the attempt at a comfortable personal connection when engaged in selling—hence the comfort food moniker.

If you were forthright in your answers on the diagnostic survey, the pattern descriptions should feel familiar to you as you reread your particular patterns. Often, even though they've engaged in sales for years, salespeople have not really ever thought about their particular selling style and are surprised to find themselves saying, "Yeah that sounds like me, that *is* the way I sell."

An interesting thing often occurs in our seminars among people who score highest in either the Driver or Engineer patterns. Sometimes those individuals suggest that they don't necessarily see themselves with those selling strategies. Their coworkers in the audience always provide a resounding reality check and give specific, and often humorous examples as to why those are precisely their go-to selling patterns.

Because decision-making in sales tends to be informed by our own personal patterns, it's important to remember there is no good or bad selling pattern. Every circumstance dictates which pattern or patterns will work the best when engaging a single customer, couple, or committee. Therefore, to be ultimately successful, a salesperson doesn't have the luxury of relying exclusively on one pattern.

What your personal diagnostic results tell you is that you have an established pattern you follow for sales, as indicated by the highest number results. The other patterns tend to be less dominant, with the lowest numbers indicating a selling pattern in which you probably lack familiarity and comfort.

For some, there is a wider discrepancy in their pattern numbers. For others the numbers are closer in value. Interestingly, in all of our years of administering this diagnostic, only one person has scored the exact same number for all four patterns. The good news is that you now have enough information to reinforce and strengthen those selling patterns that will give you the chance of creating a higher level of customer satisfaction, which in turn will reward you with greater sales opportunities.

Buying Pattern Vocabulary

It is estimated that there are approximately 171,500 words in the English language. Of those words, writer Robert Charles Lee estimates that "just 3,000 words will cover 95% of everyday writing, including emails, newspapers, and so on."

We have provided you with information regarding the four buying patterns. Upon first read through, it might appear daunting to try to track all the different attributes and to think about building these concepts into your selling routine. But just as relatively few words make up the bulk of how we communicate, the buying patterns can be distilled down to their essence. Here they are, simply put:

- Drivers buy for the thrill of the *deal.*

- Actors buy for the exciting *features.*

- Managers buy for a *safe and defined process.*

- Engineers buy for well executed *efficiency and detail.*

As is the case in English, in which knowing more words gives you a greater command of the language, knowing more information and concepts about the buying patterns gives you greater access to more selling capability.

Still, understanding the basic idea of the patterns—and taking the time to see and understand the world through the customer's eyes—gives you a huge advantage over your competitor who likely approaches selling as a singular experience, operating under the impression that how they sell is automatically in sync with how their customers like to buy.

It will take some time to assimilate all the buying pattern information into your daily routine. That is perfectly okay. For now, focus on gaining a basic understanding of the difference between the four patterns. As we proceed we will introduce more tools for building up your buying pattern vocabulary.

Below, we've included a sample of key connecting words as they relate to the buying patterns. These words are not an exhaustive list, as there are countless more words that elicit similar emotions. We suggest that you familiarize yourself with these types of words to identify those that help create a positive experience for each buying pattern. Language is key to communication and using words that are more surgical in their pattern connection is an easy way to incorporate the buying pattern concepts as you move towards a higher level of sales.

Actor	Manager	Engineer	Driver
stunning	considered	accurate	deal
beautiful	thought through	precise	unique
exquisite	safe	exact	cutting edge
gorgeous	secure	perfect	advanced
attractive	protected	clear cut	exclusive
elegant	working together	specific	matchless
respected	measured	fixed	limited
luxurious	planned out	correct	superior
polished	process	approved	special
superb	method	strict	exceptional
fabulous	progression	defined	sophisticated
outstanding	guidelines	rigorous	distinctive
wonderful	rule	careful	one of a kind
brilliant	procedure	meticulous	sole
magnificent	thorough	hand-crafted	valuable
splendid	careful	thorough	priceless

Diagnosing Your Customer's Pattern

We have detailed the buying patterns, and established that they offer a way of connecting with your customer by leveraging the customer's own habit for decision-making. It follows then that to be a Sales Genius, you must diagnose your customers' patterns and then become the chameleon, effortlessly dropping into their pattern. Your own natural pattern must be temporarily jettisoned in order to connect with your customer on their terms.

But how do you know which pattern your customer has?

By now we're assuming you've taken the survey and determined your own pattern. It would be a relatively easy task to determine your customer's buying pattern if your customer also took the survey, but the idea of making your customer take a brain-related survey prior to engaging with you is just not in the cards, for a myriad of reasons you can probably imagine.

Is there a quick way to determine your customer's pattern right off the bat?

I often think of the buying pattern diagnostic process much like a detective game. When I first meet the customer, my radar is up and I ask myself, "how does this person like to be sold?" Like a good detective, my next step is to look and listen for clues. And where do those clues come from? The questions your customers ask. In the same way that body language of physical gestures gives us a window into how your customer is feeling, your customer's questions actually reveal a lot about how they like to buy.

This is why the first job of a salesperson is not to jump right in with a sales pitch, but rather to actively listen in order to determine the most direct path to your customer's brain. The good news is that you have an advantage. Just as ancient Greek scholar Hippocrates figured out, your customer is going to bias towards one of the four patterns, and their questions to you will direct your next course of action. Amazingly, unbeknownst to your customer, within roughly 90 seconds you will most likely be flooded with clues as to their buying pattern.

For example, perhaps your customer's first question is, "How much does X cost?" or "How competitive are your prices?" These first clues suggest you might be working with a Driver.

On the other hand, maybe your customer's first question is cloaked in anticipation like, "I was watching the Food Network last night, and I saw the most amazing X, do you have those in stock?" That excited windup suggests you might be working with an Actor pattern.

A customer who focuses on questions like, "How long will this take?" or "What are the steps involved?" or "What happens if....?" is concerned about processes and their outcomes. This line of questioning would point to a Manager pattern.

Questions revolving around intricacies, particularly detailed questions like, "What is the composition of X?" or "What is the tolerance of X, or the holding strength of Y?" are the kinds of domain-specific questions we would expect from the Engineer pattern.

I once worked with a customer who happened to be a scientist at Fermilab, in Batavia, Illinois. Fermilab is one of the premier laboratories in the United States, specializing in high-energy particle physics. This customer also, perhaps not surprisingly, happened to be an Engineer pattern.

Our company had done some design work for this customer's new home. We had not been part of the general construction, but this customer was sorely disappointed to discover that the screws in the light switch cover plates had not all been oriented so their final resting places were all vertical and perfectly aligned. Most people wouldn't even notice this, and that kind of alignment would be nearly impossible if the goal of the electrician was to have the screws as tight and firmly set as possible. Yet this high bar of expectation is the nuanced approach to the world that is common for the Engineer pattern. Questions of mechanical tolerance, symmetry, and material composition are among the kinds of questions you might encounter depending on the products or services you represent.

Drivers are going to ask more value-related questions, particularly questions that will ensure they get a good deal or guarantee the end result will be a high value transaction. Actors will generally ask more feature-related questions, designed to guarantee an exciting emotional reward for their purchase. Managers will ask process questions designed to ensure that mistakes are minimized, and function is maximized. Engineers will ask specific questions to guarantee that quality and high standards were attained in the building of the product with an eye on long term durability and trouble-free usage down on the line. With active listening and a little practice, it won't take long for you to be able to pick up on these clues.

For example, in a car dealership, a customer might come in asking pointed questions about the deal they saw advertised on TV, such as if that price is negotiable or whether it's a limited time offer. You have a few clues you might have a Driver customer. Another customer might come in and tell you they weren't really shopping for cars but that the exquisite metallic blue car out on the lot grabbed their eye, and want to know all about it. Sounds like a possible Actor customer.

The next person might come in having a lot of questions after reading *Consumer Reports* about the new car designed with the safe but easy to adjust child friendly seats, and they'd like to see that model in person. That would be a clue that you're talking to a Manager customer.

Another customer wants to know all about the charging system necessary for the new electric car in addition to its specific maximum horsepower rating, and driving range. Could you be talking to an Engineer customer?

In those lines of questions, you hear the *deal* of the Driver, the *features* of the Actor, the *safe and defined process* of the Manager and the *attention to detail* of the Engineer pattern. It can really be that easy.

Sometimes, after an initial exchange, you might need to ask some follow-up questions to get a little more information before you decide on the pattern. Take the customer who was mesmerized by the metallic blue car color. Following up with a few stats from *Consumer Reports* about the child seats and then gauging their body language and verbal response will help you eliminate or reinforce your assumptions about their pattern type.

Again, in the early stages of the meeting, it's all about your detective abilities to suss out what is at the heart of the customer's basic interest. The more you actively listen and respond with careful follow-up questions—holding off a bit while you figure out the customer's buying pattern—the more likely you'll be able to orchestrate the rest of the exchange to the customer's liking.

This is important because the customer is not obligated to pay attention to you simply because you happen to be the salesperson they encounter. Overload and boredom are two of the more common reasons why you can lose a customer. Your personal effectiveness is inextricably linked to the customer's perception of you, your ability to deliver pertinent information, and their sense of whether what you have to say is resonating with them. We can't say this enough: it's all about them, or as we've indicated from a brain science perspective, their pattern.

When the goal is not a sale, but rather figuring out the roadmap for the best individualized customer experience you can provide, you will likely have to do way less "selling." Way less selling means way less negative stress for you and the customer, and as a result, perhaps ironically, you'll be rewarded with the final payoff of a sale. It's the natural outcome of a more personalized approach.

Working with Couples

There is at least one wrinkle in all this, and that happens when your encounter is with a couple rather than a single customer.

Old school sales would suggest that when confronted with a couple, your best bet is to sell to the dominant individual, once presumed to be the male. Today, we know that good salesmanship is not based on gender and the buying patterns are not gender-specific. Literally anyone can be a Driver, Actor, Manager, or Engineer.

But with a couple you have to understand two patterns as opposed to one. Does this make it tougher? In a word, yes. Because in addition to the two patterns, there is a dynamic between those two patterns which is important to know as well.

So, when confronted with a couple, how do you proceed? Again, it's back to your work as a detective, following all the clues, only now recognizing you have to discern both patterns. Because of their bold approach and willingness to dominate the conversation, you'll figure out pretty quickly if you're dealing with a Driver. (Drivers practically announce themselves when they walk through the door) You'll need to do some careful questioning of the partner to figure out their pattern.

Driver/Driver

When both customers demonstrate the Driver pattern, you should be prepared for fireworks. Because of their level of commitment and willingness to win at all costs, you might witness some real verbal knock-down drag-out encounters between them.

A word of a caution: when you are confronted by a double Driver couple and one of them in the heat of battle turns to you and asks for your opinion, recognize that you are in a no-win situation and should seek to find a diplomatic way of declining to engage.

Should you engage, one of the couple will likely feel that you have joined the opposing side. Where they may recognize their personal dynamic and be quite forgiving of head-to-head confrontations, as it's part of how they operate and continue to stay together, you will not have immunity for your response. Drivers tend to have long memories when it comes to who won and who lost a discussion point. Forget about dominance between the couple. You will need to win over both members of the couple to win the sale.

Actor/Actor

A couple composed of two Actor patterns can be a lot of fun. As they compete for each other's attention and your attention as well, it's generally a love fest, where either of the couple is more than willing to take you down some rabbit hole of conversation. While Actors are fun, it's all on you to keep making progress, documenting decisions as you go, and recognizing that should mistakes occur, the Actors are quite capable of turning on you and letting you be the fall person for whatever has transpired.

They are generally not buttoned up in their approach, so make sure that you are. Upgrading is exciting for Actors, so it's important that you've identified budget constraints. Do the couple a favor: don't let them get out ahead of their skis and make upgrade decisions that later they will have to scale back. Eliminating upgrades tends to leave a bad taste in customers' mouths.

If you don't orchestrate the sale carefully, you will find yourself in a world of changes and redoes, and the chance of a final sale becomes less sure. Once their emotional excitement has hit its peak, selling an Actor couple will be one of the easiest sales you will make, provided you recognize the timing. Keep in mind the danger that comes with not getting all the facts nailed down in writing.

Manager/Manager

In our estimation, much like the double Actor pattern, Managers are a ton of fun to sell. They are similar to selling Actors, but without all the drama and superficial backslapping. Managers tend to be buttoned up and are comfortable following a process, especially Justification. You generally don't have to sweep up behind a double Manager couple when it comes to decision time, unlike double Drivers where the knives might come out. Managers are all about consensus and will go out of their way to make sure their partner is happy with the final decision. This need for consensus can at times lead to some decision paralysis.

Should the Managers solicit your opinion for resolution, feel free to give them your two cents' worth. Unlike Drivers, the Managers' goal will be to break the stalemate so both parties felt like they won. In the eyes of a Manager, if the outcome produces a clear winner and loser, then something has gone wrong. When consensus has been reached, you are at the gateway to a sale.

Engineer/Engineer

Working with a double Engineer couple is a study in patience, especially if your own pattern is one of a Driver or Actor. There will be a great deal of discussion and a lot of back and forth where options are endlessly compared for their pros and cons. Because Engineers pride themselves on their thoroughness and are loath to make mistakes, analysis paralysis is a common occurrence.

If solicited for your opinion, feel free to give it without reservation. In fact, if you are asked for your opinion, take this as a sign of trust; the Engineer pattern is just as likely to leave you out of the decision equation. The double Engineer couple will often attempt to resolve an issue by seeking even more information, setting up a perpetuating circle of reassessment, which can make it even more difficult for them to discern the signal from the noise. If one of the couple comes to a point of clarity and the other partner has not yet reached that point, be prepared for a stubborn showdown.

Sometimes, this situation can feel like working with two Drivers, although it frequently involves less of a show of animosity towards each other when it is two Engineers. Justification, ripe with domain knowledge and backed up with fact-based information, is one of the best ways to steer a double Engineer couple through the rough waters of selection, and on towards a successful sale.

Driver/Actor

In this relationship, you have the buying strategy of the Driver, based on a cooler emotional tendency and eye towards cost/value/quality opportunity, and the warm "people person" orientation of the Actor pattern.

When it comes to product selection, you may see a tag team effect—a sort of good cop, bad cop situation where the "good cop" Actor's excitement for product features drives a huge list of upgrades, all the while trying to buddy bond with the salesperson. Then the "bad cop" Driver, who sees their job as the final arbitrator, works the salesperson for the best deal, feigning less interest and a willingness to walk away.

The Actor's strategy is to try to keep the nature of the encounter light, to offset the Driver's sometimes aggressive, seemingly less than friendly attitude. Keep in mind the Driver's negotiating persona is often more tactic than reflection or condemnation of the salesperson. Depending on the Driver/Actor couple, the Driver will frequently have the last word, but it's also not uncommon for that final decision to largely coincide with the Actor's wants.

As a salesperson confronted with the Driver/Actor pattern, a powerful strategy is to respond positively with the Actor, keeping their excitement stoked up at a high level, while at the same time showing respect for the Driver's opinions and, when appropriate, acknowledge their expertise and the fact that they are getting the very best deal available.

Driver/Manager

With a Driver/Manager couple you have the cool emotional tendencies of the Driver and the warmer more relationship-driven Manager. The Manager partner seeks to connect with the salesperson and is looking at the product to safely improve some aspect of life. This sets up an interesting dynamic with the Driver aggressively pushing for the upper hand and a deal, and the Manager generally less concerned about bragging rights for securing the ultimate bargain and more concerned about all parties feeling good with the outcome.

I once had a particular couple come to me for a kitchen design. The husband was a Driver and the wife was a Manager. The Driver started right in and explained how his wife was an excellent cook and had wanted a new kitchen for years but he had determined that a new driveway and garage came first. Now, though, it was time to make her dream come true. He pointed out that she had definite ideas of what she wanted and I should sharpen my pencil and not fool around with the price. He went on to make it clear to me that I was to give her exactly what she wanted. When I turned to her to hear about her dream kitchen, without skipping a beat, the Driver continued, "--and this is what she wants," as he proceeded to list out a series of features.

The wife sat patiently until the Driver ran out of gas, and then quietly laid out exactly what she actually wanted. In this case, we see how the Manager "manages" the situation. She astutely lets the Driver speak his mind to establish his importance in the transaction, and then quietly lays out the product and the improved efficiencies she was hoping for in the new kitchen design.

The working dynamic between a Driver and Manager is often obvious where the Manager lets the Driver be the Driver, and at the same time manages to get what they want and keep the peace. A balanced strategy from the Manager's viewpoint, and a win from the point of view of the Driver. In terms of partnerships with a Driver, the Manager is generally the best fit because of their ability to compromise, and at the same time make the Driver feel like they won the day.

As a salesperson, when confronted with a Driver/Manager couple, a great process is to follow the same strategy as the Manager: letting the Driver have their say and then quietly making sure to bring the Manager into the fold, soliciting their point of view as well.

Driver/Engineer

When it comes to the Driver/Engineer couple, it can be tricky to identify each of the parties involved. The stubbornness of the Engineer means that after careful analysis, they believe they are correct in their final assessment. At the same time the Driver, who for the most part eschews careful analysis but nevertheless operates from viewpoint that they are always correct, can appear to have the same pattern.

Listening carefully for clues in conversation and asking specific and directed questions, especially about product detail, should make it apparent whether that sense of correctness you're observing from either of the couple is based on strong factual analysis (Engineer) or just the greater belief in self (Driver).

In terms of who is likely to make the final decision with this particular couple, it can really go either way. A Driver who decides to go to the mat against an Engineer who believes that the facts bear out their decision can lead to a formidable standoff, and one where it's best for a salesperson to avoid offering their opinion.

Your best bet in this situation is to provide the data when requested by the Engineer pattern, and at the same time, honor the Driver, listening with intent and keeping in mind their need to not seem diminished in any exchange. After that, get out of the way and let nature take its course.

It's been our experience that if the Engineer presents a strong enough case for their selection and/or buying decision, the Driver will often find a way to save face and bow to the Engineer's point of view. If this seems counterintuitive, consider that if the Driver makes the call and later finds out they made the wrong decision, the fact-equipped Engineer can take them a long journey down "I told you so" lane. Since Drivers hate to be wrong, that's a particularly uncomfortable journey. For the Driver, it makes sense sometimes to hedge their bets and not push too hard, especially if they aren't really all that invested in the decision. Interestingly, many Drivers would save face and not describe this as a loss, rather depicting it as a case where they didn't really care about the outcome.

However, if the Engineer has not figured out how to manage or mitigate the high-intensity emotions a Driver is capable of accessing under duress, then we've seen instances where the Engineer might feel like it's not worth the struggle and concedes to the Driver, who will relish the sense of victory. It really comes down to the determination level of each member of this couple as to how this might play out.

For a new salesperson, much like a Driver/Driver couple, the Driver/Engineer couple can be a real "indoctrination by fire" into selling. We should also mention that we've seen this couple pattern work through selection and the final decision to buy in a totally amicable way without any fireworks whatsoever. Such is the beauty of the sales process; every day presents new opportunities and challenges. It's best to be prepared.

Actor/Manager

In the Actor and Manager couple, you have a warm drive meeting warm drive. Both of these patterns are relationship-driven, where the Actor is looking for the quick connection and the Manager is thinking longer term, investing in meaning and less about the moment.

The Actor will be excited about the latest features, the visual and "wow" effect, and what's hot right now. Selection is often based on whether an enhancement makes them feel good in the moment. The Manager, as is their nature, will look at features as they relate to practical use and safety. In a purchase decision about a car seat and whether to upgrade or not, while both patterns will recognize that safety is important, the Actor might be willing to pay a little more for a fashion-forward color—something trending right now—and the Manager may be willing to pay a little more for ease of taking the car seat in and out of the car.

Neither of these patterns is combative; an Actor and Manager couple is one of the easier couples. In this couple, you see the Actor's excitement during selection and a "more is more" philosophy, and the Manager's "less is more" philosophy. Together, they tend to balance each other, and with the Manager, who is interested in fairness and compromise, you see the groundwork set for a sale. This is opposed to an Actor/Actor couple, who, although fun, may take a "no one minding the store" approach.

With the Actor and Manager couple, you often have the Manager to help keep track of the details, taking a little bit of the onus off the salesperson, and reducing the general level of stress. The combination of these two patterns is often a favorite among salespeople because of their dual warm drives and pleasant disposition.

Actor/Engineer

The Actor and Engineer couple is one of those couples that prove opposites can attract. With the Actor, you have the happy-go-lucky approach in which excitement and discovery seems to follow them around every corner. An Actor has no problem communicating to you about what they like. Actors actually sort out their ideas as they speak, and so you can get a sort of running freeform dialogue as they verbally work through their ideas. This can complicate the act of helping them narrow down their selection, because as they talk, their editing process can be tough to follow, especially for Engineer and Driver salespeople.

The Engineer in the couple, on the other hand, often holds their thoughts close to the vest because they don't feel comfortable sharing until they've taken the time to think through what they might say. And what they might say depends upon their knowledge and comfort with the subject matter. The less domain knowledge, the more the Engineer will seek factual information to bolster their decision. This can stand in stark opposition to the Actor, who is operating and speaking out to a large extent based on how they feel.

In terms of selling an Actor and Engineer couple, you will need to balance two balls at the same time. One ball will be about keeping the Actor excited about features and the emotional payoff they will be rewarded with through the purchase, and the second ball will provide the Engineer with the cool logic and facts proving the material value of said features. Often with these kinds of oppositional patterns, you see a couple that has somehow established a unique system that works for them, allowing them to work together despite their differences.

For the salesperson, this couple will be a test of your flexibility. Without the ability to step out of your own pattern and accept the cognitive dissonance between the couple necessary to make this sale, your task will prove to be challenging. Where you do see symmetry in selection is when the Actor falls in love with a product or feature on the emotional level, and the Engineer can justify the same product or feature from a material quality level. In this instance, you see shared agreement even though each party got to the same conclusion from a different angle.

Manager/Engineer

A couple consisting of a Manager and Engineer is an interesting mix. The Manager has a warm drive, looking for compromise and connecting through meaningful relationships. The Engineer has a cooler drive, which generally makes them less people-oriented, and puts a lot of importance in structural quality and symmetry. However, the Manager and Engineer share a lot in common. Both put their trust in the process. The Engineer takes the process to its logical conclusion, with a seemingly endless fascination for minute detail and precision, beyond what even the system-oriented Manager requires.

Manager and Engineer couples like to approach a problem systematically, with a unifocus strategy where they work on a single aspect at a time. Unlike the Actor pattern, they don't like to bounce around in the selection process. They prefer to tackle decisions in a step-by-step manner.

The salesperson needs to include a detailed explanation ahead of time on the agenda for a sales meeting. Providing this couple with a written copy of your process, the steps you follow, and what they need to know will likely enhance your bona fides and lay the groundwork for trust. Likewise, verbally walking the couple through your process at the start of a sales encounter is also a prudent move. Managers and Engineers do not like to be surprised or rushed, and if pushed, can easily walk away from a sale.

The Manager and Engineer couple tend to do their homework ahead of time, so don't be surprised if they ask you highly detailed, well-thought questions for which you might not readily have answers. They will take a low-key approach to a sales situation, demonstrating great sincerity and focus, and expect the same from their salesperson. Neither of these buying patterns respond well to the superficial friendliness sometimes displayed by Actors or the aggressive behavior Drivers can exhibit. They don't like to be told; they would much rather be shown, and taking the time to physically demonstrate a product's full range of capabilities with a total hands-on approach is key to winning them over.

As with each of these patterns individually, the Justification process is a must. As the salesperson, be prepared to go much deeper during Justification than you might with the Driver or Actor pattern. Any time you can show factual proof to support your claims, you are much better off.

The level of interpersonal cooperation between the Manager and Engineer couple tends to be high. Although it might take them longer to reach consensus due to their strong need for proof and a thorough understanding of the product, they are nevertheless likely to reach consensus. Aside from the need for the salesperson to make sure they've crossed all their t's and dotted all their i's, Manager and Engineer couples are relatively easy to sell, largely thanks to the Manager's ability to compromise and offset the Engineer's capacity to dig in and/or slow-walk a decision.

Becoming the Buying Pattern Chameleon

Let's suppose that you as a salesperson are either a Driver or Engineer pattern. And in this experiment, let's further suppose that you encounter an Actor/Manager couple who seek to buy a new range hood to go over their kitchen range. The couple explains to you that the Actor has her heart set on a beautiful wooden old world look for the range hood, after a recent vacation in Italy where she fell in love with these kinds of embellishments in manor homes. She wants to recapture that feeling for their range makeover.

The Manager explains that their challenge is that he enjoys cooking with a wok, and his experience with their current range hood is that it doesn't have nearly enough CFM (cubic foot of air movement per minute) to exhaust properly. As a result, he's tired of cleaning up the greasy mess after cooking. He believes the answer to his problem is a modern high CFM unit designed for restaurant use. All the units he's looked at seem to be stainless steel, which is in direct opposition to his partner's visual preference for an antique wooden hood look. This problem as presented is a clear impediment to a sale.

In our scenario, let's assume that the Driver or Engineer salesperson doesn't have the flexibility yet to drop into the pattern of either the Actor or Manager before them. Taking a purely Driver selling approach, problems will mostly be seen in "black and white" terms. Using a Driver selling pattern runs the risk of boldly agreeing with the Manager customer, recognizing the effects of wok cooking, and thus suggesting the restaurant hood is the way to go. In the Driver mind of the salesperson, someone is going to win and someone is going to lose, and unfortunately the Actor customer's dream for an old-world hood will have to be abandoned.

At the same time, the Engineer salesperson reaches the exact same conclusion, but for different reasons. For the Engineer salesperson, it isn't about winning and losing, it's about science. CFM is CFM; if you don't have enough you can't achieve proper exhaust. Anything less than what is necessary renders a new range hood useless.

The Driver or Engineer salesperson feels justified in their responses and conclusions, and it's highly likely that either would lose this sale. In this instance by not taking the emotional value of the Actor customer into account, and being more mechanically and problem focused, our salesperson fails to see they are myopic in their overall approach and failing to create rewarding customer experience for everyone.

Conversely, let's assume this time that the salesperson has demonstrated mastery of the patterns and has recognized the range hood impasse of the Manager/Actor couple. As a result of their buying pattern knowledge, and selling flexibility, the salesperson chooses to drop into the mindset and buying patterns of their customers. Here is how they see the problem: one of the couple is looking for visual beauty and a connection back to a meaningful experience in her past, and the other is looking for a practical solution to a vexing exhaust problem.

This understanding of the situation leads the salesperson to ask the big question, "Is there a solution that might solve both problems?"

The enlightened salesperson in this scenario knows that a defining characteristic of both Actor/Manager patterns is that it's not about winning and losing; both of the couple are looking for a rewarding customer experience where neither feelings trump practicality or vice versa.

One solution to the problem is to offer the couple a high-quality stainless-steel level blower unit with adequate CFM, shrouded in an old-world wooden hood cover. The Manager customer, completely comfortable with compromise, finds this solution acceptable. The Actor got the visual effect she was looking for, too. (By the way, this is a real-life example and the solution offered above led to a sale.)

The point of this exercise is to point out that flexibility is at the heart of finding selling solutions, but getting there often necessitates stepping out of the comfort of your own pattern and understanding the world through the eyes of your customer. In the beginning, this will take work, patience, and imagination. For some more than others, you will find the need to push the limits of your flexibility, and you will make some mistakes. That's okay, it's part of the necessary learning curve—remember Growth Mindset.

For those veteran salespeople reading this, it's a worthwhile exercise to do a postmortem on some of the sales you can recall that got away. Think back to the encounters and where there might have been solutions that were not readily apparent at the time, based on your viewpoint and more singular selling approach back then. Doing this kind of assessment can lead to greater insight, eliminate similar problems, and gain more sales in your future.

Buying Patterns for Enhancements

Imagine that you are employed by a home builder, working as a sales consultant in a selection center. You are tasked with selling enhancements to prospective new home buyers. Let's say you are trying to sell crown molding to your customer. Crown molding is a decorative element often used at the top of cabinets, columns, doorways and the junction of wall and ceiling in a room. It is purely a finishing embellishment and gets its name from the crowning effect it has when displayed as a capping element. Builders use crown molding in homes to invoke a sense of elegance.

Since it is only a molding detail, you might think that the buying patterns wouldn't come in to play. But the better acquainted you become with the buying patterns, the more you will see that delivering a tailored message can occur even when selling a simple enhancement.

If you were talking to a Driver customer, with their keen sense of the price/value relationship, you might explain how crown molding, for a relatively small sum, can create a disproportionately larger more powerful image of a high-end home. This automatically suggesting greater value, especially to a future buyer, making it look like you spent more money on its construction than you actually did.

For the Actor customer, whose purchases reflect an emotional connection to feeling, you might suggest how crown molding instantly transports the mind to the grand estates of Europe, which once symbolized the pinnacle of beauty and created the feeling of home as your family's castle. Seeing it every day and feeling that you are surrounded in elegance just makes you feel good.

For the Manager customer, where process is important, you might explain that without the crown molding there is something about the home that feels incomplete, like a skipped step in the building process—not what you would expect from a new house—and the kind of feeling that lingers on long after you're moved in.

Finally, for the Engineer customer looking for balance and symmetry in design, you might suggest that just like a hat on the head and shoes on the feet, having base molding where the floor meets the walls but not having crown molding would destroy the sense of symmetry and balance throughout the house.

What does this tell us?

Something as mundane as decorative molding can be presented in such a way as to invoke the buying patterns in the brains of Drivers, Actors, Managers and Engineers, helping them project the enhancement through the lens from which they see the world. This is why a one-size-fits-all approach to selling will not be effective across the board, and diminishes the chance for increased opportunity through enhancements. Understanding that buyers are not monolithic in their viewpoint and accommodating them based on their own sense of what is important is why speaking the language of the buying patterns consistently pays off for sales.

The Hired Consultant

What do you do when confronted by a couple and their design consultant? Will the buying patterns still work as a strategy?

The answer is yes, with a couple of caveats. You essentially follow the same logic we have laid out where your job is that of the detective, figuring out each individual pattern. As with your customers, the consultant's buying patterns tend to reveal themselves in short order through their speech and body language, aided by a few strategic probing questions from you.

When a couple has hired an outside consultant, be aware that the consultant is in a high-stress situation where they need to justify their worth. They will frequently serve in the devil's advocate role, challenging your information and recommendations. It is their own form of putting you through a mini Justification session.

Understanding this ahead of time allows you to avoid taking these challenges personally, therefore bringing a high level of professionalism to the encounter. Once you've discerned the pattern of the consultant, you'll know the best way to put them at ease and get them working in conjunction with the collective goal of a superior customer experience.

If the consultant is a Driver or Actor pattern, acknowledging their expertise and/or dispensing some honest praise—where appropriate—will serve you well. This will go a long way towards smoothing the selling process and reducing any relational friction.

If the consultant is an Engineer or Manager pattern, it's important to understand and ask questions about their own process, and then acknowledge and emphasize where you see overlap between your process and theirs.

In all cases, it's important not to delegitimize or attempt to usurp the consultant through a show of greater expertise.

In essence, you have to approach the situation from the point of view that you are working to sell all three parties. Although this seems to create a greater challenge, if you understand the consultant's pattern and use it to get them on your side, they frequently will end up doing some of the heavy lifting for you by being a like-minded advocate. When this happens, it makes the sale all the more likely.

Decision by Committee

If you are in outside sales, you're likely to encounter a situation where you are given a set amount of time, often between 15 minutes and an hour, to present your case for selling your product and or services. Depending on the size of the prospective buyers' organization, your audience can range from 1 to 10 people. We've covered how to sell to a group of up to three so far, but what do you do when it's closer to 10 people, and you've only got 15 minutes of presentation time?

If you have more time, one tried and true method for assessing buying patterns in a hurry is to start the meeting by asking this question to the participants: "What do you hope to come away with from this meeting?" It's a slightly subtler question than "what's important to you?" The specificity of the latter question can make people feel on the spot; the first question feels more aspirational, and less personal.

With this kind of question, you can quickly go around the room and get a fast reading on what pattern is driving the respondents. It's not perfect, but it can give enough insight to determine how you orchestrate your informational delivery. In a large group setting, if there is some consensus in your mind about which way the respondents tend to lean (i.e. majority of buying patterns) you can tilt the information towards what you've observed.

When this isn't possible, you'll need to carefully tailor your presentation to include all four of the patterns. Statistically your odds are better with this strategy than the old school approach of presenting from a singular point of view, where you might be reducing your chances by up to 80% depending on which pattern you don't adequately speak to.

Based on thousands of hours and thousands of people attending our seminars, the following graph represents the breakdown we see regarding buy/sell patterns. This data represents attendees that are salespeople across a wide variety of industries. The rough breakdown: Drivers make up 20% of the group, Actors are 35%, Managers are 25%, and Engineers are the final 20%. These numbers can vary slightly from industry to industry, but we believe they represent a fair cross section of salespeople. The data shows a higher percentage of Actors, but generally all four patterns are sufficiently represented. That's why to be effective you need domain knowledge for all four patterns.

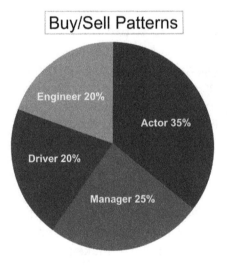

Assuming you've done your homework, you have the flexibility and comfort level to engage all four patterns. Leaving time for a question and answer period is vital because post-sales presentation, it provides the opportunity to go back and reinforce key points brought up by your audience.

Outside Sales, Hunting, and the Buying Patterns

If you are in outside sales, on the hunt for new business customers, how can you use the buying patterns to your advantage?

When building your customer base and sales territory, you can leverage the buying patterns to create a comprehensive "whole system" selling strategy. If you think about trying to attract a new customer—whether they are a manufacturer, wholesaler, or some other combination of business-to-business partner—the first thing to remember is that they are most likely already doing business with some other competitor. It's rare that you will find yourself with a totally new and unknown product and/or service that you're introducing to the world. It's possible, but unlikely. What is more likely is that you have some version or variation of what your competitor is already selling to your prospective customer.

As a result, if you are in outside sales, you are really in the relationship replacement business, or perhaps the adoption business if the opportunity is to add your product or service to the ones your prospective customer is already buying. So why, for example, would a wholesale customer drop their current vendor relationship to invite you into their business? The answer, perhaps unsurprisingly, has to do with the four buying decision patterns that we've already identified.

Opportunities for new vendor partnership arise when one or more of the following four tipping points are triggered and a business is forced to rethink their buying strategy.

The first tipping point occurs when the business perceives a failure by a current vendor in the category of price or value. This is where the customer believes that what they are currently paying for an item exceeds the value the item brings. When whatever they buy doesn't seem like it is worth it, or a competitor offers up pricing that beats their current price model, a tipping point is exposed. There is particular vulnerability for vendor change if the buying decision maker is a Driver. This is especially true because price or value is really their thing, and working a vendor for pricing is, from the Driver's point of view, both a necessity and often an enjoyable part of their job. For the Driver buyer, price or value can easily trump an existing relationship, even one that has been in existence for years.

The second tipping point occurs when the business perceives a failure by a current vendor in the features or benefits of the product or services their current vendor is supplying. If features or products seem old, outdated, or no longer relevant, a tipping point presents itself. Because of the fast-paced nature of innovation and invention, products and services that have been cash cows—industry mainstays—can seemingly become obsolete overnight. Smartphones with their built-in high-quality camera technology killed much of the photography industry in a handful of years.

But by the same token, it doesn't require groundbreaking change to expose the vulnerabilities in a product line. If the buying decision maker is an Actor, then just the sense that a product "feels tired," or a little less flashy than what they've seen displayed elsewhere in the marketplace, can put a current vendor at risk for a change. Keep in mind that the current product might still be garnering a fair amount of sales, but the Actor buyer believes change will do their business some good and that even more sales will be possible when they flip over to the new and improved model X.

Even a company or CEO's image, outside of the actual product, is a factor in today's more culturally aware society. A vendor might have the most cutting edge and cool product in the marketplace, but if that vendor's image is not in sync with the customer's values or what is considered to be acceptable from a cultural standpoint, they can find themselves quickly on the outside of the business looking wistfully back in. Again, this is especially true when a company decision maker is represented by the Actor pattern. The Actor is all about perception and how things look. On top of that, the idea of change is not an anathema to them. Change represents excitement, and excitement is in some ways what Actors crave.

The third tipping point occurs when the business perceives a failure by a current vendor in the category of operational performance. This can include supply chain breakdown, ordering issues, customer service problems, a lack of training on the part of the vendor, poor sales servicing, a lack of marketing materials or samples, and so on. A host of tipping points are possible, and under the broad heading of "process" we can begin to see how the decision to jettison a current vendor presents a scary number of possibilities, and opportunities.

Which one of these process problems is more likely to do a vendor in and lose them the business? It's tough to say, but what is clear is that if the buying decision lies on the hands of a Manager whose focus is on process breakdown and process improvement, any one of the problems outlined are enough to tip the business away from the current vendor.

The fourth tipping point occurs when the business perceives a failure by a current vendor in the category of product quality and/or construction. This tipping point is different from the obsolete feature or benefits we see with the Actor buyer. The problem is often identified by an Engineer pattern buyer who puts great emphasis on product quality. The perception of cheapening a product, as a result of price, supply, or specification change is high on the Engineer radar. Another problem can simply be that the product doesn't hold up under current operating conditions due to overall construction issues or flaws in workmanship. Product failure, as in actual systematic failure, is one of the fastest ways for the vendor to lose their customer, especially if any kind of litigation is thrown into the mix and it looks like expensive legal fees will be involved.

We can effectively sum up the four tipping points that will generate a vendor change out as:

- price/value

- feature/benefit

- process

- quality/construction

Since these are the four decision-making biases, we can see how their manifestation in the real world makes up the reasons why a vendor might either be eliminated or added.

Growing your territory and increasing your customer base starts with carefully assessing customers who would be a potentially good fit for your type of business. With the preponderance of information on the

Internet today, with the exclusion of retail customers, it's likely that you can compile such a list by defining a given territory and doing some research. Once you've identified your potential new customer opportunities, the next step should be familiar to you. You need to do a little detective work about the status between your target customer and their current vendor.

In other words, using the four categories we've outlined above as benchmarks on a scale of 1-5, where 1 is outstanding and 5 is failing, what is the level of service that is currently being provided by your competition? This information can be gathered through phone calls, reading reviews online, or personal visits.

Having attained enough information to have a clear idea of your competitor's strengths and weaknesses as it relates to the tipping points allows you the flexibility of designing a plan for the best use of your time.

For example, should you determine that your potential customer's current vendor is doing a fantastic job and hitting it out of the park in all four categories, then it makes sense to introduce your company if you can secure a meeting but to avoid going in for the hard close as it will likely have little impact.

If, however, the decision maker is a Driver and engages you in negotiation, that might be an opportunity. Short of that, other than making your presence known and staying current with the target customer, this potential customer is in the "wait and see" category. It doesn't make much sense to devote your finite energy towards a weak prospect.

The good news is that given the fast pace of business and all the inherent possibilities for hiccups paving the way for any of the four tipping points, the chances are relatively low that a competitive vendor is hitting it out of the park in all categories. And if they are, like the weather, things are always changing. A weak prospect this month might be a strong opportunity next month.

Should your sleuthing detect a tipping point for your target customer, you should try to secure a meeting with the potential customer as soon as possible. Begin initiating a strategy that incorporates some of the following elements where appropriate:

- Build a sales presentation with a strong emphasis on your solution to solving their problem—the tipping point you've identified in their current vendor. This should be done for each tipping point that's been triggered. Remember to build a presentation that addresses the key three selling points of your product or service from an emotional standpoint and reflects the appropriate buying pattern of the decision maker. (Be careful not to denigrate their current vendor in the meeting; this will not play well, especially with the Manager pattern.)

- If the buying decision is made by a committee and you are unable to ascertain the patterns of all the buyers involved, build a presentation that addresses the key three selling points of your product or service from an emotional standpoint and reflects *the four buying patterns* as a way of hedging your bets. Remember, relying on only your go-to selling pattern will likely reduce your chances of selling by anywhere from 65-80%, depending upon the makeup of the committee.

- As the number of tipping points increase, so do your chances of making a sale. If there are two or more tipping points in play, you should maximize your energy and follow either strategy point #1 or 2, depending on whether you're talking to a single buyer or a committee.

- When presenting, keep the following ideas in mind for increasing brain receptivity of your audience to what you have to say;

    a. When possible, deliver your selling presentation on your feet. It will improve your own memory recall and command greater attention.

    b. Save the "company brag," a description of your company's bona fides, until the end of the presentation.

c. Try to keep your presentation to around 15- 20 minutes in order to maximize the short-term and working memory of the participants.

d. Since the brain is a visual processing machine, use visual content and involve physical hands-on demonstration to capture a greater memory share.

e. The most important thing to a listener is WIFM, also known as "What's In It For Me?" Be sure you're addressing the respective buying patterns and your specific customer concerns.

f. Move as quickly as possible to content that explains how you intend to help your customer solve their problem—the tipping point that doomed your competitor.

g. Remember signs of interest such as pupil dilation; constantly monitor your audience's attention level and modify your content if attention wanes.

h. Keep in mind that the brain follows the ghost curve; remember to include a definitive dynamic beginning and end in your presentation.

i. Midpoint summation is a way to bring the brain back on line by hitting the key points again in the middle of the presentation.

j. The order of presentation effectiveness is:

   1. Real life story relevant to your content and selling goals

   2. Demonstration, most powerful when it is hands-on by the audience

   3. Graphs, figures, and data, as the brain struggles to hold on to this kind of information in a presentation format

k. The brain will only remember 3 key points in the context of a story. Make sure you tie emotional value to each of your 3 key points.

l. The brain needs to hear things 3 times to lock down the information in the hippocampus, where memory lives.

m. People respond more powerfully when you engage them by name.

n. The brain absorbs roughly twice as much information when it is asked to recall that information, so be sure to engage your audience with easy follow-up questions, which helps the responders feel a connection to you and the information.

o. Your audience will partly judge the presentation by their perception of your energy level; be sure to keep it high.

p. Make sure you leave time at the end of your presentation to solicit feedback.

q. Always leave your audience with some tangible handout that reinforces your messaging.

• When using a PowerPoint-type tool:

a. Follow the 10/20/30 rule: 10 slides or less, 20 minutes or less, and no font smaller than 30. This holds attention and make it easier to read.

b. On each slide, aim for only 3-4 bullet points.

c. Whenever possible, drive the point home with a relevant picture instead of text. Pictures serve as better memory markers for recall later.

d. Make sure all slides are easy for the viewer to read; avoid graphs and spreadsheets with unreadable stats which will tend to cause your audience's attention to wane.

e. Keep verbiage per slide to a minimum; remember that you are delivering the relevant information, the slides are merely a backdrop. They should read more like billboards, seven words or less.

f. Should attention wane, you are not married to the slide deck. It's better to skip slides or speak off the cuff as opposed to losing your audience to daydreaming.

g. You should be able to deliver the entire presentation sans the slide deck. If you can't do this, then your presentation is either too content-heavy or you don't know the material well enough.

h. The slides should serve as an enhancement to your talking points; they shouldn't be used as a recall crutch for the speaker.

i. Ending a presentation on the same highly visual slide you began with will create the important feeling of continuity in the minds of your audience.

Pattern-selling Tips

Tips for selling the Driver buying pattern:

- Keep information in short bursts (think bullet points).

- Specifically acknowledge their expertise early in the conversation.

- Use descriptive words like *excellence, superior, distinctive.*

- This is not a relationship-focused pattern; don't let that bother you.

- Drivers buy based on value; prove your product or service is "worth it."

- Drivers learn through challenge, it's not personal.

Tips for selling the Actor buying pattern:

- Be enthusiastic; your attitude and energy pumps up their excitement level.

- Use descriptive words like *outstanding, wonderful, brilliant,* and *exquisite.*

- Flattery and constant positive feedback are the lifeblood of the Actor.

- Engage them by letting them direct the conversation, win them over with your response.

- The Actor is a relationship-focused pattern; superficial sometimes, but you come first—your idea or initiative second.

- Actors learns by talking things out.

Tips for selling the Engineer buying pattern:

- Engineers want as much verified information as they can get.

- When delivering information, don't skimp on the details.

- This is not a relationship-focused pattern; they make their decision after a careful assessment of all the information and the process can take some time.

- Use descriptive words like *accurate, precise, clear-cut.*

- Talk about things with a fine focus, such as pros vs cons. Keep it black and white, avoid grey.

- Engineers tend not to be overly impressed by the latest and greatest features and are generally more interested in quality and construction.

Tips for selling the Manager buying pattern

- Talk about your continual attention to the process; your message should be "I'm here for you no matter what."

- Keep track of past interactions, remembering customers' family names for instance; avoid superficiality, they seek real connection.

- This is a relationship-focused pattern and will pay dividends over the long haul if you build upon that.

- Managers are impressed when you prove you have everything thought through and the process buttoned up; your goal is to remove hassle from their lives.

- Don't surprise the Manager; always let them know what is coming next and exactly what to expect.

- Use descriptive words like *guaranteed, planned out, procedure, careful.*

- Managers learn through a careful and thorough talking-through of ideas.

Buying Pattern Experiment

We conclude the buying pattern section with an example of the power of biasing towards decision patterns. Often in one of the sales seminars we conduct, we'll give everyone the buying pattern diagnostic, and once we have their results, we'll break the room up by highest scores. Each pattern goes to their own individual corner of the room. With that accomplished, we then supply a handout to the participants detailing a 10-step problem for each respective group to solve, with strict instructions that they need to work together as a team.

After about 15 minutes, I proceed to make my rounds to see how each group is progressing with the ten-step problem. I always start with the Driver group. "How are we doing in solving the problem?" Invariably someone speaks up without a moment's hesitation. (We're talking about Drivers, after all).

"Whose idea was this exercise, was this your idea?" asks the Driver participant.

I smile and say, "Yes, it was my idea, is there a problem?"

"Yeah, there's a problem, we don't really see the point in doing this. I mean we live this stuff every day. I'm not sure there is a whole lot more for us to learn. I've been doing this for twenty years. We've decided to work on our own 10-step process, or maybe 8-steps. I haven't decided, but I guarantee whatever it is it will make a whole lot more sense than what you came up with."

"Have you reached consensus on this?" I ask.

"Yes," says the Driver participant, but the ensuing comments make it clear that indeed there is no consensus. The group devolves into back-and-forth banter as many of the group members try to speak at the same time and grow progressively louder in an attempt to be heard.

I say, "Good luck, it will be interesting to see what you produce." From the distance, I hear the unofficial spokesperson of the Driver group shouting back to me, "Don't worry, I'll get them to understand..."

With that I move on to the next group, the Actors.

"How are we doing in solving the problem?" Someone speaks up, again without a moment's hesitation. (We're talking about Actors, after all). What comes next is something along these lines:

"Robb, wow, this is so cool. I mean when I was told I had to go to a class on selling I thought, "Okay, just poke my eye out with a sharp stick." Let's be honest, sales classes are usually pretty unbearable, but all this brain-related stuff, it turns out to be really interesting. I can't wait to go home and share what I've learned with my partner..."

"That's great," I say, "but how is your group doing on the 10-step problem?" At this point there is an uncomfortable silence where all eyes suddenly find somewhere else to look. Eventually, someone says quietly,

"Yeah, we haven't really had a chance to get started. We all started talking and the next thing you know somebody pulled up this crazy video on their phone. But don't get us wrong, we love this class. It's so awesome! We're probably going to need a little more time to knock this thing out. There's a lot of detail here, so we may need to skip a couple of steps to get this done. By the way, that color of shirt looks really good on you."

I say, "Good luck, it will be interesting to see what you produce." With that, I move on to the next group, the Engineers.

"How are we doing in solving the problem?" I ask. Invariably no one speaks up. There is hesitation. I repeat my question again. (We're talking about Engineers, after all).

"Hmm," says one of the group. "We have a question. Was this exercise your invention, did you come up with this?"

I smile and say, "Yes, it was my idea, is there a problem?"

"Hmm," says the spokesperson, "So we've taken a look at this and I think it's fair to say that somehow this shouldn't be a 10-step process. We can't be definite yet, but our early observations suggest this is more like a twenty-step process—perhaps more, perhaps a few steps less. In any event, without doing some more digging we just don't think it makes sense to proceed until we get more data. Don't get us wrong, we are not trying to be difficult, but had you come to us ahead of time, we might have been able to steer you towards a better outcome. We'll do our best, but we aren't prepared to sign off as a group with our solution."

I say, "Good luck, it will be interesting to see what you produce." With that, I move on to the last group, the Managers.

"How are we doing in solving the problem?" I ask. Invariably no one speaks up. There is hesitation as eyes scan each other, each waiting patiently, not wanting to hog the attention. I repeat my question again. (We're talking about Managers, after all).

"Oh," someone says. "We've been done for a little while. The other groups didn't look like they've finished yet so we've just been biding our time, talking about some of our takeaways from the seminar. Are there notes to this seminar online, by chance?"

"You're completely finished?" I ask.

Someone else speaks up, "Yes, we really enjoyed the exercise. We split the group into a couple of smaller teams, worked through the individual tasks, came back together, talked through the results, tweaked our findings with some really good ideas from the group and that's about it. Having the exercise already defined out in terms of a 10-step process made it pretty clear as to what we needed to do."

I look around the group and everyone is nodding in unison. If this had been a campout, the Managers might have been holding hands, roasting marshmallows, and singing Kumbaya.

To be fair to the other groups, starting the exercise with a 10-step defined process biases the experiment towards the Managers, who thrive in a process environment. The greater purpose of the exercise is not really about outcomes as much as it's about helping the participants recognize just how ingrained their decision patterns are when confronted with a fixed set of parameters. It's the same exercise, administered the exact same way, and yet because of brain biasing we get four distinct pattern-related results in the execution of solving the problem.

The Drivers immediately assume their knowledge level exceeds the problem and the experiment is therefore unworthy of undertaking. One of the bolder Drivers assumes for some reason that they are in charge, and the rest of the group should pay attention to them.

The Actors, having already sat through the beginning of the seminar with patience frayed and focus gone, find relief in an unrelated online video. They also assume a shortcut will help them through the project by skipping a couple of *unneeded* steps. Lastly a compliment is thrown my way for good measure by one of the Actors who wants to stay in my relationship good graces.

The Engineers proceed as if they are building a moon landing module for NASA, and perceiving a lack of information, have concluded they can't complete the project. Notice the Drivers ended up in the same place, but not for lack of information; from their viewpoint, they had plenty of information, and that information told them the project was a waste of time. Here we have two different patterns with the same end result based on different reasons.

And what about the Managers? When confronted with a problem that neatly fits their skill set, they proceeded in an orderly fashion, neither dismissing the information nor believing they needed more. The Managers' teamwork helped them distribute the load, reducing the overload effect and stress level of undertaking a new project. The end result: they systematically completed all 10 steps, and were able to keep the working atmosphere cordial.

If the exercise would have been designed to make a quick and bold choice, then the Drivers might have fared much better. A deeply detailed exercise would have been a boon to the Engineers, and an exercise stressing spontaneity would have most likely let the Actors shine.

The point is that when a problem is linked with the right skill set, solving the problem becomes a much easier task. And in that light, when confronted by a specific buying pattern, the salesperson who brings a matching selling pattern to the task is going to rise above the rest, ultimately providing a better-quality customer experience, increasing their chances of the encounter culminating in a sale.

Soundbites and the Rule of Threes

Once you determine your customers' buying pattern, how can you maximize your impact?

Soundbites, those catchy idea morsels, are ubiquitous. From billboards to tweets to political slogans, we are awash in them. Soundbites are the rhetorical currency of the 21st century.

They're powerful for a couple of reasons. First, delivering information in small doses means the brain doesn't have to work as hard saving energy. Second, like a pop earworm, they tend to stick in your head. Third, they convey a ton of meaning in a small package. If you tailor your soundbites to a particular buying pattern you begin to see just how much power they have.

Our brains rely on our network of prebuilt beliefs to help maneuver us through our day. Unfortunately, this kind of system means that we bias towards simple black-and-white answers, often choosing not to examine the nuance of a decision or argument that might put our belief at risk.

This is why soundbites are so popular; they cater to the brain's entrenched understanding of the world. We decide quickly but shallowly: this political party is the good guys and the other is the bad guys.

It takes more energy and an even more complicated reasoning process to seek out the grey area of a decision or argument. The only way to teach your brain how to do it is to actively question your own beliefs. That can be a messy business, which can lead to uncertainty—one of the very things your brain system is designed to help clean up.

This is why black and white answers are so terribly seductive. It's what our brains are hardwired to do. For many of us caught in the swirl of our day, relying on preconceived beliefs just saves time and energy. Who has time to spend digging into the reasoning, or lack thereof, behind our decisions?

Our locked-in answers have allowed us to flourish and populate a large portion of the planet. Yet as a species, the over reliance on unexamined beliefs is also our collective Achilles' heel.

In our current media landscape, a politician who can't express their ideas in a series of short, punchy phrases probably doesn't stand much of a chance. In the mind of the average voter, a lengthy, detailed policy explanation will generally lose out to a slogan, especially if that slogan can rhyme.

The "rhyme-as-reason effect," also known as the Eaton-Rosen phenomenon, is a cognitive bias in which a saying is generally found to feel truer if it rhymes. For instance, "a stitch in time saves nine" is somehow easier to grasp and believe than "a stitch in time saves eight."

Although you probably aren't thinking about creating a sales pitch built around a series of rhymes, it's helpful to understand that short impactful soundbites with repetitive sounds carry the day. "Built Ford

Tough," for example, is a slogan Ford Motor Company relied on for 35 years to tell their story in just three words.

These quick, appealing messages are incredibly appealing to the amygdala, the emotional processing center of the brain. We might assume that the prefrontal cortex, home of executive control and rational thinking, might overpower or at least subdue this powerful emotional drug. Frequently, it does not.

In fact, research shows that if a soundbite is repeated often enough, the prefrontal cortex lets go of the steering wheel altogether, allowing the amygdala to slide into the driver's seat. The message plays directly to your feelings, free of logical scrutiny. This is part of why politicians obsessively repeat their talking points—and why it works. They capitalize on a fundamental human brain flaw. It's the same in sales.

Statistically, immigrants commit fewer crimes than the rest of the population. Statistically, you are more likely to be killed by a falling flat screen TV than a terrorist attack. But nobody is arguing the real Trojan horse inside your home is your flat screen TV, waiting to topple and kill you when you're not looking. And people continue to insist that an immigration ban is a straightforward precaution, as common sense as locking the doors on your house. Plain and simple, the "lock your doors" analogy targets your amygdala's fear response, potentially deceiving you, your friends, your neighbors, and your family.

So why would otherwise rational people fall prey to flimsy emotional arguments? Because individually, our brains aren't designed to hold, understand, and display a depth of knowledge in every area of our lives. Overwhelmed, we lean on the amygdala, part of our emotional System 1, developed to save time and energy via quick gut judgments in areas where we lack expertise.

But there is a price to be paid for relying on decision shortcuts. We might be an expert in a given area or field, but mostly we operate within the *illusion of depth*. That is to say, we rely on soundbites to cover the areas we pretend to, but don't really understand.

Most achievements have been driven by a handful of brilliant people.

You might be a whiz on your smartphone, but could you build one from scratch? The same holds true for just about every piece of technology that you come in contact with. The ugly truth is that a society's technical and cultural achievements are no guarantee of the wisdom, intelligence, or rationality of its individual members.

The bottom line? *You and I are probably not that smart.*

Soundbites allow us to navigate the areas we only pretend to understand. From complicated health care bills to how microwaves work, most of us are basically ignorant. Soundbites provide the illusion of plugging the ignorance gap.

This is where a new sales team who have learned the Rule of Threes and practiced them accordingly can outperform veterans with significantly more industry experience. By keeping the delivery short and sweet, the newbies gain an advantage by not overloading their customers' short-term memory.

The newbie's Achilles heel is the customer who seeks considerably more depth of knowledge. But statistically, this is the less likely outcome. A veteran salesperson can gain the upper hand by both practicing the Rule of Threes along with leveraging years of industry-specific knowledge.

A Sales Genius follows the Rule of Threes while at the same time always seeking to add to their knowledge bank about their product line and ways to engage their customer. That way, no matter the circumstance or customer, they are prepared. This relentless pursuit of effective methods to deliver key information in a simple and digestible way is one of the central tenets of being a Sales Genius.

The problem for many salespeople is that over time, they get complacent and stop looking for better ways to deliver information. Instead, they come to settle on a handful of increasingly dusty metaphors. Complacency is a dangerous state to find yourself in, and often difficult for a veteran to recognize. The book *Peak* by Anders Ericsson and Robert Pool provides an excellent case in point—and a cautionary tale.

Ericsson and Pool cite research from Harvard Medical School finding that out of 62 studies, 60 found that a doctor's performance over time tends to either plateau or, worryingly, to get worse. "The older doctors knew less" write Ericsson and Pool, "and did worse in terms of providing care than doctors with far fewer years of experience, and researchers concluded that it was likely the older doctors' patients fared worse because of it."

The older doctors were even attending professional education seminars in an effort to keep their skills sharp. It's just that most professional education is the least helpful kind in terms of actually building skill. We don't tend to learn well from listening to lectures; we need hands-on experience with instant feedback so we can tell right away if we're succeeding or failing.

In contrast to the doctor studies, Ericsson and Pool also discuss research carried out by a group led by Andrew Vickers of the Memorial Sloan Kettering Cancer Center in New York City, examining the results of almost 8000 prostate cancer patients who had their prostates surgically removed. Vickers and his team found that the more experience a surgeon had, the less likely the cancer was to recur. Carrying out more surgeries made surgeons better, not worse.

Ericsson and Pool point out that one crucial difference between medical doctors and surgeons is that surgeons get immediate feedback as to how each case is going. If a surgeon accidentally nicks a vein, they will instantly, unambiguously know. This real-time feedback gives them a much better picture of where they need to improve.

Even if your instrument of choice is not a scalpel, there are lessons to be learned from this. Probably surprising to many sales veterans is that, just like the doctors in the study, they are not a "fine wine" getting increasingly better with age. Rather, as time goes on, they tend to be more like professional athletes whose advancing age signifies a lost step.

The good news is that unlike an athlete whose natural aging is out of their control, a veteran salesperson can stay at the top of their game by continually monitoring their progress with a constant eye towards improving their communication level with customers. The Rule of Threes is a great way to endlessly hone and refine the power of your soundbites and emotional talking points.

Binary Selection

The Rule of Threes, like the buying patterns, is an essential sales tool in building the ultimate customer experience. When it comes to the selection process, another indispensable tool is a concept called binary selection. It is based on the idea that since the brain is generally trying to conserve energy, then during product selection you should avoid overtaxing your customer's brain.

Binary selection is an efficient, simplified process for making selections. Its premise is to limit choice to comparing only two items at a time.

To imagine binary selection in action, think about an optometrist matching up a person with a new glasses prescription. Most of us are probably familiar with the process in which a prospective glasses wearer is offered the choice between just two lenses, and then a different two lenses, and so on. *Can you see better with this one or that one?*

Through the process of elimination, eventually the appropriate lenses are chosen for a pair of glasses. At no time does the optometrist offer three, four or five choices at the same time. And as a result of binary selection, it takes only a few minutes to accomplish the task.

While even choosing between two lenses can be tough, this is a far superior method compared to the brain overload that is currently a mainstay in countless other areas of life. You can imagine how difficult eyeglass selection would be instead if the optometrist offered you a selection process like you see for faucets in a big box store: row after row of different lenses to assess at once. You could be staring at hundreds of lenses for days, trying to discern which ones would work the best.

It's unlikely the average optometrist is aware of how their selection process caters perfectly to the idiosyncrasies of the brain, but that really isn't important. What is important is that they have settled on an amazingly brain-friendly way of making decisions that can easily be copied for just about any product selection.

This is not to say that product offerings should be limited to only two products like chocolate and vanilla. You can offer 33 flavors of ice cream, or even more for that matter. We only suggest that, when introducing product offerings, you limit the choices to only two at a time. The customer eliminates the least desirable of the two, and then a new offering is placed in that slot. You keep repeating this process over and over again until you've run through the entire gamut of product offerings.

To facilitate binary selection, you can speed up the process by staging product with like product. For example, if you were selling granite, you would stage all the dark color selections together and the light color selections together. If a customer knows they don't want a dark color, they can skip the dark grouping altogether and move immediately to the light colors. In this way, you can more easily work through binary choice.

If you worked in a lighting store, you might sort all of your contemporary lighting in one grouping, your arts and craft style lighting in another grouping, your traditional lighting in another grouping, and so on.

Imagine going into a paint store looking to find a suitable color to paint your bedroom. You're thinking some sort of blue would be nice, and as you enter the store, your attention is quickly consumed by the enormous wall of color offerings. Unfortunately, there is no pattern to the choices. You notice some blues in the middle of the wall, at the top of the wall, in the lower right corner of the wall, and so on. The various shades of blues are haphazardly mixed in with all the other colors, making selection and comparison almost impossible.

Luckily, paint stores figured this problem out a long time ago. They presort the colors for you, staging like colors from lightest gradient shade to darkest. If you desire to paint your bedroom blue, you simply go to the blue section and make your decision.

This pre-sorting aspect is an inexpensive key to ease and improve customer selection. Allowing a customer to bypass an entire category in which they lack interest saves their brain glucose, improves attention, and significantly reduces overload while increasing the chance of purchase.

If those weren't reasons enough, binary selection cuts down the amount of time a customer spends in the selection process, thereby allowing the salesperson to maximize their own selling time.

Given the benefits, you would think that this binary process would have already been institutionalized everywhere by now. Unfortunately some ideas, despite their merit, can take a while to catch on. Case in point: the concept of doctors washing their hands before examining patients didn't start to take off until the mid-nineteenth century.

I once led a seminar in a kitchen and bath store for about fifty sales representatives. The store was still open to customers during the seminar, and so while I was relating the advantage of binary selection, a past customer came into the store.

One of the salespeople attending my seminar immediately excused themselves, saying this was their customer and he needed to attend to her. This salesperson also made it clear that he wasn't all that happy to see this customer return.

It seems that the customer was having a great deal of trouble picking out a plastic laminate countertop for her laundry room. It was a small top and as such there wasn't a lot of profit in the sale. Nevertheless, the salesperson was duty bound to help her. The customer apparently had made repeated forays back and forth between her home and the store, struggling to choose a color that would ultimately make her happy.

Although the salesperson recognized the woman was in a state of brain overload—who wouldn't be, with easily over 150 laminate color options to choose from—he was at a loss to solve the problem. He was only now being introduced to the power of binary choice.

Someone in the sales seminar group suggested that I should demonstrate binary selection in real time to help both the struggling customer and salesperson. The roar from the seminar group made it clear that they all agreed. If you've ever been in a sales seminar and the speaker is suggesting you consider a new approach to your sales process, there are bound to be more than a few skeptics, especially when the new approach is significantly different than your own well-worn strategy.

I was delighted at the opportunity and the skeptics were eager to see the results. It was no longer a hypothetical; things were getting real.

The laminate sample boards were at the back of the store, and so as the woman headed in that direction, the entire seminar group of fifty began to follow her. She turned around, just in time to see this mass of humanity descending on her like a herd of buffalo. To say she looked surprised would be an understatement.

"What's going on," she demanded.

I explained that we were in a sales seminar, and that I'd been told she was having a tough time making her final choice out of the sea of colors. She agreed.

I asked her to show me where she was in the process. She reached into her purse and pulled out the seven laminate sample chips she'd managed to narrow it down to. Keep in mind, it had taken her nearly a week of countless trips back and forth from her home to the store to make this much progress.

I asked her for the chips, she complied, and then I began to hang these samples back up on the board.

The woman let out a gasp. "No, no," she interjected, "what are you doing?"

I said, "I'm going to make this easy for you. Tell me, do you like dark colors or light colors better?"

"I definitely don't want a dark colored top in my laundry room," she said. "I want to keep it light and airy."

That single binary decision allowed me to eliminate half of the entire board from selection. At this point I could focus on only light colors, and so I asked the next binary question,

"Do you like light greens or light yellows?"

She said, "I don't want a green countertop."

You get the idea. I continued to propose binary choices between colors, and with each choice she was eliminating large swaths of colors from the selection process. We quickly got down to a single row of light beige, and I simply pulled two samples from the beige row, let her compare, eliminated the one that interested her less, and then repeated this until we were down to a single beige sample, her final choice.

A week of agonizing had gotten her nowhere. With binary selection, from start to finish, the entire selection process took less than 90 seconds. (Literally. One diligent seminar attendee had timed it on his watch.)

If there were super powers in sales, binary selection would be one of them. And the beauty of the process is that it's not relegated to only sales situations. Any time you have a choice to make, a little pre-sorting and a few rounds of binary selection makes for among the fastest and surest ways to reach a favorable outcome.

Good, Better, Best

Binary selection has been around since the dawn of humanity. There is something breathtakingly elegant about the brevity of "this versus that". It doesn't resign your decision-making to status quo; consciously using binary selection to weigh many choices will yield less biased results.

But what can you do when you're not comparing SKU's or even categories? What do you do when you want to compare complex products with other complex products containing a myriad of pieces or parts? How do you compare multiple houses with each other, or automobiles and their seemingly endless array of options?

For complex product selection, we turn to the tiered pricing strategy.

Writing for *Harvard Business Review*, consultant Rafi Mohammed explains that

tiered pricing isn't new. Over a hundred years ago, Alfred P Sloan, CEO of General Motors, used what was touted as a "pricing ladder" to differentiate between their Chevrolet, Buick, Oldsmobile and Cadillac brands. This strategy was credited with GM finally putting Ford Motor Company in their rearview mirror.

You probably followed a simplified version of the price ladder the last time you pulled up to a gas pump and had to make a choice: a lower price ethanol blend, Regular, or Premium. It's a decision you've made thousands of times. In fact, far beyond the gas pump, you're asked to make that very same kind of three-tiered decision over and over again, whether you're picking airplane seats or you're at the local car wash.

The ridesharing company Uber started out with a single entry, their UberX service, which was a direct-to-location midsize sedan ride. In 2014 they launched UberPool, a bid to increase revenue by attracting more price-conscious riders. The discounted but less direct ride included multiple pickups and drop-offs. The dual price tiering caught on quickly. Reportedly in some cities, UberPool made up as much as 50% of Uber's total rideshare.

Uber decided to go even deeper into discounted ride sharing with another option called uberExpress, which required the rider to do a little walking to meet up at a pre-arranged site. Tiered pricing has been a boon to Uber's business model.

Good, Better, Best is a classic technique for bundling features or services into a trio of packages for customers to choose from. "Good" is the basic budget-friendly option, "Better" includes some bells and whistles at an intermediate cost, and "Best" is the most expensive and premium offering.

In a fast-changing world where the options seem to multiply every day, there is something comforting about Good, Better, Best bundling as an easy navigation tool. Your brain has adapted so well to this strategy, you likely don't even think about it. It's just another heuristic—also known as a mental shortcut.

When the brain drops into the Good, Better, Best heuristic, a customer with domain knowledge will likely move through a review of all three tiers. On the other hand, if they're not well-versed in a product or service category, they often default to, *"Well, I probably don't want the cheapest one, and I probably don't want the most expensive. Middle option it is."* It feels like the savvy, responsible thing to do when you aren't quite sure of a product or service.

And it's not just the way consumers often hedge their buying bets. Store clerks will use the same shorthand to quickly narrow the customer's selection, thereby saving themselves a lot of time and effort. But when faced with a wavering customer, a salesperson might capitalize on the uncertainty to move the sale along, saying something like, *"You probably don't want the cheapest one, or our most expensive one, right?"* With that type of framing, they are wittingly or unwittingly biasing the customer away from the full range of choice.

This is a huge problem for a vendor, because despite all their research, development, manufacturing, and marketing effort towards their higher priced product, they just got outflanked by the salesperson before the customer ever really had a fair chance to shop and compare.

Mohammed writes that in William Poundstone's book *Priceless*, Poundstone tells the story of how the famed Williams-Sonoma company stumbled into one truth about the "Better" price category. It seems that they were having only moderate selling success with a bread making machine that retailed at $279. They decided that perhaps what their customers really wanted was a more upscale model with more features, so they introduced a premium bread machine for $429, creating a new "Best" category in their lineup.

The assumption was that this new "Best" tier would be their ticket to more revenue and profit. That did pay off in a way; sales on the upscale model proved to be lackluster, but they discovered that sales on their

$279 offering took off. In fact, the sales on that model soon doubled after their deluxe model was introduced.

What happened?

Once the customers compared the two models, their brains quickly established that $429 was too much to pay for the product. However, with $429 as a reference point for what an expensive bread machine cost, suddenly a $279 machine sounded much more reasonable, and this confirmation drove up buying confidence and in turn additional sales.

This is a good example of how a careful examination of price and differentiators can alter buying tendencies one way or the other in a tiered strategy. Clear-cut differentiation in marketing, pricing, quality and features are all key in creating a viable tiered strategy.

Good, Better, Best is really the "Goldilocks rule" in disguise: not too big, not too small, but just right. But what if the bargain bin option is actually of better quality? What if paying the extra money for the pricier version is worth it in the long run? When your brain slips into heuristic mode, it runs that bit of neural code without deliberation. That's the beauty of it—and that's also how it can get you into trouble.

One common objection Mohammed encounters when advocating for Good, Better, Best is that the seller is afraid arranging one's offerings in this format will automatically push all customers to the cheapest choice with the lowest level of profit.

However, Mohammed asserts that a well-constructed Good, Better, Best overcomes this by being strategic about what features or services are present at each level. Many customers are willing to pay a little more for amenities that feel essential. All in all, Mohammed says that at the end of the day it's still not uncommon for 40% of customers to opt for the "Better" choice.

Again, those features must be chosen carefully. If those bells and whistles are not deemed essential or the price is just out of reach, you might find yourself right back in the middle like the Williams-Sonoma bread machine, which may or may not work out.

Providing a fancy "Best" bundle designed to grab the interest of luxury shoppers can still be lucrative, provided the brand offering is truly perceived as luxurious.

We should note that product or service quality can play an important role in the upscale buyer's decision as well, but that the psychological linkage between emotion and status is tough to underestimate. Higher price and upscale branding provide a powerful one-two punch. It goes back to the emotional tipping point we introduced earlier: "it makes me feel special."

At the opposite end of the tiered spectrum is the stripped down "Good" version which, when carefully managed, can help attract a whole new segment of budget-conscious customers. We saw this with the UberPool option.

Mohammed posits that one can take the "Good" version to its logical conclusion by offering a "fighter product," a low-priced option that simply exists to match competitors' cheapest offerings in an effort to stay competitive in the marketplace. In reality, the goal is *not* to sell a whole lot of this fighter product due to inherent low profit margin.

Sometimes the fighter brand strategy is seen as a softer version of "bait-and-switch." True bait-and-switch is technically fraud, when you promise one product and deliver another inferior product in its place. In the actually legal version, the "Good" option is actually available and designed to get the customer in the door, but the salesperson works hard—and is sometimes incentivized—to push the customer towards the "Better" or "Best" offering.

This is a common practice in new tract home construction sales, where there are a dizzying number of product choices and options. In this situation, the tract home builder uses a bundling strategy ripe with fighter products in an attempt to make the overall price of their homes appear to be amazingly affordable. That is, provided the new home buyer doesn't stray too far from the fighter products during their selection process.

This is not to say Good, Better, Best is a scam. On the contrary, when it comes to complex sales, bundling is much easier on the customer's decision process and can be advantageous when trying to minimize option overload, provided all tiers are fairly and honestly represented.

The simplest version of this strategy can be seen pretty much anywhere a product is being sold. In the United States, Good, Better, Best is firmly embedded as a selection strategy, and a heuristic that most of us employ without a second thought. It is a tool inextricably linked with our daily habits of how we buy.

Justification

When it comes to selection based on one main attribute, we can think of Binary Selection as the standard go-to process in sales. Good, Better, Best allows products and services to be bundled together when there is a little more complexity in choice. But what do you do when the choice involves a whole subset of mini-decisions inside an ultimately larger decision? This brings us to the decision process known as *Justification*, explaining how all the parts and pieces come together in a final design to create an emotionally rewarding experience.

When I first began selling designs in the kitchen and bath arena, I quickly became aware of how overwhelming the decision process becomes. Ignoring appliances, countertops, flooring, lighting, and wall covering, and just concentrating on the design layout of kitchen cabinetry, you recognize the enormous number of mini-decisions each single cabinet requires.

There are colors, material choices, wood species choices, design elements, hardware, door and drawer configurations, rollout trays and shelves, internal pull-out apparatuses like slide-out recycling and waste containers, and so on. Needless to say, with such a tremendous array of options and possibilities, working the customer through the mini-decisions necessary to make their final decision concerning the design makes kitchen sales a tough industry to excel in.

Imagine that you are tasked with "justifying" your design to your prospective customer. Is there a way to leverage what we know about brain function for better results? Of course, the answer is yes.

For our purposes, we will continue using our kitchen design example because of its intrinsic complexity. But the rules that we are about to lay out work with just about any complex sales built out of a myriad of components.

Think Big Picture

A complex design is composed of a lot of smaller components. Your job is to help the customer see that when all those subcomponents come together, the design is greater than the sum of its parts. To do this, you must start by detailing the individual parts and how they fit into the big picture.

Earlier in the book, we discussed how important it is for the brain to understand what it is sensing as a *complete* story. If you were in the kitchen design business, you are in essence selling a complete story with the end result being an aesthetically pleasing and highly functional work area.

To do this, you must spend time detailing each and every separate cabinet, making sure to cover all of the features and benefits that you've incorporated in each single cabinet offering.

For example, you might talk about an 18-inch wide base cabinet with a drawer on top and a roll-out shelf positioned at the midway point behind a single door below. The features could include the superior dovetailed drawer, a drawer construction method that's been around for centuries that ensures even if the glue holding the drawer should fail, the drawer will not come apart due to its locking angled joinery. And you could talk about the roll-out shelf which grants you better visual access to the contents on that shelf. But as we've discussed, feature/benefit selling doesn't necessarily appeal to the emotional part of the brain, the part of the brain where the decision to purchase is likely to occur.

In Justification you would tie emotional values to the details described above. For example, you would start by inviting the customer to open the door below the drawer on our 18-inch base cabinet, and roll out the shelf. We know the more senses the customer engages the more powerful their experience, so in this case you are sure to engage their sense of touch in addition to seeing and hearing.

Once they've had the experience of feeling the easy glide mechanism of the pull-out shelf slide out, you might say something like, "Imagine how nice it will be in the future to not have to get down on one knee to hunt down that can of green beans hidden on the back of the shelf; that's the beauty of roll-outs." With this explanation, you are offering a cool solution to a less-than-desirable knee-bending ritual that's rooted in the customer's past experience.

Here is where you can take advantage of the brain's love of soundbites and propensity to store unique memories. Advertisers spend billions of dollars every year in an attempt to cement their product or service with a notable memory marker that will stay lodged in your brain. Their goal is that this will serve as a trigger for a future purchase down the road. Marketing is awash in jingles, weird mascots, notable characters, and catchy slogans all in an attempt to maximize your memory's ability to hold on to their products' imagery. As such, name brands can carry disproportionate weight in your customer's decision process because the brain is easily tricked into tying emotions to artificially constructed ideas.

It's why you might cry when watching a movie scene, even though you know intellectually you're watching a film with actors who have been paid to follow a script.

Your goal in Justification is to drive home the value associated with your design and one way to do that is to take advantage of the marketing and advertising that's already out there. In other words, piggyback on existing advertisements. We gave the example of moving beyond a mere listing of features/benefits by incorporating an experience such as the act of bending with the pull-out shelf. Since your goal is to create a vivid picture, you can boost the customer's mental experience by inserting a name brand to take memory retention up another notch.

Using our prior example, the new enhancement might be more like, "Imagine how nice it will be in the future to not have to get down on one knee to hunt down that bag of Nacho Cheese Doritos hidden on the back of the shelf; that's the beauty of roll-outs." Your goal is not product endorsement; your goal is to jiggle the customer's memory in a way that keeps you, your product, and or services top of mind.

In this regard, it doesn't matter whether the customer is fond of the brand or not. It's about painting a colorful image that the customer is likely to associate with, and that will stick in their memory. A lot of money has been spent to create a vast library of advertisement memory markers you can co-opt for a more powerful selling story.

Once your customer has had the chance to self-demonstrate the pull-out shelf and to ponder the idea that they can eliminate the chore of bending and accessing snack foods, you ask this question: "How does that 18-inch base with the pull-out shelf *feel* to you?" Notice the question isn't, "What do you think of it?" or "Don't you think roll-out shelves are cool?" By inserting the word "feel" in the question, you are tapping into areas in the customer's brain like the amygdala where emotions are processed. You are in essence speaking to the customer's emotional buying brain.

Red Light, Green Light

This moves us into the "red light, green light" phase of Justification. If the customer feels happy with the 18-inch base cabinet, consider that a green light and move on to the next cabinet. If the customer isn't satisfied with the configuration of the 18-inch base cabinet, that's a red light, and you need to stop and offer change solutions that will make them happy. It is key that you get a "green light" on each cabinet and or component in order to move on to the next one. We will see that skipping a cabinet or component can introduce the element of doubt about the overall design, and that tiny shard of doubt can be enough to doom the design in the eyes of the customer.

As you work your way through the act of justifying all the components, know that it's easier on the brain if you proceed in a clockwise fashion, systematically moving through your explanations and using the green light, red light methodology. The brain is partial to patterns and seeks them out even in the most curious settings. Thanks to our collective learned habit of reading a clock, a clockwise pattern carries with it a certain level of comfort; it feels natural.

It is important not to skip any of the components during Justification, so in our example, this means taking time to focus on each pertinent part as you traverse your kitchen Justification in a clockwise fashion. This is where you'll likely find any objections hiding within the design that otherwise might have gone unspoken by your customer, but might have also silently doomed the sale.

Once when I was working a customer through a kitchen design Justification, we came to the corner base Lazy Susan cabinet. Up to this point in my career it had been my experience that Lazy Susans, much like center islands, were extremely popular. As such, I was breezing through its attributes, especially highlighting the efficiency of a turntable's ability to maximize storage in an otherwise difficult blind corner situation. Having done what I thought was a thorough explanation of the Lazy Susan, I asked the customer, "How does that feel to you?"

She responded with, "That won't work because I have a cat."

Intrigued, I asked her what the problem was. She went on to explain that her cat loved, to scurry into an open Lazy Susan cabinet and hide in the back of it. The configuration of the Lazy Susan turnstile mechanism apparently made it difficult to access the cat in the back corner of the cabinet and shoo it out with her preferred method, a broom. My forward progress had been stopped by an unexpected red light, due to a little feline interference.

I was in luck because the cabinet brand I was designing in at the time built their Lazy Susan base cabinets with a curved back, and like a revolving door in a department store, when the Lazy Susan turnstile turned, whatever was in the space was swept along with it, including a grumpy cat. Once the customer understood there would be no corner for the cat to take refuge in, she was on board and greenlit the cabinet.

This example makes clear the mistake of assuming that what normally is a highlighted key selling point doesn't need Justification. Only by taking the time to discover what is considered beneficial from the customer's standpoint can you ensure that you are truly speaking to their values, and therefore creating the best customer experience possible.

The Justification Meeting

What happens when you are selling a complex design—be it a new corporate insurance program, a remodeling project, or a kitchen design—and you don't take the time to fully justify? In the heat of sales, it might seem like full Justification is overkill, and that just hitting the highlight reel will be enough to sway the customer.

In some cases, the highlight reel will get the job done. Yet for customers who are detail-driven and fear making a purchasing mistake, not fully justifying is likely to cost you the sale as well as hamper your referral pipeline.

Suppose you have just that cautious customer and you took a chance with them on their kitchen design Justification by only explaining the key components. Or perhaps you've done all the hard work of design, and in light of a Justification appointment, you've left the finished design for the customer to pick up at your receptionist's front desk at their discretion. You've instructed the receptionist, in your absence, to make sure that if the customer has any questions or concerns, they can call, text, or email.

Emailing a customer a design or leaving it for pickup sans Justification is a fairly common occurrence in the world of design, especially with today's hectic pace. Unfortunately, following this strategy is likely to dramatically reduce your chances of a sale.

In this scenario where you don't take the opportunity to explain how you achieved the customer's vision based on your deep domain knowledge, your design's brilliant selling points can either be overlooked, misunderstood, or become the fodder for the weekend design warrior who lives next door.

We've all encountered the weekend design warrior, who having just remodeled their own kitchen believes they are now an expert on all remodels henceforth. (It's lucky that self-dentistry isn't a thing.) Your customer, lacking Justification and still not sure if the design is satisfactory, will open it up to outside criticism. This is where their neighbor comes in with something like, "Since our kitchens are similar, I'll tell you what I did. I decided to move the range to the other side of the kitchen..." and so it goes.

It's not even that your customer necessarily trusts their neighbor's design chops as much as this second opinion plants a seed of doubt leaving your design is teetering in your customer's mind. They can either decide to get yet another opinion and make a trip to your competitor, or if you're lucky they may call and ask you to redraw the kitchen based on "tips" from their neighbor. Neither of these last two options probably serve you well, especially when both scenarios could likely have been avoided.

The way to avoid getting caught in this drama involves an upfront orchestration of the sale. When you first meet with the customer, that's the critical time where you also set up the specific Justification appointment including time and date, thoroughly explaining the process and why it's necessary for you to help the customer understand how you've captured their vision in person. The day before the meeting, a co-worker—not you—gives the customer a courtesy call to remind them of their Justification appointment.

This keeps the customer from jumping right away to an emotionally-driven price question, and guarantees that your hard work and domain knowledge will have a chance to shine. For a customer experience to be of value, it's important that the customer be a full participant; it can't be a one-way enterprise. The strategy we've outlined gives everyone involved the best opportunity for a fair and honest chance at achieving a rewarding experience.

Over the years I've had a chance to work in the financial sector and done a fair amount of consulting with credit unions. If there was ever a field that benefits from Justification, it's institutions that deal with people's finances. There is a fair amount of anxiety surrounding financial institutions and it makes sense given that people's mortgages, loans, college savings, and retirement funds are at stake.

Internal credit union research has shown that people are not always comfortable asking a lot of questions for fear of looking less informed than they think they should be. Couple this with the fact that monetary policy can be extremely confusing and you have a situation ripe for the brain to operate on edge where fear and anxiety are at a tipping point.

Understanding this and working the customer through the Justification process, making sure that you have secured green lights before moving on, is one of the surest ways to change a customer's perspective and lessen their anxiety load.

If for some reason the idea of meeting in person is not in the cards with your customer, then the next best thing is to tap into any one of a myriad of options afforded by the Internet to have a virtual meeting. The key is to recognize the importance of the Justification process for your customer's amygdala (the brain's fear center), so they can be assured that all the jigsaw pieces are in place, leaving zero room for doubt that they will be happy with the final outcome of product or service. This is why Justification is a necessity and not optional.

PART 3

Closing
Techniques
and Brain Bias

part

4

Brain-driven Quotes and Proposals

We turn now to another form of Justification for closing called Quote Justification. It's likely that part of your selling strategy includes some form of written documentation that lays out the terms of your sales agreement. This often takes the form of a proposal or quote, and included are the options available to your customer from which to make their final buying decision. This might seem like one of those necessary pieces of boring bureaucracy, but understanding how the brain decides can turn this dry piece of documentation into an effective selling tool, helping you do some of the heavy lifting for finalizing the sale.

In order to explain the theory of quote science, we need to begin by building a foundation. Some of the concepts we've already introduced, while others will be new to you. It's important that you understand the "why" behind the concept so that you will be able to better tailor your proposals specifically to your industry. All of the concepts in Quote Justification leverage brain biases, or cognitive processing errors found in humans.

Self-importance

A defining trait of Homo sapiens is the level of importance each of us imbues in our self. This makes sense because the brain's main job is to keep you alive, thus making us all somewhat prone to me-driven decisions. This also might be why individuals who are able to transcend this behavior and show genuine empathy towards others are considered by many to be heroes. When it comes to a buying experience, recognizing the customer's importance and then finding a way to communicate it to them is a selling fundamental.

Your name is the chief identifier by which you make yourself known. Taking the time to learn and use the customer's name is one way of making a transaction more personal. As a salesperson, the underlying message is that it's all about the customer, and you want them to clearly see they are not simply a means to an end or just one more notch on your sales belt.

Anchoring Effect

Once the brain encounters specific information, it will then use that data as a reference point for making a decision—even if that data doesn't necessarily have any pertinent value.

To better understand this, we turn to an experiment that was done with University of Oregon students by famed psychologists Amos Tversky and Daniel Kahneman. For the experiment, the psychologists had rigged a spinning wheel like the one used on *Wheel of Fortune*. It was numbered from 0 to 100, but unbeknown to the students, when spun it would either stop at 10 or 65.

As part of the experiment, the students were asked to spin the wheel and record their number. Then the students were asked a barely-related question like, "Is the percentage of African nations among UN members larger or smaller than the number you just wrote?"

Kahneman points out that the spin of a wheel should have no bearing on this kind of question. After all, what does spinning a random wheel have to do with UN membership? Nothing.

But the answers the students generated were strongly linked to the number they had spun and recorded. Among students that hit the number 10 on the wheel, their estimates of the percent of African nations in the UN came in at 25% on average. For those students that hit 65 on the wheel, their answers to the same question averaged about 45%. That's a whopping 20% difference in answers, with the only variable being a random spin of a wheel. In other words, the students' brains were being biased either high or low based on a flick of the wrist.

A whole host of experiments have proven this time and time again. This is what we call the anchoring effect.

When you're facing a decision and given information—particularly numeric information, the brain will attempt to incorporate that information into its calculations regardless of whether or not the information is actually relevant to the subject at hand.

Anchoring can have dramatic effect in negotiations. In real estate sales, this is especially true. Generally speaking the party with the strongest negotiating power is the one who has a chance to set the price. When the seller artificially sets the price extremely high, the prospective buyer anchors on that number and is unknowingly influenced towards a higher bid price. It's like the seller had a wheel of fortune that they rigged ahead of time in their favor.

The opposite is also true: when the price is set low, this can in turn set off anchoring to drive the price downwards. The bottom line is that if you give the brain a number before some sort of question involving other numbers, the brain is thrown for a loop by this unrelated information. It will anchor on the first number and use it as a jumping off point for its next set of calculations. In quote science, the anchoring effect carries enormous opportunity.

Von Restorff Effect

Way back in 1933, psychologist Hedwig von Restorff made an important discovery regarding bias and perception. Modern marketing and advertising capitalizes on her findings every day. She discovered that in a list or group of items the brain will recall an item that is different and stands out more often than items of a generic nature.

In 1978, psychologists Shelley E. Taylor and Susan T. Fiske followed up on this notion and showed novel, unique, and surprising information held more salience in the brain when compared to other stimuli. It makes perfect sense that things that jump out and grab our attention are more likely to be cemented in memory and recalled later.

Cathedral Effect

You might be surprised to learn that even architectural design can be built on the back of human bias. But that's exactly what anthropologist Edward T. Hall figured out in the 1960's while studying the way people reacted to stepping into small cozy chapels versus stepping into large, inspiring cathedrals.

When you enter a new space, the brain creates a kind of wire diagram map, locating key points of reference for reference and to orient you in that space—think human GPS. This is why you can do something like walk across a room and find your seat without running into walls or banging into other furniture. Your brain tracks your location visually using surrounding reference points of walls, floors, and other objects, and then calculating your distance to those points. All of this is done below consciousness which is why you have no sense of these calculations taking place.

As a result, one of the first things you do when you arrive in a new space is to glance upward, starting at the top and working your way down and around the space. When you encounter words on a written page, your brain applies a similar sort of logic, starting at the top of the page and working down. This is something we do naturally and weren't taught in school. We will see how this impacts our quote construction when we begin building out a neuroscience-based strategy.

Illusion of Depth

You're probably already familiar with one flaw or bias: the illusion of depth. Any time you stare into a deep body of clear water, you recognize that it's really difficult to tell just how deep it actually is. What looks like something twelve feet down can really be more like three feet down. Unfortunately, this bias has caused more than its share of cases where people have misjudged pool depth and suffered diving accidents.

In science, the illusion of depth refers to the tendency for people to believe they have far greater knowledge in a given subject than they actually have. You can try this experiment yourself. Take a bicycle, or toaster, or any modern product that has working parts that you might use on a regular basis, and attempt to draw it from scratch without actually looking at it. You might be surprised to find that although you have a general idea, when you get to the specifics of your working knowledge your ability to create a viable blueprint is shockingly inaccurate.

Illusion of depth is not limited to our belief about objects. It also extends to history, politics, other professions and so forth. Skim a Wikipedia article about the Civil War and suddenly you feel like a military expert.

As a species we tend to be generalists, relying on soundbites to mask what we don't know—which for the most part works well, until we are exposed by questions of a much deeper nature. As we've seen, the brain is driven by an energy-saving strategy, and doesn't tend to invest more energy learning huge amounts of detail without the promise of some sort of payback. System 1 ensures that habit-producing shortcuts carry the day, which makes brevity and simplicity in quote science a critical component.

Overload Paradigm

We have devoted much of this book to the bias of brain overload. In fact, it is one of the central tenets behind the use of neuroscience to enhance your ability to sell. Avoiding overload plays into so many aspects of creating a rewarding experience. If you were to look at defining characteristics of Sales Geniuses, the ability to avoid overloading their customers with too much information is a key goal at all times.

This constant level of vigilance, always observing the customer's reaction and adjusting—simplifying if needed—is one incremental aspect of how Sales Geniuses achieve a superior result.

In quote science, the goal is to present information to the customer in a written format that is as clean, simple, and easy to read as possible, eliminating any unnecessary information, detail, or distraction that might weigh them down. All clutter needs to be excised from the document, following the principle that "less is more."

Short-term Memory

Hand in hand with the overload paradigm is the function of short-term memory. You will recall that short-term memory is like the scratch pad your brain uses to keep track of immediate information. It typically can retain that information for around 15 seconds before it is erased from memory. This is why you might be able to retain a phone number just long enough to punch in the call, but you'd be hard pressed to remember that same series of numbers an hour later.

For most people, short-term memory is like a post-it note that holds between 4-7 bits of information. This is why, when dispensing information verbally, it's important to be as precise and succinct as possible. Verbal information is fleeting.

Written information, because it affords one the opportunity to review it later, allows for greater dissemination of detail. Nevertheless, it is a good idea when creating a quote or proposal to follow the rules of a good speaker and likewise be as direct, precise, and succinct as possible. It is difficult for the brain to hold emotional impact for long-winded written documentation that requires the deep analysis we associate with System 2 decision-making.

Binary and Good, Better, Best

We've talked at length about the power of binary contrast and how easy it is for the brain to make decisions when they are framed in a *"this* or *that"* scenario. For more advanced decisions we've laid out the structure of Good, Better, Best: the idea of group packaging to simplify decision-making. When it comes to creating quotes and proposals, these two methodologies are the perfect tools to employ because they cater well to avoiding mental overload. An endless list of options is not an enhancement, but a detriment almost ensuring your customer will be bogged down in information overload.

Readability

In order to stress the customers' brains as little as possible, it's important to create a quote document that is extremely easy to read. On his website, successful entrepreneur Sol Orwell discusses what he's learned about maximizing readability for his online content. Some of this is common sense—for instance, make sure there's a high contrast between your paper color and your ink color so the words stand out.

It's also important to allow for some white space around the lines of text. Orwell recommends that when typing, make sure the line height is set at 150%, what he considers the sweet spot between too much space and not enough.

What about font style? Consider serif fonts--where the letters have little lines at the ends, like Times New Roman--and sans-serif fonts--where the letters lack these adornments, like Helvetica or Arial. Orwell writes that people tend to score higher on reading speed when reading sans-serif fonts, but at the same time, they also tend to prefer serif fonts, which are considered to be more trustworthy. You'll have to decide for yourself what is best.

In legal documents we've all been admonished to beware of the small print. There is a legitimate reason for this beyond being difficult to read. It's also taxing on the brain. As a result, small print in quotes and proposals should be studiously avoided. Use at least 12-point font.

Priming

In psychology, priming is the name for the phenomena where a stimulus is introduced that triggers an associated thought or memory. Priming occurs below an individual's conscious awareness and can take different forms.

For example, hearing the word "boat" will grant you quicker access to the word "coat" in memory because of the close *perception* of the way the words sound. Hearing the word "desk" might cause you to retrieve the word "chair" faster from memory because desk and chair share the same *conceptual* category. And Pavlov's dog came to associate the ringing of a bell with the arrival of food due to the *repetitive* nature of the stimuli.

In all cases, the brain is using a concept known as schema, a cognitive framework that helps the brain create more efficient organization, interpretation, and speed of recall for content stored in memory.

Priming can effectively steer thinking and decision-making in the primed direction because it happens below conscious awareness; people are generally unaware that it's happening.

Here is a priming experiment you can try. Answer the following three prompts:

1. Write down the name of the individual who brought us the iPad and iPhone.

2. Write down the color of a stop sign in the USA.

3. Write down the name of the first fruit that comes to mind.

By answering the first question we get Steve Jobs, for the one who brought us the iPad and iPhone. The second question's answer is red, for the color of a stop sign. It is statistically probable that your final answer for a fruit was primed to be *apple*.

If priming worked for you in this example, it is because of the associative links between Steve Jobs, the company Apple, and the color red, which is the color most associated with apples. In seminars doing this experiment both nationally and internationally, we've found that this priming example generates the answer "apple" about 70% of the time.

When it doesn't work, we've discovered it is often because the individual has a particularly close habitual attachment to another fruit like orange, such as drinking orange juice every morning as part of their daily routine. In that case, the brain's storage/retrieval system is more readily primed and tuned to a higher alert for orange as a result of their regular routine.

As a weird side note, in just about every seminar, there is always at least one individual whose answer to the fruit question is banana. For this I offer no explanation, nor can I explain why it always gets a laugh.

Emotional Appeal

Poetry, literature, and song lyrics can be extremely evocative and generate such deep levels of emotional attachment that they are capable of producing tears of sorrow or joy. While our goal in quote science is not to bring your customer to tears, the words you choose, much like the paint choices an artist makes, will color your proposal for better or worse.

In marketing, the ability to write copy that stirs the soul is highly coveted, and brands go to great lengths to implant emotional markers wherever possible. A running shoe is no longer just clothing that cushions your foot. The Nike Air VaporMax Plus "looks to the past and propels you into the future."

Individual words can carry enormous weight, especially in a quote or proposal. Let's examine the word "option." This is a word commonly used to depict choice. Even a mundane word like option can be substituted for a far more powerful word like "enhancement," which has greater emotional selling.

"Option" simply means choice, an add-on if the customer so desires. Not only does "enhancement" mean guaranteed improvement but it carries a second hidden benefit. If the customer chooses not to take advantage of an enhancement, then they are in essence refusing the chance to improve the quality of their product or service. Walking away from an enhancement is likely to alert the System 1 emotional part of the brain, kicking in loss aversion.

Now eliminating an enhancement takes on far more meaning, and makes the stakes much higher than simply declining an option or choice. This is but one example showing that word choice is paramount in creating a higher level of emotional experience, and thereby improving the likelihood a customer will tip towards a greater level of purchase.

Loss Aversion

As we have seen, loss aversion can be triggered by carefully curated words like "enhancement" in your sales proposal. Loss aversion is the brain's way of making sure that you are not missing out on something important by short shrifting your current opportunity.

We've stated that the brain feels loss at twice the rate it feels a win, and so it is particularly guarded when it comes to the thought of losing its chance at a win. Sales promotions that have a time deadline promote loss aversion as well as key words like enhancement, or phrases like "limited time only," "while supplies last," "only X amount left in stock." All of these phrases have one thing in common: if you don't act soon, you will forever lose the chance of their benefit.

Cognitive Dissonance

Cognitive dissonance is the brain's ability to hold two conflicting ideas at the same time. If the brain was a purely rational structure, cognitive dissonance would be impossible because logic would dictate that two opposite thoughts are in conflict and demand resolution.

For example, you might keep money in a bank, and as such, be very much concerned with the bank's security and their ability to keep your money safe. At the same time, you might be fascinated by Henry McCarty, the real name of the infamous outlaw, gunfighter, and bank robber known

as Billy the Kid. That would be an example of cognitive dissonance where you're both a proponent of bank security and at the same time admire a bank robber.

We will see how this brain flaw can be leveraged when it comes to the way a buyer's brain processes pricing. In fact, this one bias has unwittingly cost a lot of salespeople the chance at a sale simply because of the way they've presented price in quotes and proposals.

Ghost Curve

As previously mentioned, the ghost curve is the brain's tendency to most vividly recall the beginning and end of, say, a list or conversation. Attention drops out in the middle.

Quote Template

In the sections above, we have outlined a wide collection of brain biases. Now we will take these concepts and build a sample quote, using what we have learned. You can think of this quote as a template, keeping in mind the exact layout is not absolutely critical. Your industry's unique qualities might call for alterations to this template. More than the layout, what is important is that you understand the concepts underpinning this template so that you are then able to implement these ideas for your own purposes in the future.

Take a look at the next page and you will see a proposal built using the brain biases discussed thus far. At first glance, it might not seem all that unusual, but turn to the next page and we will break this proposal down, pointing out the quote science contained within.

After identifying each of the biases we've leveraged in this quote format, we will then explain how you would verbally go about justifying the quote to your customer. Remember that this step, during which you walk the customer through the proposal, is a critical step. This is your opportunity to fix any issues and put all the puzzle pieces in place for the customer's peace of mind.

Carter Cabinets
591 Ellis Blvd
Columbus, OH 43210
Rowan@CarterCabinets.com

Quote: 10228
Sold to: Ben and Tori Cho
355 Park Blvd
South Bend, IN 46614

Ben and Tori's New Kitchen

Cabinetry choice: Carter Custom
Heirloom Maple (full overlay, shaker door style) Cashew finish
Island: Heirloom Maple Morel Finish

BASE PRICE	$	7,145	
Enhancements:			
Clear Glass Mullion Door, Finished Cabinet Interior	$	154	
Top Mount Dbl Bowl SBKR377			
& Top Mount Food Prep SBK-R16			
	$	1,191	
Classic 2"/16" Large Crown Molding/Arts&Crafts	$	541	
Sinc-motion FX Drawer Guide Upgrade	$	150	
10 Slide-out Shelves for Utility Cabinets	$	715	
Decorative Appliance Panels / Refrigerator and Dishwasher	$	513	
Range Wood Hood and Liner/Blower Unit	$	885	
	$	11,294	
	$	790	tax
	$	12,084	total

This offer expires at 12PM on November 21 of this year

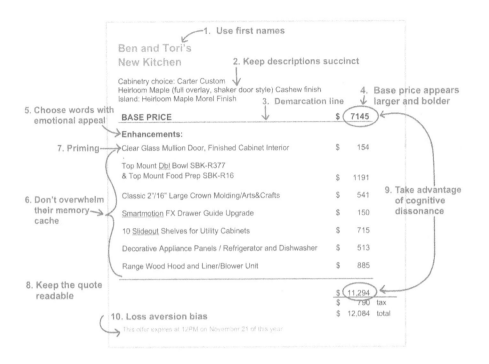

1. Use first names

Ben and Tori's
New Kitchen

2. Keep descriptions succinct

Cabinetry choice: Carter Custom
Heirloom Maple (full overlay, shaker door style) Cashew finish
Island: Heirloom Maple Morel Finish

3. Demarcation line

4. Base price appears larger and bolder

5. Choose words with emotional appeal

BASE PRICE $ 7145

Enhancements:

7. Priming

Clear Glass Mullion Door, Finished Cabinet Interior $ 154

Top Mount Dbl Bowl SBK-R377
& Top Mount Food Prep SBK-R16 $ 1191

6. Don't overwhelm their memory cache

Classic 2"/16" Large Crown Molding/Arts&Crafts $ 541

9. Take advantage of cognitive dissonance

Smartmotion FX Drawer Guide Upgrade $ 150

10 Slideout Shelves for Utility Cabinets $ 715

Decorative Appliance Panels / Refrigerator and Dishwasher $ 513

Range Wood Hood and Liner/Blower Unit $ 885

8. Keep the quote readable

$ 11,294
$ 790 tax
$ 12,084 total

10. Loss aversion bias

This offer expires at 12PM on November 21 of this year

1. Starting at the top, notice the names of the customers. Their *first* names are large and prominently depicted. Why no last names? The use of first names is less formal. The receptionist at the doctor's office might call me Mr. Best, but my friends all call me Robb. Using first names in the quote says this is personal and it's all about *you*. This speaks directly to the **self-importance bias**.

2. Look at the description below the names. It is short and to the point, carefully crafted to avoid overload. In less than a paragraph, it gets to the essentials: the manufacturer of the product, door style, wood species, and finish color. It follows the Goldilocks rule: not too little and not too much information, just the right amount to keep the brain satisfied and moving forward and engaged.

3. Notice under the words **BASE PRICE**, you see a horizontal line. At first glance, this looks to be simply a design element consistent with a similar line at the bottom of the page. And it is a design element, but it is also there to serve another purpose.

By introducing a horizontal line, your visual perception is momentarily interrupted, and as a result of this imperceptible pause, your brain is forced to increase focus. And what does it focus on? The $7,145 price depicted on the right.

4. The **$7,145** seems to jump out at you in the quote. Upon closer examination, you will find that the number is both one font size larger than the other numbers on the page and is also the only number that has been bolded. This font size choice and bolding isn't random; it adheres to the **Von Restorff Effect**.

    Your customer's brain hangs on to the highlighted number and affords it additional importance. Also, because this brain highlight occurs at the top of the page, we take advantage of the **Cathedral Effect**, bestowing even greater importance due to its positioning.

    As a result of all this cognitive attention, your customer's brain will use this number to anchor on. As Amos Tversky and Daniel Kahneman discovered, **Anchoring Bias** means that this base price number of $7,145 will now be seriously factored into your customer's decision to buy. Since the base price is significantly lower than the final price, the anchoring effect gives your customer the emotional feeling of comfort, helping to justify the purchase in their mind.

5. Below the horizontal demarcation line at the top of the page, we find the bolded word "enhancements." This **emotional appealing** connection word implies higher quality by definition. It is far superior to the word "option" which only signifies add-ons, with no qualitative guarantee. Enhancements as a category header trumpets that more delighters are coming your customer's way. Any decision to eliminate a particular enhancement means your customer runs the risk of loss aversion. In the throes of loss aversion, losses loom larger than gains, and avoiding loss works towards a greater likelihood of your customer choosing "yes" on each enhancement line item.

6. Not only has the enhancement category prepared your customer's brain for the coming list of delighters, but notice the number of enhancements that have been broken out. Seven is the number at the high end of what **short-term memory** can handle before it tips into overload and stops recording information. For this reason, we've limited the enhancement breakout to seven.

Again, we are attempting to follow the goldilocks rule, with just the right amount of enhancements to give greater definition to the project without overwhelming and sending the customer into the **overload paradigm**. Seven might not always be achievable, but it is a worthwhile goal to shoot for, and it's important that you attempt to honor the brain's short-term memory limitations.

A single price for the entire project might seem like a good idea. We've certainly touted simplicity from a brain-friendly point of view, but not breaking the price into small increments or not providing enough detail is just as dangerous as overwhelming detail. A lack of detail can create insecurity in the customer's mind because they are not sure exactly what they are getting when they purchase. This can push your customer into the arms of your competitor, who might be offering a lower price with far less than your quote includes. Because the customer isn't clear on what comes in your package, they might be tempted to walk away from the sale after comparing apples to oranges—or bananas as the case may be.

Moderate breakout of pricing (close to 7-line items) provides a comfort level, and also serves to protect you if the customer decides to shop your offer. In that case, you're more likely to get an apples for apples comparison since the customer has specific knowledge of what you've included in your proposal. That said, breaking out every single piece and part puts you right back in overload territory.

If you overload with too many line item breakouts, it's likely the customer will say something along the lines of, "Okay, I'm going to need to go home and think about this," because on some level they are aware that they can't comprehend all the information you've provided in one sitting. This means that time and your competitor have a chance to weigh in and reduce excitement and buying from your sale.

If you provide a scant amount of information, fear will drive a customer to get another bid as an insurance policy. Relying on the Goldilocks' rule—just the right amount of information—increases the chances your customer will feel enough comfort to make their buying decision during the Justification meeting.

7. **Priming,** setting the brain to tilt in a buying direction, is used in at least two ways in this quote document. First, the word **enhancement** begins to entice and prime the brain towards a buy by promising good things to come. And of those good things, it's important that the first enhancement you record is at the top of your customers' wish list of "must-haves." Those must-haves are at the core and central to why they want to do the project in the first place. By listening carefully and determining one of their most desired must-have enhancements, then positioning it at the top of the list, you begin to prime your customer's brain towards a "yes" decision for the rest of line item enhancements you've identified.

8. What about **quote readability**? Notice the type font in this template is Arial and the font size is no smaller than 12 points. Also notice that the background is white to make the contrast between the dark print and white background easy on the eye. There is no small text in the document, and no distracting unneeded patterns.

9. At the bottom of the right-hand corner in our template, we come to the final price. If the quote is executed correctly, this is where **cognitive dissonance** on the customer's part takes effect. Cognitive dissonance is the ability to hold two divergent ideas at the same time. What are those two divergent ideas? The two prices: the base price at the top of the page, which the customer's brain has biased towards and anchored on, and the actual final price spelled out at the bottom. There is a big difference between those two prices, and yet as we will see in our Justification phase, the base price will carry surprising weight in the final decision.

10. Lastly, we call on the **Loss Aversion bias** once again. Notice there is a time-oriented end date when this quote will no longer be in effect, and it is specific right down to the hour. This last bit of information is crystal clear: the opportunity you are affording the customer will not last forever. As a result, your customer's amygdala is sending messaging to their prefrontal cortex, "Don't make a mistake and lose out on this opportunity." Because this statement appears at the end of the document along with the final price, we are able to avoid the **Ghost Curve**, and take advantage of placement and the gravitas the brain automatically applies to this end positioning.

Quote Justification

Having explained the biases and how they've been applied in this quote template, we are now ready to employ the Justification process. Even though we've been able to apply a lot of brain research in the construction of the template, it is not meant to be a free-standing entity to be left at a front desk for pick up, or emailed to a customer. To maximize your chances for a sale, you need to orchestrate the delivery of this document verbally.

In prior chapters, we've pointed out the value of conducting your Justification meeting in an open area and presenting standing next to the customer in the passenger seat as opposed to across from them. Your goal should be helping your customer feel that it is more of a team meeting where everyone is working towards their goal of a rewarding experience, as opposed to an adversarial one where they are battling you for a fair price. All of these suggestions are valuable incremental steps to creating a more positive outcome for everyone involved.

You would start by making sure each person that will take part in the buying decision has their own copy of the document to help personalize the experience. Then you would begin the document walkthrough, which might go something like this:

Ben and Tori, we're excited about your new kitchen and we want to make sure we've got everything just the way you want it, so feel free to jump in with any questions or changes you're interested in making.

As we discussed we've built the quote around Carter cabinetry, Heirloom series, in Providence Maple, full overlay, shaker door style with the cashew finish. For your island we are using Providence Maple Morel, in the heirloom finish.

How does that feel to you?

This is your first greenlight opportunity. Showing the customer samples of exactly what you are referencing is a must to guarantee you're all on the same page. If they give you the green light, you move to the next section. If they red-light you, you need to adjust the details as necessary to secure a green light. Assuming you got the green light, you move to the BASE PRICE:

We can do this beautiful set of kitchen cabinets for $7,145, but we've added some enhancements to really take it up a notch and achieve the kitchen you were excited about when we first met.

Notice the power of the statement above. By stating the base price and affirming the kitchen can be completed for this price, $7,145, and because of the anchoring effect, this base price will be fixed in the customer's brain. As such, this becomes the price of the kitchen from the customer's emotional standpoint.

At the same time, because of cognitive dissonance, you are also saying there are enhancements needed to achieve the kitchen of their dreams, the driving force behind their initial idea to purchase.

What has just happened?

You have provided a lower comfort price on which the customer's brain locks. Enhancement variables also make it clear that $7,145 isn't necessarily going to be the final price.

This very important aspect of how the customer's brain will process this pricing information isn't something that will naturally occur with a dry reading of the quote on their own. This is where you, the salesperson, need to verbally establish what is at stake. By adding your verbal explanation as you take the customer through the proposal step by step, you create additional sensory impact. At this point they have seen, touched, and heard the quote explained, leveraging three key memory senses on behalf of fulfilling their aspirational new kitchen dream, which helps to bring them that much closer to a purchase.

The next step is to walk the customer through the enhancement opportunities. Begin with the first enhancement, the one that you have purposely selected because of the importance the customer has bestowed upon it. Having carefully listened through the selection phase and recognizing key details your customer has shared with you about a purchase they made on their honeymoon, you might say something like:

I know you're excited about the Clear Mullion Door, with the finished cabinet interior. It's such a great way to show off your antique tea set from Ireland that you found on your honeymoon, especially in the evening when the amber light washes down around it. We can make that happen for $154, how does that feel?

Listening and understanding your customer's goals and aspirations is critical to being able to deliver the emotional experience they are seeking. You are not just providing a cabinet with a glass door for display, you are providing a touchstone to an important honeymoon memory. If that seems a little corny, keep in mind that the emotional part of the brain is the brain area that buys the mushy Hallmark greeting card and tears up at parades. Once the customer feels the connection between their honeymoon, the tea set, and the glass door, rationalization kicks in and $154 seems like a small price to pay for the emotional payoff.

As you work your way through each enhancement, you follow the same strategy of connecting each line item to an emotional payoff. Justification requires that you verbally address each item, securing a green light in the form of a yes. As the confirmations stack up, the effect is that each yes provides a priming effect for the next one, and you start to get yes momentum moving down the line, adding more confirmations along the way.

When you break out the line items as indicated, the customer is much more likely to buy the enhancements one by one as they go, rationalizing each single enhancement as not that much more money. In other words, the brain is much more likely to buy the entire enhancement package if it only has to make buying decisions one piece at a time.

Remember to ask the customer how they feel after each enhancement line item description.

What happens if the customer decides that they don't want a particular enhancement?

That's fine. Your goal is not to sell them anything in which they truly are not interested; that would be counter to creating an emotionally rewarding customer experience. Your sales lifeblood of referrals is dependent upon satisfied customers.

What happens if your customer asks you, the salesperson, for your opinion about whether or not they should buy a given enhancement?

This is an interesting phenomenon that can happen, especially with Sales Geniuses, and generally indicates a level of trust since, as the salesperson, you have a vested interest in the sale. If your opinion is legitimately solicited it's okay to give your opinion. Again, this is where you should be totally transparent in your answer and give them the benefit of your expertise, helping them to understand the pros and cons of their choice. It is important that in the end, the customer is the final arbiter for deciding what they will. Also keep the buying patterns in mind, as we have learned that some patterns will be more or less positive towards your insights.

After you've walked the customer through the entire process—making certain that they recognize the time stamp on the bottom of the proposal—and you've totaled everything to get the final purchase price, it's important to ask them how they feel about the final price. This is an important gauge on their willingness to purchase, and will help direct your next set of actions.

This is where your focus is critical. You should be gauging things like body language and pupil dilation. If they lean towards you after the final price has been established, that's a great sign. If their body language suggests leaning away from you after you've reached the final price, that can be a valuable indicator that they are not comfortable with the final price. This is regardless of whether they are saying positive things which sound like they are interested in making a purchase.

Keep in mind that their body language is generally far more honest and accurate then what they may be verbalizing to you out of embarrassment or as part of their exit strategy. If you notice facial distress or gestures of fidgeting, often signals of discomfort, those can be indicators that you have more work to do to create some level of comfort for your customer, the precursor to a sale.

Now consider how to respond if your customer seems verbally tentative and says something like, *"Wow, that's a little more than I thought it would be."*

Keep in mind this is a reasonable response, especially if the product or service you provide is not something the customer is wholly familiar with. Don't despair. With this type of response, your next line of inquiry should be to determine where they thought the price might come in at.

For example, let's assume that the customer loved all the enhancements, complete with green lights along the way, which brings the final price in at $12,084. But they thought the price would be closer to $11,000. Recognizing that your goal isn't to browbeat the customer into a price that's higher than their comfort level, you might consider this approach:

"I totally understand where you are coming from. If $11,000 feels more comfortable; let's see how we can get you there. It looks like if we eliminate the Classic crown molding and the decorative appliance panels, we would save a total of $1,154, bringing us in just under our goal to $10,930. How does that feel now?"

Notice you are now working on their behalf, and your goal has become their goal to hit at or below the $11,000 number. Interestingly, what often happens after you've justified a quote proposal, carefully created emotional connections to the enhancements, and had the customer greenlight them, is that the thought of losing those enhancements kicks loss aversion back in and the customer decides they don't want to eliminate anything. It's not uncommon to hear the customer say something like:

"I don't want to eliminate the crown molding or the wood appliance panels, how would that look?"

Your response might be:

"It's true the crown molding really sets the kitchen up, along with the appliance panes for a truly elegant look, but if price is the absolute arbitrator we can do it without them."

With this kind of response, you are being both truthful and at the same time reminding your customer what is at stake. This often helps them determine where their true priorities lie. Frequently the emotional sense of lost opportunity rules supreme, causing them not to abandon the enhancements.

Now, consider how to respond if your customer simply says:

"I've been shopping around and I can get a better price down the street."

At all costs, avoid dropping the price to get a sale. If you are offering fair pricing and your profit margin is reasonable, then some of the ways to legitimately reduce price are through the elimination of line items as we've stated, or a reduction in model/styling choice.

To simply drop your price to accommodate your customer's price goals suggests that you have been less than scrupulous in your original pricing. In other words, there can be the perception of price padding or gouging on your part, and over time, this can seriously damage your reputation in the marketplace, even if you chose to arbitrarily drop your price on a whim just that once. Word of mouth spreads fast.

It is also perfectly acceptable to reiterate what benefits you are providing to the customer and it's important that you convey to the customer that they make sure they are getting an "apples for apples" bid, that your competitor is providing equal product or service. If your customer chooses to purchase elsewhere, be gracious and never leave the customer with a bad taste in their mouth. They will remember the experience long after it is over, and judge it largely by how they felt in the end. (More on this in Part 5.)

Sometimes the threat of going elsewhere is simply a ploy by the customer to test your resolve and satisfy themselves that they are getting a good deal. If the customer should walk away, don't be surprised if you find them returning at some later date after realizing your competitor wasn't providing quite the same experience they were hoping for.

Remember that a customer that walks away and then comes back to you, provided you give them a stellar buying experience, tends to generate some of the best word of mouth you will ever get. That said, it is statistically impossible to sell each and every customer you encounter, even for a Sales Genius. As my high school math teacher would say before a test, "Do your best and miss the rest."

Now for some key takeaways from employing the quote science and Justification we've described above. By starting from a base price, which anchors the brain, and proceeding to an enhancement line item strategy, you'll frequently cause the customer to actually internalize the *base price*, not the final price, as the price of the kitchen.

How is this illogical phenomenon possible, especially when the customer is going to write a check or use a credit card to pay the actual final price? Emotional value setting and the brain's frequent reliance on compartmentalization, plus a little cognitive dissonance thrown in for good measure set up the brain for its own unique take on reality.

If you were to ask the customer after it was all said and done:

"So how much did that new kitchen cost?"

Their answer might be something like:

"The kitchen cost, $7,145.00, and then we added a few enhancements on top of that."

Notice the discrepancy in how their brain has recorded the event. The real answer to the cost of the kitchen question is $12,084.00. That's what the customer actually paid. In the customer's mind, their memory has recorded the event not as an accurate entry on a financial spreadsheet but as a base price, plus enhancements *experience.* The brain is built to understand the world through experiences, not spreadsheets. It's a way for the brain to essentially trick itself and take the emotional sting out of the actual price. It just *feels* better to think of it that way; such is the quiet power of System 1 at work.

As a salesperson, should you encounter a customer who has been to your competitor, and if your competitor is working off of some form of a base price strategy, be careful to recognize that even though your customer has no intention of deception, the price they are suggesting they can get elsewhere is not an accurate representation of the entire product or service package at stake. Once again, this is why it's a must for you to help your customer understand the importance of them getting an "apples for apples" comparison before they make a buying decision. Many a sale has been lost to misperception, and the desire to capitalize on what seems to your customer like an extraordinary deal from your competitor.

Your
Customer's
Experience

part

5

Theory of Mind

There's another important tool to keep in mind when it comes to maintaining a connection with your customers, and it's one you might not expect.

Theory of Mind is the skill involved in seeing life from another's perspective. Do you want to strengthen your ability to see things from your customers' point of view? Do you want to be able to put yourself in their shoes and better anticipate their wants, worries, and objections? Luckily, like any skill, Theory of Mind can be developed and improved with practice.

As "me-driven" individuals, our first inclination is generally to assume the way we see the world is universal. I assume my likes and dislikes, for example, will coincide with yours.

As a salesperson, this can be problematic. I might like contemporary furniture and therefore be more likely to spend time touting its attributes, while you on the other hand might be firmly entrenched in the Arts and Crafts tradition and bored by my enthusiasm. Quickly, your brain will move into daydreaming mode, taking the opportunity to save a little energy as my opportunity to sell you dissipates. This is one of the reasons why we introduced the buying patterns earlier, to help mitigate the feeling of disenfranchisement from your customer.

At the same time Theory of Mind goes beyond buying patterns. For instance, I might assume that we share the same political or religious beliefs and make a joke which I consider to be a completely innocent icebreaker, but which you find insulting.

Theory of Mind is not about political correctness, where the goal might be simply not to be seen as offensive. Theory of Mind goes to the deeper idea of understanding the emotional values underpinning thoughts and ideas. Sales Geniuses recognize that Theory of Mind is at the core of building trust with their customer.

One important way that you can develop your Theory of Mind is to first

244 | Selling To The Brain

focus your attention on what the customer is saying. Although much of language is imprecise and repetitive, often there are highlight words that can grant the salesperson crucial insight into their customer's desires.

Declarative words from your customer that convey strong positive or negative emotions like love and hate are among those highlight words. For example, if you were in the kitchen design business, your customer might say, "My current kitchen has a center island and it's always in the way. It's such a hassle every time I'm under the gun trying to get a meal on the table, I hate it." A few seconds of active listening will completely change your thinking on the design parameters for your customer's new kitchen. Since center islands are usually in hot demand your usual go-to design strategy might have to be significantly altered.

The important thing to understand is not just that the island from this customer's point of view is a physical impediment, it's how this affects their System 1 emotional decision-making. The island is causing the customer frustration and stress, which she is verbalizing as hatred.

Once you've taken the customer's concerns into account, you will be able to demonstrate how you not only removed the island as a physical impediment, but more importantly gotten rid of the hassle factor. Eliminating the customer's emotional stress is the real job you are performing. This is a big deal to your customer's System 1, the engine of the buying decisions.

Heightening your awareness of the powerful emotions that guide people's buying decisions will not only lead to a superior design, but also create a much deeper value in the mind of the customer. This is the essence of an exemplary customer experience.

Deep listening might sound like a no-brainer, but when you have worked in an industry for a long time, your habits solidify and you begin to believe, "I know what people want." This kind of thinking, while quite common, is in direct opposition to Theory of Mind. In Theory of Mind, your goal is to start from a place of neutrality and base your behavior and next steps in the selling process on reading the customer's emotional cues and then acting accordingly.

Much in the same way that "flow" is a deeper level of understanding rooted in knowledge and practice, Theory of Mind is rooted in a deeper ability to interpret what your customer is feeling and then create a positive experience out of that.

Surprisingly, one way to build your Theory of Mind chops doesn't even involve selling. But when practiced properly this method can give your selling technique a notable boost. It involves cracking open some literary fiction. That's right, literary fiction.

Many of us get out of the habit of reading literature once we graduate high school English class, or finish our Lit requirements in college. However, research by David Kidd and Emanuele Castano finds that consuming literary fiction is linked to an immediate increase in Theory of Mind performance[22]. We're not talking about picking up the nearest airport thriller; literary fiction is the fancy stuff, the stories with complex, nuanced characters, where getting into their heads requires some work.

Doing this work, however, soon yields its share of rewards. Reading high quality fictional narratives gives you a glimpse into other people's mindsets. It affords you the chance of living vicariously through points of view perhaps far different than your own. This kind of risk-free experience helps grow and broaden your general understanding of people. And even though the characters are fictional, you still have the potential to gain a deeper understanding of the role emotions play in people's decisions. Emotional intelligence is a core component of Theory of Mind.

If you're too busy to sit down every night and read for an hour or two, consider investing in an audio book for your morning commute. Incorporating deep reading or listening into your life will be worth it.

Sales Intelligence

How do we measure sales intelligence, or intelligence in general?

The ancient Chinese had some of the first tests designed to evaluate a person's smarts: a game called tangram and another game called jiulianhuan. You can still play them today, if you're a fan of puzzles or humility.

In 1905, Alfred Binet, Victor Henri and Theodore Simon needed a way to assess mental disability in school children. They created their own system, the not-very-cleverly-named Binet-Simon test.

This eventually morphed into the Intelligence Quotient test, more commonly known as the IQ test. It analyzes your applied knowledge of math, as well as verbal and spatial recognition skills. At the end of the test, you get a number between 1 and 200. This number tells us how smart you are, or so conventional wisdom went. (In fact, Alfred Binet himself described the number as something that could be often improved through effective studying and practice.)

Most of us hummed along happily with this notion until Howard Gardner showed up in 1983 with his groundbreaking book *Frame of Mind.*

In his book, Gardner argued that the standard IQ test doesn't give us nearly the whole picture. How can one number possibly give us any useful information about something as complex as a human mind? He suggested we were missing a whole boatload of emotionally-driven indicators, which had a profound effect on our intellectual process. Collectively, these additional factors became known as Emotional Intelligence, or EI (sometimes called EQ).

Many agreed with Gardner, but the question remained: what was E.I. exactly, and how could we ever measure it?

In *The Brain and Emotional Intelligence: New Insights*, author and PhD Daniel Goleman believes that work done by brain researcher Antonio Damasio and psychologist Reuven Bar-on has begun to unravel the mystery.

According to Goleman, "Damasio and Bar-on used the gold standard method in neuropsychology for identifying the brain areas associated with specific behaviors and mental functions: lesion studies. That is, they studied patients who have brain injuries in clearly defined areas, correlating the site of the injury with the resulting specific diminished or lost capacities in the patient."

Goleman describes one particularly striking case. An exceedingly sharp lawyer had a brain tumor that was successfully operated on and removed. Subsequent testing after the surgery showed that the lawyer had no signs of I.Q. damage or attention deficit. Curiously though, the lawyer was suddenly unable to function in society.

The problem was decision-making. The lawyer could still easily list all the pros and cons of a situation—System at work. He was just unable to ever take the plunge. From choosing a legal course of action to picking out his tie, the lawyer was in a constant state of indecision. It didn't just screw up his ability to grocery shop; it ruined his life. Ultimately, he lost his job, house, and his marriage.

What in the world had happened? Damasio explained that during the operation, the surgeon snipped connections between the prefrontal cortex, the brain's executive control, and the amygdala, the brain's emotional processor.

This was the heart of the lawyer's problem. Emotion allows us to create a kind of stack ranking of what we care about and therefore what should come next—System 1 at work. Without connecting our thoughts to our feelings, we can't prioritize, and so we are paralyzed.

Goleman's concept is much like Theory of Mind, but instead of applying it towards understanding how my customer *feels* and *thinks*, Emotional Intelligence applies the same concept towards "self." How do *I* personally feel and think?

And most importantly, how does that affect my behavior towards my customers? At its most basic level, it asks you to actively apply your System 2 analytical decision-making to better understand your System 1 emotional based decisions. Hopefully with newly gained insight, you can more clearly see the linkage between your thoughts, feelings, and actions, thereby improving your personal interactions.

Goleman's Emotional Intelligence model breaks the concept down into four elements:

1. **Self-awareness**

    Self-awareness is the ability to understand how your feelings are having a direct influence on your actions. If I know that I am cranky before my first cup of coffee in the morning—and this is liable to show up as me being short with my customers—then I can plan accordingly. At the core of self-awareness is working on your ability to stop and ask yourself, "why am I feeling this way, and how is that affecting my behavior?" Often, we find ourselves, as a result of habituated behavior, repeating actions without question that are fundamentally detrimental to us.

    How many of our decisions fall into this category of regular behaviors that aren't rooted in logic and haven't been evaluated on their own merit for a long time? Stopping and allowing yourself to consider how your feelings—from a long time ago, or experienced moments ago—are impacting decisions can lead to tremendous personal growth opportunities.

    One way to improve your self-awareness is to make a detailed list of your strengths and weaknesses. Getting assistance from someone you trust and who really knows you can be helpful. Then keep a sales journal where you identify and track how your strengths and weaknesses are affecting your customer interactions, and subsequent sales. This gives you the chance to dial up or dial down behaviors based on real-life positive or negative feedback and outcomes.

2. **Self-management**

    The easiest way to define self-management is "staying in control of your emotions." Your feelings are your feelings, and as we have written, there is a lot of complicated neural processing, brain chemicals, and past experiences that impact how you feel. That said, as a sentient being, you have the power to monitor and manage your own behavior.

In sales, when a customer is being totally unreasonable, it's easy to allow yourself to ramp up your own negative behavior under the self-justification that you're simply matching your actions with the customer's. Unfortunately, escalation tends to lead to more escalation and matters become worse, not better.

How can you avoid this? The practice of meditative deep breathing we've discussed before can have a calming effect. Taking the time to write down your own statement of personal values and reviewing that statement regularly can also have a grounding effect, helping to combat emotions that negatively impact your ability to live those values. One example is the value of honesty. Honesty in sales is a must, and regardless of your position people who readily admit when they make mistakes and don't play the blame game are always held in the highest regard by fellow co-workers and customers alike.

It's a very common practice, especially for large companies and corporations, to create a mission statement or value statement in an attempt to codify the value principles upheld by an organization. One can argue the effect this actually has on the day-to-day worker, but nevertheless, taking time on an individual basis to examine your own underlying principles can act as a touchstone in helping establish your own code of behavior for self-management. This in conjunction with your strengths and weaknesses analysis is at the core of working on increasing your EQ.

3. Social Awareness

Theory of Mind is the very essence of social awareness, the ability to see the world from your customer's perspective. How is my customer feeling right now? This is sometimes referred to as "taking your customer's temperature," when you are consciously taking the time to be aware of your customer's words and body language, and as a result, responding appropriately to their verbal and physical cues.

Perspective taking, and showing empathy by actively imagining how you would feel if the tables were turned and you suddenly found yourself in the customer's shoes, is a great social awareness exercise that can yield surprising insights. Customers attach huge value to you and your product or service when you clearly go out of your way to help, as opposed to the indifference that's often at the core of a poor customer experience.

This proactive behavior of going above and beyond sends the message to the customer that they truly matter. For the "me-driven" Homo sapiens brain, that's a big emotional deal. Conversely, if a customer prefaces a statement with, "I know I'm probably not your biggest account," that statement can be interpreted as, "I don't seem to matter that much to you." If you are actively practicing and perfecting your social awareness skills, statements like that should never arise.

4. Relationship Management

A single word to characterize relationship management would be "fairness." The willingness to demonstrate equality in all your dealings, particularly when it comes to conflict resolution with customers, vendors, and employees is a highly prized attribute.

Another important aspect in relationship management is the outward show of appreciation. For some reason, praise is often in short supply during the onslaught of a busy sales day, and yet it shows up again and again in HR surveys where employees say they feel consistently under-appreciated. Research indicates it is one of the main reasons employees change jobs, often rating being appreciated for what they do even higher in importance than salary.

When it comes to customers, praise might not be top of mind; but in fact, it's important to be mindful of how customers are positively attempting to participate in the buying process. For example, your customer's willingness to follow up on details you've requested, or even calling to tell you they're running late for an appointment, is an opportunity for you to show appreciation for their commitment or thoughtfulness. It's easy to forget there can be a lot at stake for the customer, too.

For many of us, being free with praise falls under the category of, "something I need to do more of." This is a great example of how taking the time to consciously assess the pitfalls of one's own day in and day out behavior can lead to better emotional intelligence skills, and, serendipitously, more sales.

So how smart are you in your sales ability?

By combining the fundamentals of EQ with IQ, Goleman suggests we get a much more complex, nuanced picture of a person's intelligence. It's fair to say the same can be said about sales. Your willingness to recognize the role emotions play in selling, and then striving to improve your communication skills as a result, moves you a step closer to the status of Sales Genius.

French philosopher Rene Descartes once postulated, "I think therefore I am." If he had known about Kahneman's work on System 1 and 2 decision-making and Goleman's work on Emotional intelligence, today Descartes might amend his statement to, "I think and feel, therefore I am."

Power of Word of Mouth

Inside each customer's skull are enough neural pathways to go around the moon and then circle the earth 6 times. This web of myriad connections will decide whether or not to make the purchase.

And that decision, the one that has enormous implications for you and me, our families, the economy, and virtually everyone else on the planet, begins its journey in the future.

Whenever someone decides to purchase a product, they start with a kind of thought experiment, imagining how their life will be with their new acquisition. This can take the form of a vague notion ("Wouldn't be nice to have a new pair of running shoes?") or it might be a little more concrete ("I want Chuck Taylor All-Stars in bright orange with white laces, size 10 ½").

It is the job of a salesperson to usher our mental movies into reality, which often means helping to define that imagined experience.

Not so long ago, the first step to a sale might have begun with the yellow pages. Today, the Internet is where over half of new customers will plot the beginning and, often, the end of the journey. This is why companies large and small devote major dollars to making their websites as vibrant as possible.

So, does all of this mean traditional brick-and-mortar is going the way of the dinosaur? The demise of long-time retailers suggests that the Internet is definitely changing the purchasing landscape. Yet in 2020, Statista Marketing Research estimated that 2021's e-Commerce sales in the United States would still only account for just under 14% of total retail sales.

In his book *Contagious*, Jonah Berger lays out the truth about the power of the Internet as influencer. He points out the following: word of mouth is the primary driver of 20-50% of all sales in the US. Let that sink in. With all the media marketing targeting you every day, your personal acquaintances are still an enormous factor when it comes to your personal buying decisions.

How is that possible?

Even if you, like the average American, spend two hours of each day online, most of your life is still conducted in "unplugged" mode. Even factoring in sleep, you spend 8 times longer dealing with people face-to-face, sharing your thoughts with the 150 people closest to you. (150 is the maximum number of real relationships one can actually juggle in their life, according to anthropologist Robin Dunbar.)

Your social group is powerful. You might have read incredible things about Nike on Consumer Report's website, but if your friend told you she just bought a pair of Nike shoes and had a miserable experience, all of the carefully compiled statistics go out the window. Your friend's word of mouth trumps the feedback of thousands of media ads.

Yes, I can get up in the middle of the night half-asleep, turn on my computer, log onto Zappo's, buy a pair of running shoes, and stumble back to bed. And yes, this single item-based sale is susceptible to that sort of enterprise. Still, when it comes to making purchasing decisions, your inner circle of family and friends hold tremendous sway over the shopping center in your brain.

According to a Nielson study, 92 percent of respondents say they trust earned media, such as "word-of-mouth or recommendations from friends and family" more than any form of advertising[23].

If your best friend tells you they went to the new pizza restaurant in town and it was the worst pizza they'd ever had, the chances of you then going to that same restaurant are extremely small. Conversely, if your best friend said the pizza at the new restaurant was the greatest they'd ever eaten, your chances of dining there would be enormously high—provided you like pizza.

Interestingly, this effect is not limited to your inner circle. In a 2019 consumer survey, 88% of participants said that they trust online reviews as much as a recommendation from someone they know.[24]

The brain tends to bias towards a person-to-person account as being more reliable than some nebulous source of information; this is true even if the person, in the case of an online opinion, is someone they've never met. This means word of mouth from a total stranger can still have a big impact on your buying tendencies. (This is one reason why artificial bots are a problem, with their ability to generate "personal content" online.)

The perception that a personal opinion is more trustworthy than a whole host of other sources might appear to be illogical, but that's your emotional System 1 at work again. Family, friends, and even the opinions of strangers beat the media when it comes to believability.

We tend to overestimate the power of marketing and advertising in this regard. Not that they aren't important, but when you stack them up against word of mouth, you begin to see the real viral power that flows from human discourse and personal critique.

Going Viral

What does it really mean to go viral?

Word of mouth operates very much like a flu virus. And flu virus transmission is largely dependent on viral load. Viral load is the number of viral particles you expel when you exhale out. When we aren't sick, we expel about 52,000 particles on average. That number jumps to around 75,000 particles if we cough while we have the flu. But during a severe bout of the flu, it is possible to expel as many as 300,000 viral particles with a violent cough, thus becoming a super spreader.

The people exposed to flu victims go on to infect other individuals, creating a daisy chain of illness. And depending on the virulence of the flu and its incubation period, and because the rate of infection moves exponentially, you can go from one sick individual to as many as 70,000 in seven weeks.

One important factor in viral spread is proximity to viral load. In a study done with the COVID-19 virus, the people who had a much higher incidence of getting sick were family members, friends, and co-workers of frontline hospital workers. In fact, in Wuhan, this group made up to 75-80 percent of the people with the most severe cases.

Which brings our analogy back to word of mouth in sales. In word of mouth, the customer who has become excited about your product or service is going to tell those people they are closest to, like family members, friends, and co-workers. If the customer's experience is stellar enough, they are likely to produce a greater amount of praise (the word of mouth equivalent of viral load). If a customer was *so* impressed with you or your product that they can't stop talking about the experience, they become "super spreaders," disproportionately getting the word out, and doing the job of many positive customers on your behalf.

If the positive word of mouth experience should hit the Internet and become constantly liked and shared, then much like the flu, your message can truly go viral on a whole new level. In extreme cases, due to the vastness of the Internet environment, viral transmission can reach hundreds of thousands in the matter of a few hours.

Flu spread is, by any measure, a negative experience. Unfortunately, word of mouth can also be negative if the customer experience did not live up to or fell below expectation. The daisy chain of negative transmission we described above follows the same trajectory and soon your business is overwhelmed and sickened, with the potential of putting you out of business.

It's not easy to identify a word of mouth super spreader. It's for this reason that each customer experience you deliver is really important. Should you encounter a super spreader, your business can either skyrocket forward or fall victim to negative feedback. The spread of the flu is extremely difficult to control, but the good news about word of mouth as it relates to the customer's experience is that to a large extent, you get to play doctor.

Peak/End Rule

The brain follows a pattern when absorbing new information and weighing the value of an experience. The brain will record more data at the most dramatic part of an experience, be it the high point or low point, and again at the end of the experience. This is called the Peak/End Rule.

(Note, this is different from the Ghost Curve, which governs attention given in the moment. The Peak/End Rule is about the emotional impression once the memory has been formed.)

This means that the peak and end of an experience are given far more gravitas and disproportionately alter the way you record, view, and store a memory for later retrieval. Prior to memory storage, it's like your brain has taken the time to edit the experience, cutting out the parts that don't seem particularly relevant, and doubling down on memory markers that create a certain point of view. The brain is less concerned with being fair and accurate and more concerned with curating a highlight reel that seems to convey what the brain deems as essential in the moment.

This means memories are not always accurate recollections of what really happened. The actual recording of the memory is also highly interpretive. This is what we mean by a brain bias, a kind of glitch in your mind's processing ability that distorts your perceptions.

Why these brain biases occur is not wholly understood. One theory is that since the human brain evolved for life 40,000 years ago, many features that feel like downsides now were at that time an evolutionary advantage. One can argue that what might have served the brain well in ancient times is ill-suited and obsolete by today's standards, but we currently have no way to permanently alter the brain's makeup and adjust our decision-making mechanism for the twenty-first century. All we can do is attempt to recognize certain incongruent behaviors that show up with consistency, and to keep them in mind when we make decisions.

Today, we understand that salespeople are in the memory business; your goal is to create positive experiences that will stick with your customer and generate word of mouth. Just like the Internet, the trick is to rank as high as you can in your customer's mental search engine. To do that, you'll have to know a little bit more about how memory works.

In his book *Thinking Fast and Slow*, Daniel Kahneman discusses the many ways the human brain acts contrary to what you might expect. One example is how we record memories.

How do you decide whether to go back to the same restaurant again, buy the same breakfast cereal, or even whether to read this book one more time?

This is the beauty of the memory, which does you the favor of storing neural code from your past to rescue and remind you of the outcome of some previous experience. Like a trailer from a movie, your brain replays a snippet or two from a past event to give you context for future decisions. That seems pretty straightforward, except for a couple of minor glitches discovered by Kahneman and his fellow researchers.

Kahneman's team has learned that in an effort to both conserve energy and keep you safe, your brain takes more of a Cliff Notes approach to memory than a blow-by-blow accounting of what actually happened.

Our memory summaries seem to be guided by two principles. First, we tend to focus more heavily on the most intense moment or moments of the experience, and on the end.

If you picture a roller coaster ride at its apex on the track, you can imagine the emotionally thrilling experience at its breathless highpoint. In sales, much like the roller coaster ride, this is the moment that your brain will record for posterity.

It happens when you feel the excitement of getting behind the wheel of a new vehicle for the first time, or the smell of the warm gooey cinnamon bun, or the cushy feel of a new pair of leather boots. It's the moment when the impact of a product or service has achieved full sensory recognition.

When we consider ourselves as individuals, we tend to think in terms of a single entity with agency. In essence, I take on information through my five senses and then use my memories to inform, guide and, perhaps most importantly, predict what will happen next—or, more accurately, what *might* happen next.

So those recollections, the stories we tell ourselves to record those experiences, are what fundamentally help us both understand ourselves and the world around us.

Kahneman's Peak/End Rule says it is not that simple. That's because the two systems—experiencing and remembering—are not in sync. In a series of experiments, he and his team proved that your "experiencing self" perceives the world moment by moment, but your "remembering self" follows a strange phenomenon, recalling the extremes of a given experience without accurately recording how long it took, or how it generally felt while it was happening.

Imagine watching your favorite team play a near-perfect game, relishing every second, and then in the last five minutes, the opposition mounts an incredible come-from-behind charge that knocks your team out of contention.

If your experiencing self and remembering self worked the same way, you'd average out your second-by-second feelings—the 98% of the game you were happy and the 2% of the game you were disappointed—and record the whole affair as having been 98% a good time.

But any sports fan knows that's not how it works. The final moments of the game carry a disproportionate power, like a shadow that blots out all of your team's great efforts over the preceding hours of play.

And it's not just sports; Kahneman reports that in experiments involving colonoscopies, the final moments will totally color your notion of the entire procedure. If it's by and large painful, but the pain decreases at the end, you'll report it wasn't so bad. Conversely, if it didn't hurt that much until the final few minutes, you're more likely to consider it an exceptionally bad experience.

Our brains are wired not to give equal weight to every detail but instead to record those moments that stand out for us. Our remembering selves are therefore in the business of altering reality for efficiency by way of a neat and tidy editing job.

And the end result is a kind of highlight film bringing you "the thrill of victory and the agony of defeat." From your brain's point of view, that's the best game in town.

As a salesperson, understanding the essence of the Peak/End Rule doesn't mean nothing else matters. But what it does tell you is that your customer is going to put a whole lot more import in the abbreviated highlight reel, and how they felt at the end of the sale—the last taste in their mouth if you will. In most cases, you get to orchestrate those essential moments.

In the Jimmy Johns restaurant chain, staff are trained to make sure they thank the customer as the customer is leaving their store. It's a small gesture, but customers become aware of this bit of courteousness. Is it enough to keep you coming back? It's hard to say, but given the vagaries of the customer's emotional System 1 decision-making, it certainly can't hurt.

The Test Drive

It's common practice, when shopping for a new car: the salesperson offers you a test drive, a chance to take your prospective automobile out on the road and get a feel for what it's like to drive it. Research has shown that if the salesperson can put you in a vehicle that matches your wants—your color choice and desired package of extras—they are much more likely to sell you the car than if they put you in a random color with a package of the same model and make.

This is where your five senses come into play. While there are technically more than five –for instance, proprioception, the awareness of your body in space—we'll concern ourselves with the standard ones: hearing, tasting, touching, seeing, and smelling.

The more of your customers' senses you engage, the more powerful your messaging becomes. If you only engage their hearing, research from John Medina in his book *Brain Rules* shows that they will remember only 10 percent of the information three days later—this is one of the reasons why phone selling is so difficult! If they also see a visual representation of a product in addition to hearing about it, then their memory will retain 65% of the information. It follows the old adage that "seeing is believing." If you add the sense of touch to the equation, they'll remember even more.

It's important to stress that Sales Geniuses, the best of the best, are quick to engage the sense of touch in selling. Offering the customer a chance to experience the product by feeling it creates a significantly more powerful buying situation.

One of my first sales jobs was in a kitchen and bath showroom. As such, one of the products we sold was the InSinkErator instant hot water dispenser, a device that fits neatly under the kitchen sink and delivers hot water on demand at just-below boiling temperature. It's a real boon for coffee and tea drinkers.

Like many newbie salespeople, I would diligently go through the product's features and benefits, carefully listing out the manufacturer's suggesting selling points. Sometimes people would buy the unit, but frequently they would simply stare at me glassy-eyed, overwhelmed by our well-equipped showroom's myriad of product offerings.

It occurred to some of the sales personnel that merely hearing about a device that super heats water wasn't very compelling. We lobbied the store manager to actually hook up one of the faucets so we would have a live demo version, instantly making coffee or tea right in front of a potential customer.

One bright Saturday morning walking an older couple around the showroom, I finally had the opportunity to demonstrate the new machine for the first time. I turned that faucet handle, and a steaming jet of water gushed out as I explained,

"This is the InSinkErator instant hot water dispenser. Be careful, at around 200 degrees Fahrenheit, this water is just under boiling—"

But I had no sooner finished the word "boiling" when the husband thrust his index finger directly into the scalding water.

Pulling his finger back with a shriek, he stared at his bright red digit in disbelief.

His wife turned to him. "What were you thinking?" she said. "He just told you the water was near-boiling!"

The husband, face nearly as red as his finger, muttered under his breath, "I didn't think it could be that hot so fast."

He clearly had not spent a great deal of time analyzing the situation before he decided to enact his own test. His System 1 was calling the shots and he wanted some instant proof of what I was saying and whether I could be trusted. If he had deliberated a few seconds longer and given his System 2 a chance, he would have realized the vapors rising from the gushing water indicated the presence of extreme heat. He had seen with his own eyes what was happening, he had heard my description, but it was his own sense of touch that drove the message home.

Without hesitation, he pulled out his credit card on the spot and demanded a hot water dispenser. The combination of his three senses, along with a little humility, had tipped him into a buying experience.

What I found interesting from a social experiment aspect was that the same scenario would play out over and over again in the months to come, right down to the conversation between the couple after the inflamed finger. Importantly, when the customer invested a little flesh in the game, it almost always resulted in a sale.

It's not that I enjoyed causing momentary pain to my customer, but I soon realized how adding the sense of touch to a selling situation made all the difference in outcome. Suggesting a customer open a cabinet drawer and feel for themselves the easy glide of the self-close roller system or the cool touch of the smooth granite countertop drove more sales. I learned to no longer demonstrate any of the products we offered, but to always ask the customer to experience it firsthand.

This need for humans to actively engage products from an enhanced sensory standpoint is everything.

Smell is an incredibly powerful sense; it's the only sense of the standard five that goes directly to the brain without any filtering mechanism.

Smell is a biological adaptation designed to instantly sort out potentially dangerous situations like deadly rotting carcasses or life-sustaining ones like sweet fruit, a mainstay in the early human diet.

Back in the heyday of shopping malls, the pastry provider Cinnabon knew the key to their sales was tapping into smell. They realized that the sugary, doughy, slightly spicy and very buttery scent of their product turned people into cartoon characters, floating along, following their noses to the sweet source.

To enhance the effect, Cinnabon strategically places their ovens towards the front of their stores; sales decrease by double digits when ovens are in the back. Franchisees are advised to buy the weakest stove hood they can legally use[25]. Sometimes, when there are no buns in the oven, a Cinnabon location will warm trays of cinnamon and brown sugar, just to keep the smell going.

Not all products have a smell component, but some sellers have attempted to capitalize on scent by artificially adding it to their environment. Hotels, retailers, and gambling casinos have all jumped on the bandwagon, hoping to leverage your brain's primitive demand. Realtors will sometimes advise their sellers to leave fresh baked goods on their counters during a house showing.

A number of studies have underlined the power of smell in retail. As John Medina writes in *Brain Rules*, Dr. Eric Spangenberg, dean of the business school at Washington State University, found that he could double sales in the women's section of a store by pumping in the scent of vanilla, while the same could be accomplished in the men's section with the spicy, more masculine aroma of rose maroc[26].

One thing is for certain: when one wears cologne or perfume, over time one's olfactory sense diminishes the importance of that particular smell. This means they no longer get the same sensation they first got when the cologne or perfume was new to them, and so without realizing it they've become somewhat nose-blind, needing to add more and more scent in order to duplicate the original pleasant effect.

We've all stepped into a crowded room only to recognize what the perfume or cologne wearer probably doesn't: a little less scent would be beneficial for the rest of us. This is why if you are a salesperson, when you are in a selling situation, it is best to be odor-neutral and refrain from dousing yourself in any strong fragrance.

It might sound like a little thing, but little things can be a big deal. As we described in the beginning, Genius tip a potential customer towards a sale through a series of small incremental steps. Not overwhelming a customer's primitive olfactory system might be the difference between tipping towards or away from a sale.

What about the sense of taste? If you don't sell a food product, taste will be difficult to incorporate into your selling routine. A home goods salesperson could say, "Hey, put your tongue on this copper pot and really taste that metal," but while this would certainly create a lasting impression with your customer, perhaps even a peak moment, it's probably not the kind of peak moment that translates to a sale.

But it's not just the peak moment of the experience that drives future buying behavior; the feeling at the very end of the experience is every bit as important.

Daniel Kahneman proved the end part of the Peak/End rule to be just as potent by running a series of experiments involving peoples' perception of pain and the outcome recorded in their memories.

He successfully demonstrated the power of *the end* through a series of clever experiments. Imagine that you are given the choice between two different scenarios, and neither one of them is especially inviting.

In the first scenario, your hand is plunged into freezing cold water for 90 seconds, followed by 30 seconds of warm water. In the second scenario, your hand is plunged into freezing water for just 60 seconds. (There is no additional warm water phase.)

The results were somewhat surprising. People in the test study actually preferred 90 seconds of pain followed by 30 seconds of warm water—as opposed to just 60 seconds of icy cold water.

That's right, the test subjects were willing to endure an additional 30 seconds more of icy water, if the experiment culminated in a more pleasant warm water transition at the tail end of the experience.

So, what's going on here?

People in both scenarios remembered that the icy water hurt, but the more pleasurable warm water ending disproportionately weighed in on their memory. This created a more palatable feeling despite the fact that the pain section actually lasted longer. It was the end of the experience that took on more meaning, and generated more memory than the actual duration of the experience.

This is why sticking the landing is so important in sales. In addition to the peak, the end of the transaction is equally recorded in the customer's mind.

It's important to realize that all other customer touchpoints in the experience might have gone swimmingly. They liked your website, your demeanor, your knowledge, and ability to deliver information. But when it comes time to make the buying decision, the climax of emotion and the end of the experience have disproportionate weight on the result and a customer's willingness to generate word of mouth.

This means if everything is going great but the product arrives damaged and needs to be reordered, don't get complacent. Throw in a quick, heartfelt apology and some type of extra bonus to keep that ending an overall positive experience. That final memory of the experience is everything. It's the gateway to the all-powerful word of mouth.

The Brain Builds a Picture

Word of mouth will drive your customer towards or away from you, but how do you keep the customer once they've been directed your way? How does the customer's brain take in the information and create its powerful emotional impression?

A good analogy to understand the customer experience is the High Definition (HD) television screen. What makes HD TV a better viewing experience? In a word: pixels, the tiny dots of color that combine to create vivid imagery. HD TVs have more pixelation and more pixels means a sharper, more vibrant picture.

If you think about the formation of an experience in your customer's brain, it starts by aggregating all the tiny feelings that build into an impression, and those impressions, when combined, form an experience. The experience is stored in the brain as a hunk of useful data that allows for comparison and critique of the next buying situation.

We know that the majority of customers begin their initial buying journey by accessing the Internet, not necessarily to buy but to gather information. The look and feel of how your business is represented on the Internet is crucial. Using our analogy, it's the beginning of the brain's "pixilation" of the experience, the first few feeling points that will help shape the eventual experience.

If your website is antiquated, overly complex, hard-to navigate, or light on visual content, the content can seem a little blurry to your customer's brain—the opposite of what you seek as a first impression.

On the other hand, maybe your website has been recently refreshed and is brimming with engaging content, beckoning your customer to come and see your state-of-the-art showroom and its plethora of hands-on displays. Your site has spoken to the Driver's sense of a deal, the Manager's awareness of a well-defined process, the Engineer's need for deep content, and the Actor's excitement for all the cool products you have available. In fact, you've done such a good job that the customer, regardless of buying pattern, is so impressed with your website—and the promise of your brick and mortar experience—that they jump into their car and head your way.

Once they arrive at your store, the ease of parking, the store's signage, and the showroom's outward appearance are all creating additional emotional pixilation. Each touchpoint, just like the initial sense of your website, starts to define the quality of their new experience. And so, the picture continues to build definition with the initial greeting, accessibility and quality of the displays, friendliness of the staff, smell of the showroom, attractive lighting, and the cleanliness of the restrooms. The list goes on and on. The point is that a customer experience is made up of an incredibly large number of touchpoints, and just like your HD TV, they are creating a powerfully vivid experience.

Imagine, for argument's sake, that you're watching the Super Bowl on your new HD TV with your family and your goofy, unpredictable uncle. When his favorite team loses the game in the final seconds, he responds by coolly unholstering his Colt 45 pistol and shooting your new TV.

Amazingly, the shot leaves a perfectly round quarter-inch hole in the otherwise pristine screen, and to your amazement, the TV is still working fine. Ignoring all the family dynamics that are likely to ensue, it's fair to say that you would most likely consider getting a new TV. Watching a screen with a hole in it would be unacceptable, even though the hole makes up less than 1 percent of the total viewing screen.

This rather dramatic example drives home an important lesson: it only takes a single touchpoint to destroy what might otherwise be a great experience. A surly waiter's attitude in what otherwise was an outstanding dining experience is enough to kill that all-important word of mouth referral. A dirty restroom, outdated displays, and a poor parking experience can individually have the same effect.

It might not be fair, but a customer's experience is only as strong as the weakest touchpoint. All those pixelated touchpoints are essential for the overall experience. Like the hole in the TV, you are at the mercy of the brain's biasing towards a complete picture.

The same thing happens when you work for hours on an elaborate jigsaw puzzle only to discover you are missing a couple of pieces to finish it. Typically, that's the last time that jigsaw puzzle will see the light of day. The brain is built to see a complete and uninterrupted picture, and whether it's your HD TV, jigsaw puzzle, or customer experience, each individual touchpoint is vital.

Sales Geniuses are constantly assessing the environment they are creating for their customer, examining each touchpoint of the experience they are creating from the customer's point of view and showing dogged determination to improve all the poorly defined touchpoints.

A great way to build on this idea is to run your own customer experience mapping experiment. This can be done a number of ways.

You can map out your showroom, or media offerings, or personal sales process, or all of the above. You begin by building a list of each touchpoint (impression) a potential customer is likely to experience during your sales effort.

For example, if you were mapping your media offerings, you would include all the touchpoints that happen during the inquiry phase before your customer even meets you. This would include evaluating all forms of media, with special attention on a detailed breakdown of the content on your website. Mapping of your sales process would include a list of all the touchpoints that happen under the following categories: initial inquiry, greeting, information delivery, design, selection, order, delivery, installation, follow up, and referral phase, etc.

Whatever your sales process might entail, you can start by listing out main categories as indicated above. Then, below each category describe the various touchpoints a customer is likely to experience. Installation touchpoints could include processes like company ID badges, pre-delivery phone call protocols, installation attire and footwear, cleanup protocols, and so on. The list includes all touchpoints that will impact the customers' impressions.

Some categories might entail hundreds of touchpoints, and some perhaps only a few. The important thing is an attempt to be as exhaustive as possible. Once you've listed the categories and their subset of touchpoints, it's time to evaluate. This usually works better if you include other individuals in the evaluation of the process. A shared approach to evaluation is more likely to create a less biased process.

To evaluate, you examine each touchpoint and decide whether that touchpoint is likely creating a subpar feeling, a neutral feeling, or a positive feeling for your customer. When scoring touchpoints using this three-point system of minus, neutral, or plus, it's important to put yourself in your customer's shoes.

For example, let's say you own a restaurant, and one of the touchpoints that a customer is likely to experience would include the restroom. If your restroom was state of the art and always immaculately clean and inviting, that would score as a plus (+). If your restroom seemed clean by most restaurant standards that would be neutral (o). And obviously if your restroom sometimes fell below the standard you'd be proud of— or worse, akin to a poorly maintained roadside gas station—that would score a minus (-).

After you go through the entire list of touchpoints, you're likely to have a range of results. The first line of attack in building a better customer experience is finding solutions to address your subpar scores. For the sake of your longevity, subpar touchpoints must be addressed as soon as possible. Touchpoints in minus territory are killing your business.

But you can't stop there, because we will soon see that **even the touchpoints that fall in the neutral feeling zone can put your business at risk.**

The Homo sapiens brain, it turns out, is a tough grader when it comes to passing on a recommendation via word of mouth, and it puts no points on the scoreboard for either subpar or neutral touchpoint performance.

Interestingly, word of mouth really only thrives off touchpoints that fall in the category of exceptional, what we call "plus" experiences. If you want people raving about your business, it's imperative you give them something extra to rave about.

If you stay at a hotel and the room is clean, the heat or air conditioning is adequate, the TV and WIFI reception work, and the hotel staff is pleasant enough—all neutral touchpoints—it's unlikely you'd rave about your stay to your friends when you get home.

Here lies the rub: even if everything goes well and nobody drops the ball, merely meeting expectations doesn't give you or your business any real forward momentum. The human brain basically discounts everything that falls below exceptional performance.

One common lesson that comes out of touchpoint mapping is that in order to create the ultimate customer experience, you probably have far more work to do then you might realize.

Shep Hyken, writing for Forbes, reports that 80% of CEOs believe they deliver "super experiences," but only 8% of customers agree.[27] It is easy to get lulled into believing that your website, showroom, or even your own brand of selling is delivering top notch results, but it's the customer that gets the final vote, and they have no incentive to take it easy on you.

The Science of "Extras"

For an easy tool to understand the power of orchestrating a positive customer experience, let's look at the Kano Model, created by Professor Noriaki Kano.

While studying customer satisfaction and loyalty, Kano found that driving word of mouth requires creating an exceptional experience, or what we have introduced as the "plus experience." And this in turn necessitated fulfilling three categorical needs: must-haves, one-dimensional needs, and "attractors" or "delighters[28]. Essentially, it's Maslow's Hierarchy of Needs for sales.

Must-haves are the things your product or service *must* provide, or else the customer will be extremely dissatisfied. Often, these are needs the customer doesn't think much about beforehand. Neglect one of these and your customers will have a lasting negative story to share.

For example, stand-up comedian Riley Silverman once checked into a hotel while on tour, only to discover her room had no door. Even before the front desk clerk reacted to the news by nonchalantly assuring Silverman, "Aw come on! None of "em gonna take your stuff," the hotel had clearly lost a customer[29]. Most people don't incorporate their customer complaints into a stand-up comedy routine, but with a missing hotel door it's pretty much a given that your friends will hear about it at the next dinner party. A door on a hotel room is not really negotiable, it's a must-have.

One-dimensional needs are next. This is the category where you can increase customer satisfaction by offering more. Examples include providing more memory on a smartphone, more leg room on a plane, or a more comfortable hotel bed and extra pillows. While these needs are not the flashiest, they are an important part of your product or service's value proposition, and as such can't be neglected.

Finally, there's what Kano called "attractors" or "delighters" – pleasant surprises which go above and beyond the customer's expectations to *plus* their experience. By definition, people won't be upset if a given delighter is not present, but those little extras are what makes a customer experience special and open the door for a word of mouth endorsement. A delighter could be a free bottle of water at your local gym, or free samples in the cheese aisle at your neighborhood grocery store.

At a restaurant, serving food free of hair is a must-have. Prompt service is a one-dimensional need. An unexpected dish of free sorbet at the end is a delighter. It's the delighters that make you stand out, get noticed, and get talked about—in a good way. Given the importance of the Peak/End Rule, delighters like peak moments should be a key part of your selling strategy.

There are just a few things you'll want to remember about delighters.

Consider your Market

Just what constitutes a delighter can get a little counterintuitive. Sometimes a cheap establishment offers perks that you'd never expect to find at a ritzier place. Consider the free continental breakfasts served at most budget hotels. An extremely upscale hotel is much more likely to direct you to a pricy in-house restaurant. Complimentary breakfast is not the norm at a deluxe resort, and so we don't even consider it as a possibility.

Delighters are all about exceeding expectations, and our expectations are not an exact science. Be sure you are offering delighters in keeping with your price point and image.

Consider your Audience

When you check in at a Hilton hotel, the clerk behind the desk offers you a large free cookie, warmed by a heat drawer. For guests on holiday, this may seem like a genius move, but there's a slight problem. Some of us travel constantly, and for people trying to stay healthy, all those cookies add up. Thus, there is a subset of frequent travelers who come to view the offer of that nice warm cookie as nothing more than a test of willpower—essentially, an annoyance.

Alternately, Sheraton lets you choose between an "amenity" (usually a snack, bottle of water, etc.) or points, which can eventually be cashed in for a free stay—much more valuable to someone who knows they'll be needing another room next week. Now both the vacationers and the road travelers are happy.

Novelty is Key

As Kano himself noted, over time, a delighter can become so common that it reshapes customer expectation, moving from a fun bonus to a near-given. In other words, as the market evolves, delighters can become must-haves. For instance, private bathrooms weren't standard in hotels until after 1900[30]. Forget about free bottles of shampoo or conditioner! These days, if your hotel failed to provide your own bathroom, you might react roughly as if they had forgotten the door.

There's an element of randomness to a good delighter. It shouldn't be something that people will grow to expect. Thus, if your business depends on repeat customers, you should probably change up your delighters, or risk hard-wiring your clients to take that little extra for granted.

YOUR CUSTOMER'S EXPERIENCE

People in route sales often find themselves returning to the same customer locations again and again. You want your customers to take a break from their busy schedules to check out your latest offerings, and that means you need some kind of sweetener to buy their time. "Food bribes" are a common trick. A vendor stopping by first thing in the morning might arrive with bagels and coffee, with the unspoken agreement that the customer will now at least pay attention for as long as it takes to chow down on that special treat.

However, if your delighter each visit is that box of bagels and that hot coffee, your customers will come to associate you with a free breakfast. Now, say one week you're running a bit late and you don't have time to stop by the bagel shop. Since you're thinking of those bagels as a free perk, it doesn't seem like a big deal to you. However, your customers are so accustomed to that weekly bagel, they purposely skipped breakfast today, on the assumption that you'd provide. Now they're cranky and hungry—never a winning combination. You went from what seemed like a no-brainer win to a loss on the experience scoreboard.

Delighters Can't Fix Absent Must-haves

While it can be fun to brainstorm cool little extras to set yourself apart, that doesn't mean you can skip the fundamentals. If you show up each week with a box of baked goods but your product offerings aren't worth looking at, you risk becoming a mere "donut carrier" – a vendor who brings breakfast but no real value beyond that.

At worst, a delighter paired with a glaring lack of a must-haves can feel downright insulting. If Riley Silverman's hotel had offered her a warm cookie but still neglected to give her a room with a door, her take-home impression would not be "well, at least I got a warm cookie."

In a similar vein, it's not uncommon for a company's upper management to get excited about promoting new groundbreaking products. However, if that same company has constant problems with fulfillment and delivery, customers will likely grow annoyed at what will feel like surface improvements with no real substance.

Yet, well placed and timely delighters can have real persuasion power, and they don't have to be expensive.

A study by the Center for Hospitality Research at Cornell showed that giving out two pieces of candy with a dining bill increased the server's tip by almost 3 percent.[31] Humans are affected by what appears to be a genuine show of caring. An unexpected treat, even as small as a piece of hard candy, can pay dividends for a human's System 1 emotional brain. This is why plussing an experience is so important.

In another Center for Hospitality Research study, a server who gave out a piece of candy to each customer at the table, then seemed to "spontaneously" offer a second piece of candy, saw a jump in their tip from 19 percent (no candy) to 23 percent. On a fifty-dollar bill that amounts to an $11.50 tip, a nice return on 20 cents' worth of candy.

Another study showed that restaurant servers who either touched their customer momentarily on the shoulder, and/or squatted down to make eye contact with them as they took their order, also saw their tip values increase. The brain is impacted by moments suggesting a customer is being attended to, or more simply that the customer matters and is not seen as just another billing opportunity.

A handwritten note thanking a customer for a product or service you sold them might seem like a trifle, but because customers understand that the gesture was not required and the salesperson took the time to write and mail the note, this too, qualifies as a delighter.

You wouldn't expect a customer to respond with an additional tip after you sold them a couch, but perhaps you'll receive something far more valuable. Since word of mouth drives business, and the last thought the customer had about you was a considerate handwritten note, you've just taken advantage of the Peak/End rule. These types of small delighters can lead to positive soundbites about you or your business that can reverberate in the marketplace and create additional selling opportunities for you down the line.

Again, it's important to emphasize that what drives customer satisfaction has less to do with the size or cost of the delighter, and far more to do with the customer *feeling* that you went out of your way for them when you really didn't have to.

As we've seen, it doesn't take much for the brain to lose focus and attention in a variety of ways and circumstances, yet the emotional part of the brain seems to quietly keep a running tally of both perceived slights and acts of generosity. This System 1-driven subconscious scoreboard can either propel you and your business towards sales victory or defeat.

Keep Up with your Industry

Remember: as consumer expectations evolve, you need to evolve as well, and that means staying current with which former delighters are now must-haves. Falling behind on this score can be deadly. For instance, in our previous book, *Brain Apps*, we outlined the rise and fall of RIM, the company that brought us the BlackBerry.

At the start of the smartphone revolution, BlackBerry was ubiquitous. "At its peak, Blackberry owned over 50% of the US and 20% of the global smartphone market, sold over 50 million devices a year, had its device referred to as the "CrackBerry," and boasted a stock price of over $230. Today, BlackBerry has 0% share of the smartphone market," says J Luo, writing for the Digital Initiative at Harvard Business School.[32]

Why did Blackberry fall from grace? RIM leadership mistakenly viewed color screens and touch screens as fads—inconsequential delighters— rather than the wave of the future. As these features increasingly became must-haves, RIM's share of the market took a hard nosedive.

It's not enough to know what delighters you offer; you need to keep informed about your competitors as well, or risk becoming the next BlackBerry.

This is because you're always up against every delighter out there, not just the ones recognized in your industry. Customers don't compartmentalize their buying experiences. Once one vendor offers a delighter, it becomes the bar by which all other vendors are measured regardless of buying experience.

When Amazon came out with their one-click technology, allowing customers to order products with a single click once payment and delivery is saved, customers began to expect it from every online retailer.

The Kano model makes it clear that customer's tastes and expectations are always evolving, and it's imperative to keep up. Today's delighter is tomorrow's must-have, and word of mouth is built on those end satisfiers and high points of experience recorded in the memory.

It's easy to lose sight of this, especially when there have been problems in a sales situation. What happens when it takes several tries to make everything right about the buying experience, as a result of missing, or damaged product or an initial poor service experience?

When the sale is complete and the product or service has been completed, if there were problems, it's important to go back and *plus* the experience at the very end—even if the problems were eventually solved by one means or another,

Just finishing the job is not enough. Because it's at the point of conclusion where the customer, much like the crowds at the Roman Coliseum, will decide to give you a thumbs up or a thumbs down. A thumbs up means you live to sell again through word of mouth, a thumb down means you run the risk of becoming obsolete.

I once worked with a regional sales manager who would come back after making his rounds through his dealer territory and I'd ask him, "How is so and so dealership doing?" Recognizing that some of his dealers failed to understand the power of a positive customer experience, he would answer, "Oh they're out of business, they just don't know it yet." This really drives home a truism about the importance of managing a customer's experience by leveraging the power of the Peak/End Rule.

It's not uncommon when I am doing executive coaching with a CEO to hear them brag about the fact they really don't get negative complaints from their customers, which they believe reflects an exemplary customer experience. One study found that 96% of customers will not tell you they were unhappy with your product or service[33]. This means that not hearing from your customers is not always a silent vote of confidence.

The same source showed that 91% of unhappy customers won't contact you, and then choose to buy from your competitor next time around. In sales, silence is not necessarily golden.

Super-fixing

It comes as no surprise that when a problem shows up after a sale, nobody is happy. From the customer's point of view, a problem—whether tiny or significant—spawns a sense of dread. The idea that they might have made a mistake in putting their trust in you, your products, or your service confirms their lurking fears and feeds their sense of loss aversion.

The sad truth is that something in a sale can go wrong. Considering supply chain complexities, manufacturing defects, mishandling, human error in ordering, shipping or receiving, and miscommunication on your part or the part of the customer, a sale in today's world is a bit like a moonshot.

In the coming pages, we will examine how Sales Geniuses attempt to mitigate mistakes. But there is one thing they do at the outset which goes a long way in tamping down a customer's dread and anger. We call it super-fixing.

Super-fixing occurs when something goes sideways and the salesperson acts decisively, fixing the problem in a way that goes above and beyond customer expectations.

Nordstrom department store has long been famous for their exceptional customer service. One day in 2011, Eric Wilson, a loss prevention manager at Nordstrom, came across a customer in the women's department who was down on her knees frantically combing the floor. The clearly upset customer, Lisa McIntire Shaw, explained that she had lost the diamond out of her wedding ring while shopping yesterday.

Wilson had a host of options in dealing with this distraught customer. First, he could simply pretend he didn't see her and move on. He could furrow his brow and say something like, "I'm so sorry to hear this. I wish you the best of luck," hurrying on to his next task. However, on that day, he went beyond merely sympathizing and got down on his hands and knees, joining the search. To many, that would feel like the most he could possibly have done for a customer, even after the diamond failed to materialize.

Instead of stopping there, Wilson went into super-fix mode, recruiting two building-services workers to join the effort. These workers wound up retrieving the vacuum bags from last night's cleaning and proceeded to rake through the accumulated floor detritus by hand, bag after bag, meticulously searching for the glint of a diamond ring. As impossible as it might seem, they did indeed manage to find Shaw's diamond.

When Wilson reunited Shaw with her diamond ring, she broke down and cried.

Wilson would've been justified in shedding a few tears of relief himself. There was no guarantee, and it was statistically more likely that this problem was not going to have a fairy tale ending. That's not the point. The point is that Wilson went to extreme lengths to try to remedy a problem, and importantly, it wasn't even a problem that Nordstrom had caused.

"I tell everybody the story," Shaw said in a video later produced by Nordstrom. "I don't shop anywhere else...everything comes from Nordstrom."[34]

Aside from the notion that helping others is a basic golden rule for business, super-fixing drives customer loyalty and repeat business. When something does go wrong during a sales situation and you super fix it, sailing above the customer's expectation, the end result is a doubling effect: the customer is twice as likely to shop with you again and contribute to the all-powerful word-of-mouth, the lifeblood of any business.

Super-fixing creates a more powerful positive customer experience, even when someone in your company was initially at fault. It's no doubt a bit counterintuitive that a mistake on your part can actually lead to an improved relationship with a customer. Note that it only works when the customer recognizes that extraordinary effort went towards solving their problem.

On the other hand, if Wilson had chosen to ignore Shaw, the research is also very clear.

For reasons probably relating to the early survival of the species, the human brain tends to privilege negative information over the positive. Being able to recall, the location of a wasp nest or a den of wolves mattered more to early humans than recording the location of a good cache of berries. Negative details are more vividly remembered, and the research says they're more widely shared.

A 2017 study by American Express found that the average customer shares a bad shopping experience with about 15 people, while the positive stories are generally spread to roughly 11 people.[35] We call this the 3/2 Rule.

3/2 Rule

The 3/2 Rule says that a customer is about 30% more likely to, via word of mouth, spread a negative sales experience versus a positive one. This is a vitally important statistic to keep in mind because it means that poor quality experiences, over time, have the ability to put a company out of business, or at least do long-term damage to reputation, products or services.

On March 31, 2008, Singer/songwriter Dave Carroll and his band were flying United Airlines on their way to Omaha for a week-long tour in Nebraska. While waiting to deplane at a layover in Chicago's O'Hare Airport, Carroll heard the woman behind him shout perhaps the words a traveling band least hopes to hear: "My god, they're throwing guitars out there."

The bass player peered out the window in time to see the United baggage handlers flinging his bass around without any regard for the instrument. Carroll's $3500 Taylor guitar had already received such a treatment. Carroll searched for a United employee willing to help him, but was repeatedly brushed off, including by a gate agent who calmly told him, "But hon, that's why we make you sign the waiver." (Carroll had not signed a waiver.)[36] Finally, he was told to take it up with the ground crew in Omaha.

The trouble was, when Carroll landed in Omaha at 12:30 am, there were no employees around. At sound check the next morning, his worst fears were confirmed when he discovered that the neck of his guitar was smashed.

Carroll decided to file a claim. Thus, began nine months of a bureaucratic nightmare, as Carroll was pushed off to one arm of United after another. Eventually, he was told that United could do nothing because he'd waited more than 24 hours to file a claim. Carroll requested just $1200, enough to cover the repairs to his guitar. He offered to take the money via flight vouchers if necessary. United said no.

Carroll decided there was only one thing he could do. He attacked the problem from a musical angle: he wrote a song (and made a YouTube music video) called "United Breaks Guitars."

When the YouTube video hit 150,000 views, United contacted Carroll to offer payment to take it down. Carroll refused. (The video now has over 19 million views.) Carroll appeared on radio shows. He appeared on TV shows. Everywhere he went, he told his story.

On a Newark, New Jersey airport shuttle ride, passengers allegedly began a spontaneous sing-along of "United Breaks Guitars."[37]

While there is no way to prove a causal relationship, it is true that within four weeks of the debut of Carroll's first song about the United fiasco (yes, he wrote others), United's stock price had fallen about 10%– a value of $180 million. Given the chance, negative news can spread far and wide, especially when it's delivered via catchy song.

The Internet has democratized selling in many ways, not the least of which is the ability for a customer to share their buying experience with an untold number of people. It's estimated that 1-4 adults have left a review online. This kind of widespread recognition can launch a small basement startup into the stratosphere of sales, but just as easily knock a giant company to their knees.

There is an old political adage that all politics are local; the opposite can be said about a sale in today's global marketplace.

Orchestrating the Sale

If you hang out with salespeople, especially veterans of the industry, and you manage to gain their confidence, one of the things you're liable to hear are past sales horror stories. To be fair, many of those stories are more humorous than horror, but still there is no shortage of tales about sales that went horribly wrong, customers making impossible demands, and salespeople finding themselves in some downright wacky situations. A veteran of over thirty years of selling, I've heard my share of those stories, and told a few myself.

What I find interesting about those stories, if you listen carefully beyond the horror and humor, is a single recurring theme often unseen by the teller. While these stories are often told by customers, the theme is a loss of control by the salesperson.

You have to pass a test to drive a car, practice medicine, law, or real estate. You don't have to pass a test to be a shopper or a customer. Customers show up without any formal training in how to be a good efficient and effective shopper, and so abilities run the gamut. In many cases, shoppers come to you because they are not experts in your product. Many show up courteous, well-informed, serious, and looking for a fair shake, and then, well...and then...you get the idea.

Like an orchestra leader confronted with a bunch of unruly musicians, you can choose to let the tough customers make a lot of noise, or you can patiently work to turn a cacophony of sound into beautiful music. There are five key concepts to keep in mind when orchestrating a sale for a better customer experience.

Set Expectations

Your customers come in with an expectation of what they think is likely to happen. Sometimes they are right on the money and other times wildly off. Since the customer will judge you and the subsequent experience against their initial expectation, helping them form a clearer picture of what to expect makes sense.

Master carpenter Norm Abrams was the original contractor along with Bob Villa on the PBS TV series *This Old House.* Abrams would later go on to host another acclaimed PBS show called *The New Yankee Workshop.* When Abrams began working on *This Old House,* the pay wasn't stellar, and as a result, he continued to moonlight on the side with his own contractor business.

He told me he once got a call from a fan of the show wondering if he could build a fairly elaborate deck in her backyard. It seemed her daughter was getting married and the deck would be center stage for the ceremony. Abrams, busy with the show, inquired into the timeframe she had in mind. "No problem," she told him, "the wedding is not until later in the week." She was calling late Monday afternoon.

Abrams patiently told her that with permit, concrete footing work, materials, and so on, that timeframe would be impossible to achieve. The woman was incredulous, explaining that a couple of weeks earlier she had watched him build a large deck project on the show in less than a half an hour. Abrams had to explain that it was all done thanks to the magic of time lapse photography and weeks-long television shooting.

Earlier in my career, when I was working as a kitchen designer, I once got a call the day before Thanksgiving from a gentleman who wanted a set of "loaner" countertops so Thanksgiving wouldn't be interpreted by the kitchen remodeling project he had undertaken and in which he was currently knee-deep.

His expectation was that somewhere in a warehouse, assumedly the size of Texas, was a set of "loaner" countertops the exact size and exact color he wanted, just waiting for him to use for 24 hours and then return. He was shocked to discover that no such countertop exchange program or infinity-sized warehouse actually existed.

Taking time to understand just what the customer is expecting, and then from time to time amending that expectation to be more realistic, is a critical step to help keep the customer's experience from being doomed from the start. Some sales take the first wrong turn at the very beginning when customer expectation and reality are not aligned.

Explain your Process

Part and parcel with expectation is helping your customer understand exactly how the whole process is going to unfold. For survival's sake. The human brain is fear-oriented and as such, not knowing what's coming next, combined with a monetary outlay, is bound to result in stress.

Zeev N. Kain, MD, MBA, MA (Hon), FAAP, is a Yale and Harvard trained physician. In a *Psychology Today* article entitled "How to Mentally Prepare for Surgery and Recover Faster," he reports that, not surprisingly, surgery raises the stress level in patients, but that proper pre-surgery preparation results in shorter hospital stays, less need for pain medication, and quicker recovery.[38]

And one of the ways to reduce stress, which salespeople should note, is to thoroughly lay out a detailed explanation for what is about to happen and then prompt the patient, or in our case customer, to ask as many questions as necessary to make sure they understand what to expect. Stress reduction is always beneficial and frequently can keep the escalation of anxiety and tempers in check. Anxiety is one ingredient that seems manifest in just about every sales horror story I've heard.

Keep Them Informed

As we've stated, the unknown can send the brain down some pretty dark roads.

How can you avoid this?

The company Safelite Autoglass has built a nationally recognized business around fixing and/or replacing auto glass damage. Their market niche is to do the repair work on the spot, and in a short amount of time. They are also known for their dedication to the customer experience. Therefore, Safelite has learned to put stock in direct verbal feedback that occurs out in the field when their installation team is interacting with customers.

One bit of feedback that has proven invaluable is the idea that customers are interested in knowing, in real time, where the service tech is in relation to their own location. You can see how this would be important, especially since the customer could be stranded with a broken windshield someplace far from home.

To meet that need, Safelite has leveraged technology and adopted an Uber-like app to make the service tech's location and approximate arrival time available to the customer. App technology offers tremendous efficiency, but keeping your customer in the loop throughout the process doesn't take anything more than a text or phone call.

Even when you the salesperson might be waiting on parts or additional information to complete the job, it's smart practice to contact the customer, letting them know you haven't forgotten them and that you're still working on the solution. Not knowing is a sure-fire way to produce the stress hormone cortisol in your customer's brain. And as we've seen, mixing cortisol with sales is a dangerous concoction.

Set High Standards/Make It Personal

Starbucks is known for their extensive employee training program and their insistence on putting the customer experience first. They go to great lengths to make their stores' ambiance physically inviting. They also make sure that the drinks they deliver are visually appealing, and instruct barista's to remake drinks that don't meet visual standards, even though the taste of the drink wasn't affected. All of this is done to create an impression in the customer's mind that there is true value in the Starbucks experience.

For a business model that relies on a customer paying as much as 30 times more than a cup of coffee they could make at home, perceived value is everything. Interestingly, one of the ways they create a personalized experience goes beyond a customer's ability to order a customizable drink.

If you frequent Starbucks you're probably aware that they ask for your first name and mark it on your cup when you place your order. Seems like kind of a no brainer way to keep track of your drink, among all the other drinks in the daily morning rush.

However, there may be another clever brain related reason why Starbucks incorporates your name. By plastering it on your cup, your System 1 begins to make a subliminal mental connection between you and the Starbucks experience.

If you find the Starbucks experience pleasant, your brain starts to habituate the link between you and Starbucks. As a result, your brain rewires itself, and hitting Starbucks in the morning feels like a necessity, becoming an integral part of your unspoken routine.

Research shows that your name, the outward symbol of who you are, is incredibly important to your psyche. Starbucks is leveraging your brain's own "me driven" dynamic to create the feeling of loyalty, so necessary for your ongoing positive experience, and Starbucks' long-term future.

Winning Over an Unhappy Customer

Richard Branson, famed entrepreneur and owner of Virgin Atlantic airlines, once received a complaint letter from a dissatisfied passenger. "A complaint is a chance to turn a customer into a lifelong friend," says Branson. "At Virgin, we think that if we address a complaint well, and even involve the customer in the solution, it brings customers closer to our brand."

It seems that the passenger, flying in Virgin Atlantic's first class, experienced an extraordinarily bad dining experience, describing the main entree as a "miscellaneous central cuboid of beige matter."[39] I don't know about you, but there is something about food as "beige matter" that doesn't confer confidence.

It appears Branson agreed, and reached out to the customer, asking him if he would be interested in helping assist in a total revision of the airlines menu, and then subsequently invited the passenger to serve on Virgin Atlantic's culinary council.

In an age where the prevailing winds might suggest customers are no more than pawns in a game played by giant corporations, it's refreshing to think that a complaint letter would not be met with the typical boilerplate response of "Thank you for bringing this to our attention, your opinion matters to us," and then once again, back to business as usual.

When CEOs, responding to a complaint letter, demonstrate that they take a healthy dose of negative feedback seriously by legitimately seeking the passenger's advice and council, that is the hallmark of true believers in the Customer Experience. This is but another example of "plussing" an experience, not by providing some additional unexpected service or amenity, but by speaking to the emotional System 1 part of the brain, and through actions, conveying the powerful sentiment to the customer that *you matter*.

The five tenets listed above are by no means exhaustive when it comes to improving and orchestrating your customer's experience. Setting expectations at the outset, explaining the journey ahead, keeping the customer in the loop, making it personal, and dealing decisively and positively with negative fallout serves only as a rough outline. Sales Geniuses creatively color in the details, managing their sales-specific touchpoints along the way, in order to lead their customers' personalized journey towards a plus experience

Conclusion

There is a famous Arabic proverb where a camel loaded beyond capacity collapses after a single straw too many, hence, "the straw that broke the camel's back." The idea is a basic one: a small, seemingly inconsequential event ends up having profound effects.

"A journey of a thousand miles must begin with the first step," is sometimes attributed to the Chinese philosopher Lao Tzu, but the concept also resonates in BJ Fogg's idea of starting small with a tiny habit.

It's the compounding effect of building on a single decision, where the crucial first step overcomes inertia for creating a new habit. We understand the process: practice creates repetition, which in turn builds habit. Habit is really nothing more than neural code put into action. But, of course, knowing is not the same as doing.

Our lives are a complex dance of experience, interpreted through the lens of emotion, and it's difficult in the moment to comprehend the swirl around us. Even when our goals and aspirations are clearly defined, actually achieving them proves difficult.

It's not the knowing; for the most part, we know what we should do or want to do. The selling techniques we've shared aren't exceedingly difficult. In some way, it is the very simplicity of that initial step that lures us away from it. Can binary selection, midpoint summation or Justification really be that easy? It feels as though somehow there has to be more to it than that.

And yet, maybe there isn't. Water boils at 212 degrees Fahrenheit. At 211 degrees, all you have is really hot water. Raise the temperature one degree and steam is generated; steam has the power to run a city's electrical grid.

Someone had to lay that first stone at the pyramid of Giza. Itzak Perlman had to run his bow across a violin string for the first time. Stephen Curry had to shoot his first three-point shot. And Mark Twain had to write the first word in *Huckleberry Finn*. You will have to block time to master techniques like using brain biases to build powerful quotes, or spaced learning to lock the buying patterns into your long-term memory.

As the process plays out, tiny steps build into something much greater than merely the sum of incremental parts. Nothing illustrates this better than a bird's nest. Bits of debris, twigs, and straw, when woven together, create an amazingly resilient and viable structure that has served our feathered friends for millions of years.

The straw that broke the camel's back is a parable of warning, but it can also be reframed as the awesome power contained in a single straw.

We have spent a lot of time talking about brain research-based techniques for selling and creating an exceptional customer experience. We can't stress enough the importance of implementing your habit-building abilities. It is truly at the heart of all great performance, from music, to sports, and—yes—especially in sales. Sales Geniuses, the best of the best, are non-stop habituators. There is no getting around it. You will need to put your basal ganglia to work on your behalf to reach your true sales potential.

Good luck, and good selling.

[1] Belludi, Nagesh. "Albert Mehrabian's 7-38-55 Rule of Personal Communication." RightAttitudes.com, 4 Oct 2008, https://www.rightattitudes.com/2008/10/04/7-38-55-rule-personal-communication/#:~:text=In%20communication%2C%20a%20speaker's%20words,being%20communicated%20by%20words%20alone.

[2] Gino, Francesca. "Are You Too Stressed to Be Productive? Or Not Stressed Enough?" *Harvard Business Review*, 14 April 2016. https://hbr.org/2016/04/are-you-too-stressed-to-be-productive-or-not-stressed-enough

[3] Hasenkamp, Wendy. "How to Focus a Wandering Mind." *Greater Good Magazine*, 17 Jul 2013. https://greatergood.berkeley.edu/article/item/how_to_focus_a_wandering_mind

[4] Hamblin, James. "Buy Experiences, Not Things." *The Atlantic*, 7 Oct 2014, https://www.theatlantic.com/business/archive/2014/10/buy-experiences/381132/

[5] Frank, Thomas. "How to Remember More of What You Learn with Spaced Repetition," *CollegeInfoGeek*, 17 Jul 2020, https://collegeinfogeek.com/spaced-repetition-memory-technique/

[6] Fields, Douglas K. "Making Memories Stick," *Scientific American*, Feb 2005. https://www.scientificamerican.com/article/making-memories-stick/

[7] Maybin, Simon. "Busting the attention span myth." *BBC News*, 10 Mar 2017, https://www.bbc.com/news/health-38896790

[8] Briggs, Saga. "The Science of Attention: How To Capture And Hold The Attention of Easily Distracted Students," *InformED*, 28 Jun 2014, https://www.opencolleges.edu.au/informed/features/30-tricks-for-capturing-students-attention/

[9] Gallo, Carmine. "Neuroscience Proves You Should Follow TED's 18-Minute Rule to Win Your Pitch," *Inc*, 21 Feb 2017, https://www.inc.com/mbvans/contest.html

ENDNOTES

[10]Chadha, Saakhi, "Ditch the Keyboard & Pick up a Pen — Your Brain Will Thank You," Fit, 27 Sep 2019, https://fit.thequint.com/mind-it/why-writing-is-good-for-your-brain#:~:text=%E2%80%9CThere%20are%20more%20cognitive%20tasks,be%20better%20in%20that%20sense.%E2%80%9D

[11]Lynn, Michael. "Reach Out and Touch Your Customers," School of Hotel Administration Collection, 1998. https://scholarship.sha.cornell.edu/cgi/viewcontent.cgi?article=1111&context=articles

[12]Thompson, Austin. "When Did Shaking Hands Become a Standard Way of Greeting Someone?" *Mental Floss*, 1 Jan 2020, https://www.mentalfloss.com/article/606627/handshake-origins

[13]Rosenbaum, David, et al. "Stand By Your Stroop: Standing Up Enhances Selective Attention and Cognitive Control," *Psychological Science*, Sep 2017. https://www.researchgate.net/publication/320070495_Stand_by_Your_Stroop_Standing_Up_Enhances_Selective_Attention_and_Cognitive_Control#:~:text=Rosenbaum%2C%20Mama%2C%20and%20Algom%20(,compared%20to%20a%20seated%20posture.&text=(2017)%20demonstrated%20that%20Stroop%20interference,in%20enhanced%20selectivity%20of%20attention.

[14]Wong, May. "Stanford study finds walking improves creativity," *Stanford News*, 24 Apr 2014, http://stanford.io/211ThUt

[15]Sheihk, Knvul. "How We Save Face—Researchers Crack the Brain's Facial-Recognition Code," *Scientific American*, 1 Aug 2017, https://www.scientificamerican.com/article/how-we-save-face-mdash-researchers-crack-the-brains-facial-recognition-code/

[16]Keefe, Patrick Radden. "The Detectives Who Never Forget a Face," *The Atlantic*, 15 Aug 2016, https://www.newyorker.com/magazine/2016/08/22/londons-super-recognizer-police-force

[17]"How to improve your running? Smiling boosts efficiency, researchers find," *TheConversation.com*, 23 Jan 2018, https://theconversation.com/how-to-improve-your-running-smiling-boosts-efficiency-researchers-find-89722

[18]"Marriage and Divorce," *American Psychological Association*, https://www.apa.org/topics/divorce

[19]Essig, Todd. "The Mysterious Popularity Of The Meaningless Myers-Briggs (MBTI)," 29 Sep 2014, *Forbes.com*, https://www.forbes.com/sites/toddessig/2014/09/29/the-mysterious-popularity-of-the-meaningless-myers-briggs-mbti/#1485409f1c79

[20]Grant, Adam. "Goodbye to Myers Briggs, the Fad That Won't Die," 18 Sep 2013, *Psychology Today*, https://www.psychologytoday.com/us/blog/give-and-take/201309/goodbye-mbti-the-fad-won-t-die

[21]McDade, Dan. "What Should the Sales Close Rate Be?" Prospect-Experience.com, 29 Jan 2019, https://www.prospect-experience.com/insights/2019/1/29/what-should-the-sales-close-rate-be

[22]Kidd, David and Emanuele Castano. "Reading Literary Fiction Improves Theory of Mind," *Science*, 18 Oct 2018, https://science.sciencemag.org/content/342/6156/377

[23]"CONSUMER TRUST IN ONLINE, SOCIAL AND MOBILE ADVERTISING GROWS." Nielsen.com, 11 Mar 2012, https://www.nielsen.com/us/en/insights/article/2012/consumer-trust-in-online-social-and-mobile-advertising-grows/

[24]"ONLINE REVIEWS VS WORD OF MOUTH: WHICH HAS MORE TRUST?" Signal Interactive, 27 Jun 2019. https://signal-interactive.com/online-reviews-vs-word-of-mouth-which-has-more-trust/

[25]Shah, Khushbu. "How Cinnabon Tricks You With Its Cinnamon Smells." eater.com, 21 May 2014. https://www.eater.com/2014/5/21/6220567/how-cinnabon-tricks-you-with-its-cinnamon-smells

[26]Pemberton, Caele. "Smell Something Different At The Gym? It Might Not Be What You Think." npr.com, 15 Mar 2015. https://www.npr.org/2015/03/15/392761787/smell-something-different-at-the-gym-it-might-not-be-what-you-think

[27]Hyken, Shep. "Customer Experience is the New Brand." *Forbes.com*, 15 Jul 2018. https://www.forbes.com/sites/shephyken/2018/07/15/customer-experience-is-the-new-brand/#457888ec7f52

[28]"WHAT IS THE KANO MODEL?" *asq.org*, https://asq.org/quality-resources/kano-model#:~:text=The%20highest%20level%20of%20customer,might%20imagine%20and%20ask%20for.

[29]Door is more important than bed." *YouTube*, uploaded by Riley Silverman, 27 Jun 2013, https://www.youtube.com/watch?v=rapOAUg4gLU

[30]Engber, Daniel. "The Mystery of the Missing Hotel Toothpaste." 3 Jul 2013, Slate.com, https://slate.com/human-interest/2013/07/toothpaste-in-hotels-why-do-they-provide-shampoo-soap-and-high-end-toiletries-but-no-toothpaste.html

[31]Strohmetz, David B. et al. "Sweetening the Till: The Use of Candy to Increase Restaurant Tipping." School of Hotel Administration Collection, 2002. https://scholarship.sha.cornell.edu/cgi/viewcontent.cgi?article=1129&context=articles

[32]Luo, J. "The Rise and Fall (and Rise Again?) of BlackBerry." *The Harvard Business School Digital Initiative*, 1 Feb 2018, https://digital.hbs.edu/platform-digit/submission/the-rise-and-fall-and-rise-again-of-blackberry/

[33]Shaw, Colin. "15 Statistics That Should Change the Business World - But Haven't." Beyond Philosophy, 10 Jun 2013, https://beyondphilosophy.com/15-statistics-that-should-change-the-business-world-but-havent/

[34]Nordstrom, "Nordstrom: Diamond Story." *YouTube.com*, 30 Dec 2011. https://www.youtube.com/watch?v=LbkhEB6H8Xk

[35]BusinessWire. "#WellActually, Americans Say Customer Service is Better Than Ever." *BusinessWire.com*, 15 Dec 2017, https://www.businesswire.com/news/home/20171215005416/en/WellActually-Americans-Customer-Service

[36]Carroll, Dave. "UNITED BREAKS GUITARS." https://www.davecarrollmusic.com/songwriting/united-breaks-guitars

[37]Sentium. "A Public Relations Disaster: How saving $1,200 cost United

Airlines 10,772,839 negative views on YouTube." *Sentium.com*, 2011. https://sentium.com/a-public-relations-disaster-how-saving-1200-cost-united-airlines-10772839-negative-views-on-youtube/

[38]Zeev N. Kain, "How to Mentally Prepare for Surgery and Recover Faster." *Psychology Today*, 9 Dec 2017, https://www.psychologytoday.com/us/blog/the-anxiety-medicine/201712/how-mentally-prepare-surgery-and-recover-faster

[39]Unix Commerce, "10 Examples of Great Customer Service." *Unixcommerce.com*, 2018. https://www.unixcommerce.com/10-examples-of-great-customer-service/

About the Authors

Robert G. Best's life experience is truly an American gumbo: railroad worker, land surveyor, musician, woodworker, public school teacher, award winning sales/designer and consultant.

Robb also ran a nationally recognized company. His fascination with cognitive science led to the development of a selling and marketing system based on cutting edge brain research. Robb appears throughout the United States and abroad as a keynote speaker. His workshops and seminars are booked out a year in advance and his science blog, *Mindframewithrobb,* is regularly read in 14 countries.

J.M. Best is a freelance writer and editor, with clients in marketing and education. She also writes, directs, and executive produces the sci-fi podcast *The Strange Case of Starship Iris.*

Visit us at www.bestmindframe.com

CPSIA information can be obtained
at www.ICGtesting.com
Printed in the USA
LVHW040200300422
717195LV00002B/6